The Municipal Bond Market

Wilson White

The Municipal Bond Market

Basics

The Financial Press

Library of Congress Cataloguing in Publication Data
White, Wilson
    The Municipal Bond Market

    Bibliography: page 247
    Includes Index
    Library of Congress 85-80289
    ISBN 0-9615066-0-1

The Financial Press, Jersey City, NJ 07304

90 89 88 87 86 85

To my father,
Wilson White, Jr.,
author of
White's Ratings,
who showed me
the way to
many books.

Contents

continued

Preface

I am Wilson White, and it would please me if you the reader were to come to think of me as a bond man. I have been active in the municipal securities markets since 1954, fresh—very fresh, some thought—from Summit High School and Harvard College. I started trading bonds for Rand & Co., opened a small municipal department at Granger & Co., had my own firm for many years, and am now manager of the special situation trading department at Glickenhaus & Co., New York City. You might well wonder that such a non-academic person would try to write a book on the whole tax-exempt market, and one explanation is that I have had a lot of help. Another is that I am out of my mind. Try writing one yourself someday and you'll see what I mean. However that may be, more people than I can count properly have assisted me answering direct questions, and supplying me with all sorts of information and comment.

About 15 people have read various versions of the text and have suggested additions and revisions, particularly Norm Wright and Mike Coleman, who are in our business, and Patsy Shillingburg and Carol Rothkopf, who are not. Bill Forsyth and Jim of the same name were very helpful on the Vermont issue which Harris Trust bought in 1978. Dick Goss, Gene Shulz, and Ken Kerznar, who you may meet in the Kenosha section, provided much data on a bond sale back in 1979. And I have had the services of three exceptional researchers, Sybil Wong, Amy Lambe, and especially Emily Nolan. I have read many a book with prefaces loaded with what I had thought were unnecessarily lengthy acknowledgements, but now I think differently; so I continue to Lou Figliola, design man extraordinary, who turned a messy sheaf of papers into a real book, while remaining utterly charming about all of its, and my, oddnesses.

Because the work was rejected by several publishers, including Brent Harries of McGraw-Hill, still a friend, barely, I went ahead to do it myself, a process which I have genuinely enjoyed and recommend to any aspiring writers out there. Since I have invested my own money in addition to my efforts, I will doubly appreciate the readers' approval and purchases. When you find an error, please call me, and I will correct the next edition. Proceeding like this, on my own, reminds me of an actor or singer addressing a window open onto darkness. Who knows what audience is out there, and how they will judge?

Throughout the years I have spent on this volume, and on two more books on the subject, one on revenue bonds and one on trading, both of which are well on their way to completion, there have been dozens of others who I have cause to thank. But there has been one most constant, staunch encourager, my editor, my wife, Joyce Rudd White. We hope you will read this book with profit and pleasure.

SECTION I

Basics
Chapters 1-10

U.S. EXPENDITURES AND INVESTMENTS
1980-1984

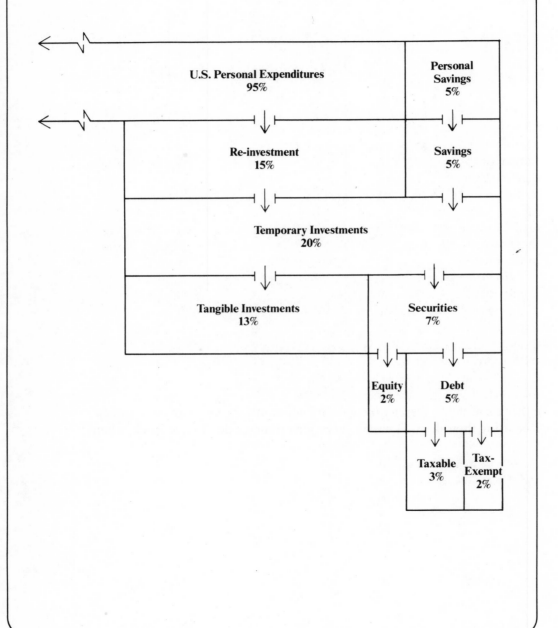

Chapter One

The Municipal Bond Market

In recent years Americans have been spending an average of about 95% of their personal income and saving the rest. This 5% remainder is available for investment, that is, for putting to work to earn a return. Part of the savings goes to buy tangible, real things, such as oil wells, real estate, or collectibles; most of the rest comes to Wall Street to buy intangibles, that is, securities. While some people are looking for ways to invest their savings, other individuals, as well as corporations and government bodies, are looking for money to finance projects of many kinds. We in the investment business work to bring these two groups together, aiming for a profit in the process.

Saving and Investing

When someone mentions Wall Street, most people think of stocks and bonds, and that boils it down simply and correctly. Stocks represent equity, or outright ownership. For instance, in 1985, an investor who buys 24,000 shares of E.I Dupont stock buys about .01% of the company, and will share in its fortunes (and its dividends) in the same proportion. Bonds, in contrast, represent debt, or a loan. An investor who buys bonds of a corporation or government unit simply lends it money, and no ownership is involved. Corporations needing to raise money have a choice: they can either issue stock, thereby increasing their equity, or they can issue bonds, increasing their debt. However, since governments don't issue stock, when they need money, they come to the bond market.

Equity and Debt

Bonds are the main form of a somewhat broader category called fixed income securities, other forms of which include bank certificates of deposit, preferred stock, and commercial paper. Unlike equity investments, the rates of return on fixed income securities are set at issuance and remain unchanged and enforceable by law.

Fixed Income Securities

In our economy, the price of money is determined by supply and demand. What is the price of money? Its interest rate. Economists call interest a form of rent, and it is expressed as a yearly percentage return on

The Price of Money Is Interest

INITIAL RESOLUTION authorizing
not exceeding $420,000 bonds
of the City of Kenosha.

BE IT RESOLVED by the Common Council of the City of Kenosha, Wisconsin, that there shall be issued the general obligation bonds of said City in the principal amount of not exceeding $420,000 for the purpose of constructing and equipping a library of said City. For the purpose of paying the various installments of principal and interest on said bonds as they severally mature, there is hereby levied on all taxable property in said City a direct annual irrepealable tax sufficient for that purpose.

Approved ___April 2___, 1979.

_____
Acting Mayor

Recorded ___April 2___, 1979,

_____
City Clerk

It was moved by ___Alderman Johnson___ and seconded by ___Alderman Madison___ that said resolution be adopted. Upon roll being called, the following voted:

Aye: ALDERMEN: Miechowicz   Kolmos   Stancato
                   Zeihen   Boettcher
                   Baker   Johnson
                   Pocan   Lambrecht
                   Andreoli   Budella
                   Andreucci   Madison
                   Birkholz   Bellow

Nay:
        ALDERMAN: Fitchett

The following initial resolution offered and read on March 5, 1979 ~~Bebousembodomsorder~~ was again read in full:

4

investment. So if the rate is 8%, a borrower pays $8 interest per year for each $100 lent. For borrowers, the lower the rate the better. If the City of Baltimore, Maryland, decides to borrow $50 million, it invites money suppliers to compete against each other to buy its bonds, just as it would ask construction companies to bid for contracts to improve its water system or fuel companies to supply its heating oil. If it receives three bids for its bonds of, for example, 9.77%, 9.88% and 9.65%, it would naturally accept the lowest one, the 9.65%. For lenders, the higher the rate the better. If an investor has the choice of buying two similar bonds, one at a rate of 8¼% and the other at 8½%, he would naturally prefer the one with the higher interest return, the 8½% bond. The interaction between bond tenants seeking the lowest possible rent and bond landlords looking for the highest, makes our market go.

Bonds and other fixed income securities are issued and traded in three separate markets—U.S. Treasury, corporate, and municipal. In many ways, the U.S. Treasury bond market comes first. The federal government is our biggest single borrower, and its bond issues promote national, rather than regional or private, interests. Backed by the full faith of the nation, they are considered our strongest bonds. In 1984, the U.S. government sold over $185 billion of new securities, bringing the total outstanding to over $1,500 billion. Most of our major corporations also borrow by issuing corporate bonds. Over $50 billion worth came out in 1984, and more than $500 billion are outstanding. Who are the municipal borrowers? State and local governmental units, such as the State of Michigan, or Westchester County, New York, or Sunnyvale School District, California. In 1984, state and local governments sold $102 billion bonds, and investors were holding over $500 billion. *The Three Bond Markets*

Through the nineteen seventies, banks, insurance companies, and individuals each held about one-third of all municipals. However, chiefly due to the current higher interest rates, this proportion has been changing rapidly. In 1984, individuals bought more than three-quarters of all the bonds in new issues, and now own over half of all outstanding tax-exempts. *Municipal Bond Holders*

Why do states and local governments borrow? To help them fulfill their primary responsibility: providing the public facilities which bridge the gaps between the national public sector and the individual private sector. Although our communities usually pay their operating expenses from current income, they rarely have enough money on hand to pay for the costs of long-lasting improvements. They may get some funding from federal or state sources, but most of the money has to be borrowed. For *Bonds for Municipal Construction*

Negotiated Offerings

The following table gives tentative dates for negotiated bond sales of $10 million and larger as reported to **The Bond Buyer** with additions and alterations each day.

Compiled by LINA GUIDO

Issue	Approximate Date of Sale	Approximate Amount	Rating	New Item in Our Issue Of
Baltimore, Md. (port facilities revenue) (Salomon Brothers Inc., senior-manager)	wk. 6/20	$30,820,000	Moody's: Aa2 S&P: t	5/18
California Educational Facilities Authority (construction revenue)... (L.F. Rothschild Unterberg Towbin, senior-manager)	wk. 6/20	$10,500,000	Moody's: s S&P: t	5/11
Harris County Housing Finance Corporation, Tex. (multi-family housing revenue)............ (Merrill Lynch White Weld Capital Markets Group, senior-manager)	wk. 6/20	$10,200,000	Moody's: t S&P: t	6/14
Vermont Educational and Health Buildings Financing Agency (revenue refunding)............ (Kidder Peabody & Co. Incorporated, senior-manager)	wk. 6/20	$38,000,000	Moody's: cA1 S&P: A+p	5/17
Vermont Housing Finance Agency (home mortgage purchase)............ (Goldman Sachs & Co., senior-manager)	wk. 6/20	$32,150,000	Moody's: A1 S&P: t	5/27
Oklahoma State Loan Authority (state loan program-II revenue)............ (Leo Oppenheim & Co. Inc., senior-manager)	wk. 6/20	$30,055,000	Moody's: t S&P: s	6/1
Quincy, Ill. (hospital facilities revenue refunding)............ (John Nuveen & Co. Inc., senior-manager)	wk. 6/20	$12,315,000	Moody's: A S&P: BBB+	6/9
St. Paul Housing and Redevelopment Authority, Minn. (education equipment revenue)............ (Miller & Schroeder Municipals Inc., senior-manager)	wk. 6/20	$17,330,000	Moody's: t S&P: t	5/19
Cleveland, Ohio (general obligation).. (Salomon Brothers Inc., senior-manager)	6/20	$27,585,000	Moody's: Ba1 S&P: BBB	6/3
Hopewell Industrial Development Authority, Va. (floatin/fixed rate resource recovery revenue)............ (Lehman Brothers Kuhn Loeb Incorporated, senior-manager)	6/20	$35,000,000	Moody's: t S&P: t	6/15
Indiana Housing Finance Agency (single-family mortgage program).. (First Boston Corporation, senior-manager)	6/20	$45,000,000	Moody's: Aa S&P: t	6/16
Dade Co., Fla. (public facilities revenue)............ (Kidder Peabody & Co. Inc., senior-manager)	6/21	$44,675,000	Moody's: A S&P: A	6/15
Idaho Housing Agency (single-family mortgage purchase)............ (Salomon Brothers Inc., senior-manager)	6/21	$35,000,000	Moody's: Aa S&P: AA	5/20
San Diego, Calif. (hospital revenue)... (Merrill Lynch White Weld Capital Markets Group, senior-manager)	6/21	$18,360,000	Moody's: t S&P: t	6/16
Harrison Sch. Dist. No. 2, Colo. (school obligation and refunding). (Dain Bosworth Inc., senior-manager)	6/22	$19,990,000	Moody's: t S&P: t	6/16
Missouri Health and Educational Facilities Authority (health facilities revenue refunding)............ (Merrill Lynch White Weld Capital Markets Group, senior-manager)	6/22	$103,000,000	Moody's: t S&P: s	6/10

Courtesy of *The Bond Buyer*

instance, in 1978, the Kenosha, Wisconsin, Common Council voted to build a small library at an estimated cost of $1.362 million. It appropriated $500,000 from a surplus in the city's general fund, voted to use some unspent money from another project, and then sold enough bonds to complete the financing. At the same time, it levied property taxes to provide for the bonds' repayment. Families operate similarly when buying a house. They make their down payments from savings, take out mortgages, and then repay them over the years. Municipal bonds help finance improvements ranging from adding on a few fire hydrants, to building a new high school, to constructing an entire nuclear power project. About 5,000 municipalities sell bonds for these and other purposes every year, and about 50,000 of them currently have some debt outstanding. We will be looking more closely at issuing bodies in Chapter Three.

The Dealers

Linking the communities and the investors is a different kind of group—the several hundred securities dealers who underwrite (buy to resell) municipal bond new issues. These dealers act as risk taking middlemen; they buy bonds directly from communities, and then try to sell them to investors. The full cycle from issuer to dealer to investor makes up the so-called primary market. The largest underwriters are organized as separate departments of publicly-owned investment firms, such as Prudential/Bache or Shearson/American Express, and of the big commercial banks such as Citibank in New York, or First Interstate in California. Most medium-sized and smaller firms, for example, Glickenhaus in New York, or Miller Securities in Minneapolis, are privately owned and specialize in municipals. Dealers work with both issuers and buyers, incurring expenses for research, sales, and administration much like the distributors of other products; their reward, when they are successful, is a profit.

Competitive New Issues

There are two distinctly different ways a municipality can float its bonds: one is at public competitive bidding and the other is by private negotiation. In a public sale, the finance experts of the municipality itself design, schedule, and advertise an issue, inviting interested parties to bid on it. At a specified hour, the proposals (usually entered by groups of bond dealers) are opened, and, provided that an acceptable one is received, the whole bond issue is awarded to the one group that bid the lowest rate. That group, called a syndicate, becomes the temporary owner of the issue, and goes to work selling it to investors in smaller lots. If the syndicate successfully places the bonds with investors, it will make a profit, but if it has misjudged the bond's value, or if the market goes against it, the syndicate may have a loss; profit or loss, its bid commitment to the issuer remains. We will be looking at two competitive sales in later chapters—one by

7

POLLOCK *v.* FARMERS' LOAN AND TRUST COMPANY.

APPEAL FROM THE CIRCUIT COURT OF THE UNITED STATES FOR THE SOUTHERN DISTRICT OF NEW YORK.

No. 803. Argued March 7, 8, 11, 12, 13, 1895. — Decided April 8, 1895.

A court of equity has jurisdiction to prevent a threatened breach of trust in the misapplication or diversion of the funds of a corporation by illegal payments out of its capital or profits.

Such a bill being filed by a stockholder to prevent a trust company from voluntarily making returns for the imposition and payment of a tax claimed to be unconstitutional, and on the further ground of threatened multiplicity of suits and irreparable injury, and the objection of adequate remedy at law not having been raised below or in this court, and the question of jurisdiction having been waived by the United States, so far as it was within its power to do so, and the relief sought being to prevent the voluntary action of the trust company and not in respect to the assessment and collection of the tax, the court will proceed to judgment on the merits.

The doctrine of *stare decisis* is a salutary one, and is to be adhered to on proper occasions, in respect of decisions directly upon points in issue; but this court should not extend any decision upon a constitutional question, if it is convinced that error in principle might supervene.

In the cases referred to in the opinion of the court in this case, beginning with *Hylton* v. *United States,* 3 Dall. 171, (February Term, 1796,) and ending with *Springer* v. *United States,* 102 U. S. 586, (October Term, 1880,) taxes on land are conceded to be direct taxes, and in none of them is it determined that a tax on rent or income derived from land is not a tax on land.

A tax on the rents or income of real estate is a direct tax, within the meaning of that term as used in the Constitution of the United States.

A tax upon income derived from the interest of bonds issued by a municipal corporation is a tax upon the power of the State and its instrumentalities to borrow money, and is consequently repugnant to the Constitution of the United States.

So much of the act " to reduce taxation, to provide revenue for the government, and for other purposes," 28 Stat. 509, c. 349, as provides for levying taxes upon rents or income derived from real estate, or from the interest on municipal bonds, is repugnant to the Constitution of the United States and is invalid.

8

Kenosha, and one by the State of Vermont.

The second method of underwriting is by negotiated sale, in which the municipality and just one dealer underwriting group cooperate in designing a bond issue and bringing it to market. Most of our largest bond issues, particularly ones with novel or special credit features, are negotiated. Sales by the New York State Power Authority and the New Jersey Housing Agency come to mind right away.

Negotiated Underwriting

Whether a new bond issue is sold competitively or by negotiation, its primary market phase is over once the underwriting dealers have sold all of the bonds. If an investor later wishes to sell his bonds, he comes to the secondary (trading) market, where dealers buy and sell bonds according to current supply and demand. The issuer continues to pay interest to each successive buyer and repays the principal at maturity. Although individual dealers vary their emphasis widely, in general, they expend about half their energy in the primary market and half in the secondary. The U.S. Government and corporate bond markets have their own primary and secondary parts, too, which work somewhat similarly.

The Secondary Market

The Federal Government taxes the interest received on U.S. Treasury and corporate bonds at the same rate it does ordinary income. However, municipal bonds are unique: the interest earned on them is not taxed[1]. Their other name says it clearly—tax-exempt securities. Naturally, this exemption, particularly now that most tax shelters have been eliminated, makes owning municipals attractive for individual people, and also for taxed institutions such as banks and insurance companies. Tax exemption also appeals to the issuers; when the Treasury can borrow at 10%, because of their bonds' tax advantage, most states usually pay only around 8%.

Federal Income Tax Exemption

The principle supporting this exemption goes all the way back to the colonists' cry of "No taxation without representation!" After the first federal income tax was levied in 1894, the Supreme Court, having heard a long and eloquently argued suit (Pollock *vs.* Farmers Loan & Trust Co.) objecting to the tax as applied to municipal bond interest, declared that "The tax in question is a tax on the power of the states and their instrumentalities to borrow money, and consequently repugnant to the constitution." The Court referred to the intentions of members of the Constitutional Convention, citing Franklin, Hamilton, and even Washing-

Mutual Tax Exemption

(1) The Federal Government cannot tax state and local bond interest; however, most states with an income tax include in it the interest received from out-of-state bonds. For instance, California exempts income from its local bonds, but taxes the interest on Arizona municipals, and vice versa. In addition, profits realized on securities, including municipals, are subject to capital gains taxes.

REVENUE BONDS	Rating	Debt*	Final Matur.	Source of Payment	Debt Serv*	Gross Rev*	Exp.*	Net Avail.*	Coverage
Franklin Co. Dist. Sch. Bd. ('63, '70, '71, '76)	AAA				Secured by escrowed U.S. Gov'ts. to '81				
Franklin Co. Dist. Sch. Bd. ('76A)	AAA	1,430	1996		Interest paid on U.S. Govts to pay				
Gadsden Co. Sch. Bd.	BBB	1,715	2000	§		172	223		223	1.30
Gainesville (E W S 2nd Ln) '67, '70, '71, '72, '73, '74, '76	AAA				Secured by U.S. Gov'ts. in escrow acct.				
Gainesville (E. W S Rev. '76)	AAA	17,950	...		MBIA insured				
Gainesville Lsd Hsg Inc.	AA	858	1992		Partly secured by HUD subsidy				
Gainesville (Pub. Imp) Ser 54, 59, 60, 66, 70	A+	1,225	1993	u		391†	3,104	...	3,104	7.93
Gainesville Pub. Imp. '75	AAA	1,235	...		MBIA insured				
Gainesville Fl Publ Improv. Rev. Certif. Antic. Notes Dtd. 8/1/82	A	4,500			Jr. lien on utility txs proceeds of a refunding util. bond				
Gainesville Spl Oblig. Ser. '76	AAA	80,000	1999	...	Secured by escrow account U.S. Gov'ts.				
Gainesville (Swr 1st Ln)	AAA				Secured by U S Gov'ts. in escrow acct.				
Gainesville (Utl 1st Ln)	AAA	8,267	1996		Secured by U S Gov'ts. in escrow				
Gainesville Utl. Sys. Ser. '79, '80 A B	AA	265,000	2014	e-w-s		21,423	76,377	42,840	32,537	1.52x
Gtr Orlando Aviation Auth. (Orange Co.) Jr. Lien Arpt. Rev's. '78	A−	263,000	2006	a		26,207	51,636†	15,901†	35,737†	1.36†
Greater Orlando Aviation Auth. Airport Fac. Bnds. Ser. '81 Due 10-1-2006 Term Only	AAA	39,575	2006	...	MBIA insured				
Hamilton Co. Sch. Bd. (3rd Ln)	BBB	860	1994	§		212	230	...	230	1.09
Harbor Court Dev. Inc. FHA Cons. Ln. Mts. '82A	AAA	1,607	1964	...	FHA ins 221(d)(4)				
Harbor Court Devel. Inc. FHA Mge. Rev. '82A	AAA	1,715	2024	...	FHA ins 221(d)(4)				
Hendry Co. Bd. of P.I. (Race Trk Tx)	BBB	1,035	1999	a		143	447	...	447	3.13
Hernando Co. (Cap. Imp. '76)	BBB	1,000	2006		Gen fund oblig ex ad valorem tax rev sharing, race trk.				
Hernando Co Dist. Sch. Bd. (Dtd 6-1-79A)	AAA	1,625	2010	...	MBIA insured				
Hialeah Hsg Dev Corp Mtg. Rev (Meadowgreen Apt. Proj.)	A−	4,395	2011	...	Partially secured by HUD Section 8 subsidy				
Hialeah W S '68	BBB+	9,335	2006	b-c-f-q-s-u-w		695	12,249	8,319	3,930	5.65x
Highlands Co Race Track '66 1st Ln.	BBB	750	1996	§		63	223	...	223	3.54

—MARYLAND—

GENERAL OBLIGATIONS	Rating	Pop*	Est. True Value* $	Gross* $	Debt		Per Cap. $	% Val.	S.P. Index
					Net* $	Overall* $			
Allegany Co.	A+	80.5	1,063,809	16,025	15,363	30,072	373	2.8	6.0
Annapolis	BBB+	31.4	570,400	12,774	12,774	27,014	860	4.7	...
Anne Arundel Co.	AA−	376.9	7,194,980	343,324	170,874	179,874	477	2.5	7.0
Baltimore	A	786.8	8,069,831	483,031	293,801	293,801	373	3.6	5.8
Baltimore Co.	AA+	655.6	13,406,000	223,472	175,019	362,096	552	2.7	5.2
Baltimore Co. Rens. Dtd. 11-1-82 Due 11-1-83	AA+	15,000			Unltd advalorem txes.-future bond sale (planned for spring '83)				
Baltimore Co Metro Dist.	AA+	655.6	12,662,236	170,975	170,975	345,404	527	2.7	5.5
Bowie (Water Sewer G.O. Bonds)	A+	33.7	486,111	13,870	5,270	24,248	720	4.5	...

Standard & Poor's Corp. publishes a white and blue booklet describing and rating about 15,000 municipal bond issues. Some of their busiest pages detail Florida's various bond types. You can see how tranquil their Maryland section is by comparison.

ton, along the way. The Internal Revenue Code of 1954, Section 103, spells out present practice, and the instructions for filing Form 1040 say, "Do not report interest on state and local bonds." By the same kind of reasoning, the interest on U.S. bonds has been declared exempt from state and local income taxes. This mutual tax exemption is deeply embedded in our custom and law; attempts have been made to overturn it, but none has come close to succeeding. If things ever did change, precedent strongly suggests that previously issued municipals would still remain exempt from future taxation.

As you see, the municipal bond market is not located on a formal exchange, or in any one place. It is an over-the-counter, over-the-telephone, nationwide operation, in which dealers bring buyers and sellers together at prices which suit all three. Until 1975, the market functioned quite well according to its own rules, but then Congress, led by Senator Harrison Williams of New Jersey, decided it should be regulated. Competition still determines municipal prices and profits, and dealers maintain the ethical standards; but now, like most businesses, we are subject to federal overview. We operate under regulations set by the Municipal Securities Rule Making Board (M.S.R.B.) with Securities and Exchange Commission (S.E.C.) approval, and these rules are enforced reasonably by our self-regulating National Association of Security Dealers (N.A.S.D.)

Federal Regulation

Now a word of caution: beware of generalizations about municipals— their diversity can be bewildering. To begin with, each state authorizes its communities to issue bonds according to the state's own specifications, which results in hundreds of different security types, and over one and a half million different bonds. Florida authorizes the widest variety: some Florida schools are financed by bonds backed by taxes on horse racing and jai-alai betting. In contrast, most Connecticut and Maryland bond issues are secured by regular property taxes. Furthermore, not only do issuers in the 50 states sell bonds, but so do Puerto Rico, the Virgin Islands, the District of Columbia, Guam, and probably some others. In addition, some bonds are issued by different state bodies in cooperation, such as the giant Port Authority of New York and New Jersey, or little Dresden School District, which extends from Hanover, New Hampshire, over into Norwich, Vermont. So, when every straightforward statement about municipals seems to have an exception, or many exceptions, and when a sizable minority of tax-exempts doesn't conform to the simplest rules, it's not surprising. Don't be too bothered by the exceptions—you will see that departures from general principles can be interesting and profitable— again, with exceptions!

Never Say Never About Tax-Exempts

Treasury Bills, Bonds and Notes

(Prices in 32d of a point, composite bill yields in basis points n-notes.)

TREASURY BILLS

-1985-

Jan 3	5.64	5.46	+0.30	5.54
Jan 10	5.94	5.82	-0.38	5.91
Jan 17	7.30	7.20	+0.34	7.32
Jan 24	7.32	7.24	+0.31	7.38
Jan 31	7.20	7.14	+0.26	7.28
Feb 7	7.33	7.27	+0.08	7.43
Feb 14	7.40	7.34	+0.05	7.51
Feb 21	7.52	7.46	+0.09	7.65
Feb 28	7.44	7.36	+0.08	7.55
Mar 7	7.60	7.54	+0.02	7.55
Mar 14	7.63	7.59	+0.03	7.82
Mar 21	7.70	7.64	+0.05	7.88
Mar 28	7.67	7.63	+0.04	7.88
Apr 4	7.74	7.70	+0.06	7.97
Apr 11	7.66	7.62	-0.08	7.89
Apr 18	7.79	7.75	.....	8.04
Apr 25	7.74	7.68	+0.02	7.98
May 2	7.93	7.89	+0.03	8.22
May 9	7.95	7.89	+0.01	8.23
May 16	7.99	7.95	+0.04	8.31
May 23	8.01	7.95	+0.04	8.32
May 30	7.96	7.90	.....	8.28
Jun 6	8.04	7.98	+0.02	8.38
Jun 13	8.03	7.97	+0.02	8.39
Jun 20	8.03	7.99	+0.02	8.42
Jun 27	8.04	8.02	+0.01	8.47
Jul 11	8.09	8.03	+0.04	8.49
Aug 8	8.14	8.08	+0.04	8.56
Sep 5	8.25	8.21	+0.03	8.72
Oct 3	8.33	8.27	.....	8.82
Oct 31	8.41	8.37	+0.02	8.97
Nov 29	8.42	8.38	.....	9.03
Dec 26	8.41	8.39	+0.02	9.08

Source - Federal Reserve Bank.

BONDS & NOTES

Source - Federal Reserve Bank.

Date	Rate	Bid	Ask	Chg.	Yield
Dec 84 n	9⅜	100	100.4	- .1	0.00
Dec 84 n	14	100.2	100.6	- .1	0.00
Jan 85 n	9¼	100.3	100.7	.....	6.39
Feb 85 n	8	100	100.4	+ .1	6.79
Feb 85 n	9⅝	100.8	100.12	- .1	7.07
Feb 85 n	14⅝	100.28	101	.....	6.22
Mar 85 n	9⅝	100.10	100.14	.....	7.64
Mar 85 n	13⅜	101.7	101.11	- .1	7.58
Apr 85 n	9½	100.12	100.16	- .1	7.83
May 85	3¼	98.7	99.7	.....	5.36
May 75-85	4¼	98.8	99.8	.....	6.27
May 85 n	9⅞	100.19	100.23	.....	8.02
May 85 n	10⅜	100.23	100.27	- .1	7.94
May 85 n	14⅛	102.5	102.9	.....	7.69
May 85 n	14⅜	102.9	102.13	.....	7.60
Jun 85 n	14	102.22	102.26	.....	8.15
Jun 85 n	10	100.24	100.28	+ .2	8.18
Jul 85 n	10⅝	101.2	101.6	- .1	8.50
Aug 85 n	8¼	99.24	99.28	.....	8.46
Aug 85 n	9⅝	100.15	100.19	.....	8.63
Aug 85 n	10⅝	100.31	101.3	- .1	8.90
Aug 85 n	13⅛	102.16	102.20	- .2	8.73
Sep 85 n	10⅞	101.12	101.16	.....	8.76
Sep 85 n	15⅞	104.29	105.1	.....	8.80
Oct 85 n	10½	101.1	101.5	- .2	9.03
Nov 85 n	9¾	100.15	100.19	.....	9.03
Nov 85 n	10½	101.2	101.6	- .1	9.12
Nov 85 n	11¾	102.4	102.8	- .1	9.02
Dec 85 n	10⅞	101.18	101.22	.....	9.07
Dec 85 n	14⅛	104.19	104.23	- .2	9.08
Jan 86 n	10⅝	101.10	101.14	- .1	9.20
Feb 86 n	10⅞	101.18	101.20	- .2	9.37
Feb 86 n	13½	104.8	104.12	- .4	9.32
Feb 86 n	9⅞	100.15	100.19	- .1	9.31
Mar 86 n	14	105.7	105.11	- .1	9.37
Mar 86 n	11½	102.10	102.14	- .2	9.39
Apr 86 n	11¾	102.21	102.25	- .1	9.48
May 86 n	7⅞	97.24	98	- .2	9.46
May 86 n	9⅜	99.22	99.26	.....	9.52
May 86 n	12⅝	103.23	103.27	- .3	9.66
May 86 n	13¾	105.5	105.9	- .2	9.56
Jun 86	13	104.15	104.19	+ .1	9.64
Jun 86 n	14⅞	107.2	107.6	- .2	9.62
Jul 86 p	12⅝	103.31	104.3	- .3	9.78
Aug 86 n	8	97.9	97.13	- .2	9.76
Aug 86 n	11⅜	102.6	102.10	- .2	9.80
Aug 86 p	12⅜	103.18	103.22	- .3	9.92
Sep 86 p	11⅞	102.30	103.2	- .3	9.93
Sep 86 n	12¼	103.18	103.22	- .3	9.90
Oct 86 p	11⅝	102.21	102.25	- .2	9.93
Nov 86	6⅛	94.8	95.8	- .2	8.93
Nov 86 p	10⅜	100.23	100.27	- .3	9.88
Nov 86 n	11	101.18	101.22	- .3	9.99
Nov 86 n	13⅞	106.11	106.15	- .4	10.01
Feb 87 n	9	98	98.4	- .2	10.09
Feb 87 n	10⅞	101.13	101.17	- .4	10.06
Feb 87 n	12¾	104.28	105	- .4	10.08
Mar 87 n	10¼	100.7	100.11	- .4	10.08
May 87 n	12	103.24	103.28	- .2	10.12
May 87 n	12½	104.20	104.24	- .2	10.20
May 87 n	14	107.20	107.24	- .5	10.24
Jun 87 n	10½	100.13	100.17	- .6	10.25
Aug 87 p	12⅜	104.18	104.22	- .2	10.29
Aug 87 n	13¾	107.15	107.19	- .4	10.37
Sep 87 n	11⅛	101.24	101.28	- .4	10.32
Nov 87 n	7⅝	93.18	94.2	- .8	10.05
Nov 87 p	11	101.16	101.18	- .5	10.36
Nov 87 n	12⅝	105.8	105.12	- .4	10.41
Dec 87 n	11¼	102	102.4	- .4	10.41
Jan 88 n	12⅜	104.25	104.29	- .5	10.45
Feb 88 n	10⅛	99.3	99.7	- .5	10.42
Mar 88 n	12	103.22	103.26	- .4	10.58
Apr 88 n	13¼	107.2	107.6	- .6	10.61
May 88 n	8¼	93.11	93.19	- .3	10.56
May 88 n	9⅞	97.27	97.31	- .6	10.61
Jun 88 n	13⅝	108.4	108.8	- .8	10.74
Jul 88 n	14	109.5	109.13	- .5	10.74
Aug 88 n	10½	99.8	99.12	- .2	10.71
Oct 88 n	15⅜	113.22	113.30	- .1	10.80
Sep 88 p	11⅜	101.24	101.26	- .1	10.77
Nov 88 n	8¾	94.4	94.12	+ .8	10.56
Nov 88 n	11¾	102.24	102.28	+ .1	10.82
Jan 89 n	14⅝	111.17	111.25	- .2	10.94
Feb 89 n	11⅜	101.14	101.18	- .1	10.89
Apr 89 n	14⅜	110.30	111.6	- .2	11.03
May 89 n	9¼	94.16	94.24	- .3	10.79
May 89 n	11¾	102.20	102.24	+ .6	10.94
Jul 89 n	14½	111.23	111.31	- .1	11.08
Aug 89 n	13⅞	109.18	109.22	- .2	11.14
Oct 89 n	11⅞	102.26	103.2	- .2	11.03
Nov 89 n	10¾	99.13	99.21	.....	10.84
Nov 89 p	12¾	105.28	106	- .3	11.12
Jan 90 n	10½	97.23	97.27	- .4	11.07
Feb 90	3½	89.28	90.28	+ .12	5.57
Feb 90 p	11	99.29	99.31	- .1	10.99
Apr 90 n	10½	97.17	97.25	+ .1	11.07
May 90	8¼	90.4	90.20	- .5	10.58
Jul 90 n	10¾	98.5	98.13	.....	11.14
Aug 90 n	10¾	98.5	98.13	.....	11.14
Oct 90 n	11½	101.2	101.10	- .1	11.19
Nov 90 n	13	107	107.8	- .1	11.28
Jan 91 n	11¾	101.24	102	- .2	11.28
Apr 91 n	12⅜	104.5	104.9	- .3	11.40
May 91 n	14½	113.19	113.27	- .1	11.39
Jul 91 n	13¾	110	110.4	- .4	11.51
Aug 91 n	14⅞	115.6	115.14	- .4	11.48
Oct 91 p	12¼	103.27	103.31	- .2	11.39n
Feb 92 n	14⅝	114.26	114.30	- .3	11.50
May 92 n	13¾	110.25	110.29	- .1	11.52
Aug 87-92	4¼	89.24	90.24	+ .2	5.77
Aug 92	7¼	79.20	80.4	- .1	11.19
Nov 92 n	10½	95.14	95.22	+ .1	11.34
Feb 88-93	4	89.20	90.20	+ .8	5.44
Feb 93	6¾	77.10	77.26	- .2	10.94
Feb 93	7⅞	81.27	82.11	+ .13	11.25
Feb 93 n	10⅞	96.26	97.2	- .4	11.44
May 93 n	10⅛	92.26	93.2	.....	11.43
Aug 88-93	7½	79.14	79.30	.....	11.18
Aug 93	8⅝	85	85.8	+ .1	11.35
Aug 93 n	11⅞	101.27	101.31	- .3	11.51
Nov 93	8⅝	84.29	85.5	+ .1	11.32
Nov 93 n	11¾	101.7	101.11	.....	11.58
Feb 94	9	86.10	86.18	- .3	11.41
May 89-94	4⅛	89.6	90.6	- .13	5.48
May 94	13⅛	108.30	109.2	- .3	11.52
Aug 94	8¾	84.28	85.12	- .2	11.28
Aug 94 p	12⅝	106.12	106.16	- .4	11.49
Nov 94	10⅛	93	93.8	- .2	11.28
Nov 94 p	11⅝	101	101.2	.....	11.44
Feb 95	3	89.21	90.21	+ .8	4.14
Feb 95	10½	94.26	95.2	- .5	11.33
May 95	10⅜	93.23	93.31	- .8	11.38
May 95	12⅝	107.9	107.17	- .6	11.37
Nov 95	11½	101.2	101.10	.....	11.29
May 93-98	7	71.9	71.25	- .5	11.10
Nov 98	3½	89.27	90.27	+ .3	4.39
May 94-99	8½	79.13	79.29	- .7	11.37
Feb 95-00	7⅞	74.4	74.20	- .6	11.44
Aug 95-00	8⅜	77.10	77.26	- .2	11.46
Feb 01	11¾	101.9	101.17	- .5	11.54
May 01	13⅛	110.29	111.5	- .6	11.59
Aug 96-01	8	74	74.16	- .5	11.47
Aug 01	13⅜	112.18	112.26	- .5	11.62
Nov 01	15¾	130.21	130.29	+ .9	11.55
Feb 02	14¼	119.6	119.14	- .5	11.61
Nov 02	11⅝	100.2	100.10	- .5	11.58
Feb 03	10¾	93.14	93.22	- .6	11.59
May 03	10¾	93.14	93.22	- .8	11.59
Aug 03	11⅛	96.11	96.19	- .5	11.57
Nov 03	11⅞	101.31	102.7	- .7	11.58
May 04	12⅜	105.30	106.6	- .4	11.57
Aug 04	13¾	116.8	116.16	- .11	11.60
Nov 04 k	11⅝	100.5	100.13	- .5	11.57
May 00-05	8¼	76	76.16	.....	11.20
Feb 02-07	7⅝	70.1	70.17	- .2	11.27
Nov 02-07	7⅞	71.24	72.8	- .2	11.28
Aug 03-08	8⅜	75.7	75.15	- .3	11.39
Nov 03-08	8¾	77.27	78.3	.....	11.45
May 04-09	9⅛	80.25	81.1	- .2	11.45
Nov 04-09	10⅜	90.24	91	- .1	11.48
Feb 05-10	11¾	101.13	101.21	- .1	11.54
May 05-10	10	87.23	87.31	- .2	11.47
Nov 05-10	12¾	109.3	109.11	- .3	11.56
May 06-11	13⅞	118.10	118.18	- .2	11.52
Nov 06-11	14	119.17	119.25	- .4	11.51
Nov 07-12	10⅜	90.22	90.30	- .2	11.46
Aug 08-13	12	103.15	103.23	- .4	11.54
May 09-14	13¼	113.23	113.31	- .7	11.53
Aug 09-14k	12½	107.24	107.28	- .8	11.53
Nov 09-14k	11¾	102.9	102.13	- .4	11.46

k - Non U. S. citizen exempt from withholding taxes. n - Treasury note, p - Treasury note and non U. S. citizen exempt from withholding taxes.

Tax-Exempt Authority Bonds

Bond	Bid	Ask	Chng
Alabama GO 8⅜s 2001	88	92	......
Battery Prk 6⅜s 2014	63	67	......
Chelan Co 5s 2013	59½	61½	......
Clark Co.Apt10½s 2007	96½	100½	......
Col SPE 3⅞s 2003	76	79	......
Del R PA 6½s 2001	66½	68½	......
Dgs Co PUD 4s 2018	41	43	......
Georgia MEA 8s 2015	76	80	......
Interm't Pwr 7½s 2018	71½	75½	......
Interm't Pwr10½s 2018	98	102	......
Interm't Pwr 14s 2021	120	124	......
Jacksonville ER 2013	88	92	......
LA. Off. Ter. 6½s 2008	62	66	......
M.A.C. N.Y. 7½s 92	92½	96½	......
M.A.C. N.Y. 7½s 95	90½	94½	......
M.A.C. N.Y. 8s 86	99	103	......
M.A.C. N.Y. 8s 91	98½	102½	......
M.A.C. N.Y. 9.70s 2008	95½	99½	......
M.A.C. N.Y. 9¾s 92	100½	104½	......
M.A.C. N.Y. 10¼s 93	105½	109½	......
Mass Port 6s 2011	65	68	......
Mass G.O. 6ps 2000	71½	75½	......
Mass Whl 6⅜s 2015	50	54	......
Mass Whl 13⅜s 2017	93	97	......
MetroTrsAth 9¼s 2015	87	91	......
Mich Pwr 10⅝s 2018	99½	103½	......
Neb PPD 7.10s 2017	69	73	......
NJ Tpke 4¾s 2006	58	61	......

Bonds	Bid	Ask	Chng
NYS Power 5½s 2010	59½	63½	......
NYS Power 6⅝s 2010	69	72	......
NYS Power 9½s 2001	102½	104½	......
NYS Power 9⅞s 2020	95½	98½	......
NYS Thruwy 3.10s 94	68	70	......
NYS U D C 6s 2013	59	63	......
NYS U D C 7s 2014	68	72	......
NC E MPA 11¼s 2018	101	104	......
Okla Tpke 4.70s 2006	65	67	......
Port N.Y. 4¾s 2003	56	59	......
Port N.Y. 6s 2006	65	68	......
Port N.Y. 7s 2011	74	77	......
Port N.Y. 10½s 2008	99	102	......
Salt River 9¼s 2020	91	95	......
So. Car. P.S. 10¼ 2020	98½	102½	......
Tx Mun PA. 9½s 2012	90	94½	......
Valdez 5½s 2007	62	64	......
Valdez 6s 2007	62½	64½	......
Wash PS 6s 2015F	8	12	......
Wash PS 7¾s 2018F	8	12	......
Wash PS 9⅞s 2012F	9	13	......
Wash PS 12½s 2010F	11½	15½	......
Wash PS 6s 2012	46	50	......
Wash PS 7¾s 2017	52	56	......
Wash PS 9¼s 2011	68½	72½	......
Wash PS 13⅞s 2018	94½	98½	......
Wash PS 14¾s 2012	104½	108½	......

THE NEW YORK TIMES, SUNDAY, DECEMBER 30, 1984

Chapter Two

The Investors

We outlined how people who have saved money can use it in order to earn themselves more income. Recently, over two-thirds of these savings has been invested in tangibles, such as land, pieces of sculpture, antique furniture, and coins and stamps, to mention just a few. Most tangibles bought for investment share two characteristics: 1.) Their individual qualities make buying and selling them relatively complex and expensive events, often requiring the use of lawyers and other professionals. 2.) They do not provide income (exception: some real estate), so investors benefit only if market prices rise. People who are skilled or lucky in buying tangibles sometimes make great profits doing so, but not always.

Tangibles As Investments

The remaining third of U.S. personal savings has been going into securities, which are quite different. First, instead of being real things, securities are pieces of paper, each one of which represents part of a whole investment issue. Since they are worth exactly the same as others of their kind, their value is easy to determine, making it possible to buy or sell them readily in small or large amounts. These and other qualities make securities suitable for many kinds of investors. Second, securities usually provide present income in the form of interest or dividends. Some (like bonds) pay out a high return; some (like many seasoned stocks) provide moderate income and some potential profit; still others (like growth stocks) offer lower income now and the possibility of substantial price appreciation in the future.

Security Investments

How do savers buy and sell securities? Through the financial markets: stock, option, bond, and many others. What we call Wall Street is actually a nationwide investment supermarket which offers a multitude of securities and other products to a wide range of customers. Some fifteen major financial markets are now in operation; a few date back to colonial days, while others have been established only recently. The U.S. Government bond market is the largest in dollar volume; tens of billions of dollars trade

The Securities Markets

New York Stock Exchange

CONSOLIDATED TRADING / WEEK ENDED FRIDAY, DECEMBER 28, 1984

12-Month High Low Stock	Yld %	P.E Ratio	Sales hds.	Week's High Low Last	Net Chg.

Continued From Page 12

(Stock listing table — dense data, largely illegible)

MOST ACTIVE STOCKS
WEEK ENDED DECEMBER 28, 1984
(Consolidated)

Company	Sales	Last	Net Chng
Phil Pet	10,221,300	45⅞	− 9
CmwE	6,136,000	27⅛	+ 1⅝
SCalE	5,373,800	22⅛	+ ⅛
AT&T	4,826,000	19⅜	+ ¼
ToysRUs	3,766,600	39⅜	− 7⅞
Bell So	3,157,700	33⅜	+ ⅝
Burrgh	3,123,600	57⅞	+ ⅜
NIndPS	2,830,800	11⅞	− 1⅜
Amrtch	2,402,100	75⅛	+ ⅜
Scovill	2,320,100	39¼	+ ¾
IBM	2,251,300	123½	− ⅛
NYNEX	2,177,600	73¼	+ .1⅝
PacTele	2,064,800	68½	+ ⅞
Mobil	2,063,200	28½	+ 1
Exxon	1,821,100	44¼	+ ⅞

MARKET DIARY

	Last Week	Prev. Week
Advances	1,063	1,343
Declines	819	663
Total Issues	2,214	2,254
New Highs	89	233
New Lows	57	106

VOLUME
(4 P.M. New York Close)

	Last Week	Year To Date
Total Sales	249,426,674	22,990,771,097
Same Per. 1983	276,597,000	21,589,576,997

E F G H

(Stock listing table — dense data, largely illegible)

THE NEW YORK TIMES, SUNDAY, DECEMBER 30, 1984

in it daily. The New York Stock Exchange is the single most visible one. In 1984, about three billion dollars worth of stocks changed hands there on an average day. The municipal bond market is medium-sized—in 1984, about three-quarters of a billion dollars traded in it per day.

We mentioned that investors can choose either equity or debt. The usual way to invest in equity is to buy common stock, each share representing the outright ownership of one fraction of a corporation. In 1984, about one-third of all new security money was spent on equities, and about two-thirds on debt. *Equities*

Investors put their money into debt securities by buying bonds and similar obligations of the Federal Government, of corporations, or of municipalities. What, exactly, are bonds? In one sense they are pieces of paper which identify the exact debt issues, the amount involved, and the holder. However, in another sense, they represent a contract between borrower and lender which specifies the sources of money pledged to repayment, the rate of interest, the rights of bond holders, and the date the debt will be repaid. This contract is the legal bond between issuer and investor, fixing their relationship until the debt is redeemed. *Debts*

To repeat, bond investors do not, like stockholders, own a part of the issuing body itself; they are simply its creditors. Owners of DuPont bonds do not benefit from chemical, or oil, prosperity, except to the extent that the company is able to pay them back. Similarly, people who buy bonds issued by the State of Alabama are just lending it some money; as creditors they expect to get it back on a certain date, with interest in the meanwhile. *Reprise*

One hundred or more different U.S. Government securities, and thousands of different corporate and municipal bonds, are available for purchase every day. After someone has decided to invest in a debt security, how does he choose among them? By finding the one whose investment properties best suit his own particular needs. We will be getting to this shortly. However, one other factor, the U.S. federal income tax, alters the choosing process, dividing the bond market into two parts, taxable and tax-exempt. *Bond Selection*

We saw that interest received on Government and corporate bonds is subject to federal income tax, and that municipals are exempt and therefore carry lower interest rates. For instance, when short-term U.S. bonds return about 8.00% and high quality corporates about 9.00%, best quality short-term municipals usually return only 5.00%. Who would be better off buying taxable bonds? Investors in low, or zero tax brackets. Since the earnings on the U.S. Steel pension funds are not taxed until distributed, their managers buy taxable, not tax-exempt, investments. Why give up *Taxables*

1983 Tax Rate Schedule

SCHEDULE X—Single Taxpayers

If line 5 is:		The tax is:	Of the amount Over—
Over—	But not Over—		
$0	$2,300	—0—	
2,300	3,400	.... 11%	$2,300
3,400	4,400	$121+13%	3,400
4,400	8,500	251+15%	4,400
8,500	10,800	866+17%	8,500
10,800	12,900	1,257+19%	10,800
12,900	15,000	1,656+21%	12,900
15,000	18,200	2,097+24%	15,000
18,200	23,500	2,865+28%	18,200
23,500	28,800	4,349+32%	23,500
28,800	34,100	6,045+36%	28,800
34,100	41,500	7,953+40%	34,100
41,500	55,300	10,913+45%	41,500
55,300	....	17,123+50%	55,300

Line 8

Interest Income

Enter your total interest income. If the total is more than $400 or you have any interest from All-Savers Certificates, first fill in Schedule B. (The instructions for Schedule B begin on page 20.)

Report any interest you received or that was credited to your account so you could withdraw it. (It does not have to be entered in your passbook.)
If you were charged a penalty for early withdrawal of your savings, see the instructions for line 27 on page 11.

Examples of Interest Income You MUST Report

Report interest from:
- Accounts (including certificates of deposit) with banks, credit unions, and savings and loan associations.
- Building and loan accounts.
- Notes, loans, and mortgages.
- Tax refunds (report only the interest on them as interest income).
- Bonds and debentures. Also arbitrage bonds issued by State and local governments after October 9, 1969. (Do not report interest on other State and local bonds and securities.)
- The discount for the part of the year you held corporate bonds or other notes first issued at a discount after May 27, 1969.
- U.S. Treasury bills.

higher rates of return for an exemption you don't need?

However, because we can't escape the fact that most income is (in 1984-1985) taxed at up to 50%, minimizing the rates can be a major money saver. One way to lower one's taxes is to invest for capital gains, because for individuals 60% of any realized gains on assets held more than six months is excluded from federal income tax. The 40% remainder is then taxable to 50%, in effect making the capital gains rate no higher than 20%. Many investors seek this and similar benefits through buying tangibles or stocks, hoping their value will rise. Other investors, however, prefer not to take the risks involved and turn to municipals for relief, lending money to our state and local governments in the process.

The Capital Gains Preference

This obvious tax advantage has created substantial demand for municipals, driving their interest rates so low that it isn't always clear when someone would benefit by buying them rather than taxables. For instance, suppose that on a certain day in April, 1983, taxable one-year maturity U.S. Government bonds were yielding 8.00%, and that similar State of North Carolina bonds were available at 5.00%. Who would have been better off buying the North Carolinas? Investors whose return on the Treasury bonds would have been reduced by taxation to under 5.00%. How do we figure this? By using the tax charts. Suppose Ms. Smithers from Greensboro, North Carolina, filing as a single individual, and having a taxable income of about $80,000, was considering investing $100,000 in either the Treasuries or the North Carolinas. Which would have given her the better income, the taxable 8.00%, or the exempt 5.00%? At $80,000 her top federal income bracket was 50%. $100,000 in Treasuries would provide her with a gross income of $8,000 ($100,000 x .08). On this she would pay 50% in federal taxes, or $4,000, and keep $4,000. However, if she had bought the North Carolina bonds, she would keep the whole 5.00%, or $5,000. So buying the municipal tax-exempt bonds would increase her spendable income by $1,000 that year, maybe enough to take her to the Caribbean for a vacation instead of Florida again.

Higher Taxable Return or Lower Tax-Exempt Return

We talked about investors who seek capital gains, but bond buyers are a different breed. For their own reasons—temperamental, budgetary, or whatever—most people buy tax-exempts to keep their principal safe, and then, after achieving this, to get the highest possible return. However, these two goals are in natural opposition to each other, for greater safety means less risk and therefore lower return; and greater return involves higher risk and less safety. Balancing risk and return is part of the art and science of recommending and buying bonds, and we have developed two specialized gauges to quantify them. The first gauge is liquidity, which measures the

Risk vs. Return

LIQUIDITY VALUE OF 1 AND 20 YEAR BONDS

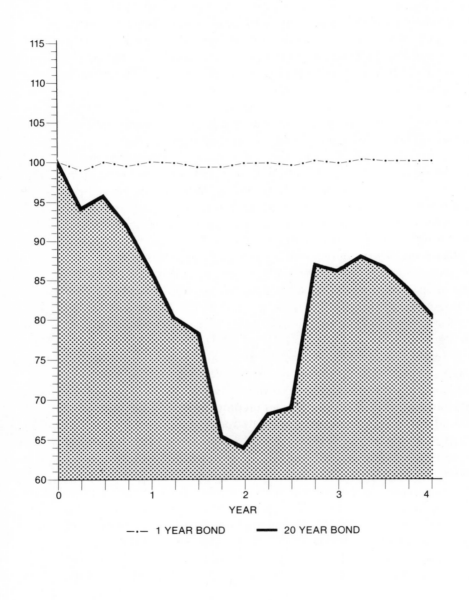

conservation of principal. The second gauge is yield, which measures the level of return.

What does liquidity mean? Cashability. Cash is a pure, face value, spendable asset. A twenty dollar bill, for instance, is 100% liquid. It can either be spent, or changed into two tens, or invested, all at face value. Slightly less liquid are U.S. Treasury bills, which are full faith and credit obligations of the United States. Several billion dollars worth of them are issued in their own market every Monday afternoon. These debt instruments seldom fall in market value by more than 1%, that is, they will stay about 99% liquid over their three or six month life, and will be redeemed at 100% of principal at maturity. Short-term municipals, called notes, provide similar liquidity.

Liquidity

We use percentages of principal amount to measure a bond's liquidity, starting at 100 for the face amount, and going down to 99, 98, 97, etc., and also up, to 104, 102, 105, etc. How is the degree of expected liquidity figured? By dividing minimum future market value by present market value. So a bond bought at 100 whose minimum expected market value over its life is 99, will provide a probable degree of liquidity of 99%. And a bond bought at 90 that now sells for 88 is in fact providing about 98% liquidity (88/90 = 97.8%). How is the minimum predicted? By referring to actual price experience under a wide range of bond market conditions. The one overriding factor is length of maturity. The degree of predictable bond liquidity of both Treasuries and municipals is usually lower on bonds with longer maturity dates, for reasons we will be examining later. Good quality five-year maturity bonds usually provide a probable minimum liquidity of 80 to 90% over their life span, and 20 to 30 year bonds usually less, ranging down to about 60 to 80%.

Dollar Prices

Why try to predict an investment's liquidity? So its cash value can be matched to obligations coming due. Suppose that in early 1983, our Ms. Smithers had received, in addition to her income, an insurance payment of $300,000, of which her accountant estimated she would owe $100,000 to the IRS the following April. We saw that at 5% the State of North Carolina bonds due 4/1/84 provided her a higher return than did U.S. Treasuries. Suppose, at the same time, that North Carolinas due in 20 years (2003) were available at a 8.50% return. Which of these two would be a more suitable investment for the $100,000 part of her cash, the one year bonds, or the long bonds? Definitely the short ones. Why? Because their liquidity characteristics matched them well to the date of her tax obligation. Even if the short-term bond market dropped by a record amount, and the value of the one year North Carolinas fell to as low as $99,000 by July '83, and to

Investing for a Specific Liquidity Need

NET MUNICIPAL BOND PURCHASES—1983
(BILLIONS OF DOLLARS)

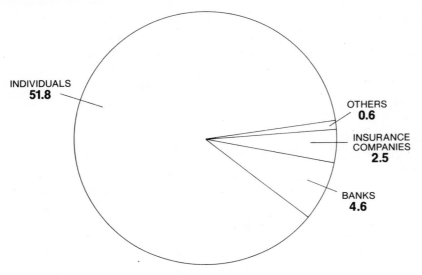

INDIVIDUALS
51.8

OTHERS
0.6

INSURANCE
COMPANIES
2.5

BANKS
4.6

HOLDERS OF MUNICIPALS—1983
(BILLIONS OF DOLLARS)

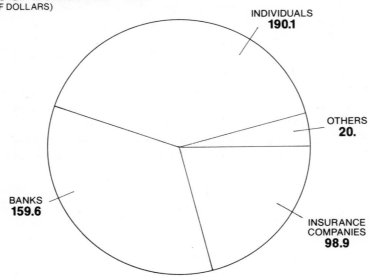

INDIVIDUALS
190.1

OTHERS
20.

BANKS
159.6

INSURANCE
COMPANIES
98.9

Source: Public Securities Association

$96,000 by August (providing 99% and 96% liquidity) they would come due at 100% on 4/1/84, in time to pay the tax due. If, instead, she had bought the long-term bonds, hard-won experience shows that within one year she could lose up to 25% of her investment, leaving her $25,000 short on taxes ($100,000 x .25, or $25,000), too high a risk for that $3,500 in extra income. Other factors, including price, credit rank, and size, also affect liquidity, but by far the most important is maturity.

Why would an investor take the chance of buying bonds with lower liquidity? Because of pressure from the other side of the investing equation—income. Generally speaking, the more liquid an investment, the lower its return; and the less liquid, the greater. In early 1983, at the same time that one-year governments were yielding 8.00%, three-year government bonds were around 9.75%, and the longest bonds at 10.50%. If an investor won't need the money in the near future, he might consider buying longer term, less liquid bonds, if they provide a sufficiently higher income. We quantify income with the second bond investing gauge, return, which expresses it in one average percentage rate, like 8.00%, 8.05%, 8.10%, 8.25%, etc. For more on yield, as we call it in municipals, see Chapter Ten.

Going back to Ms. Smithers, we saw that she invested in a one-year bond against the $100,000 tax liability. However, assuming the remaining $200,000 was relatively free of such constraints, and that her other investments were reasonably balanced, she might look around for municipals yielding more than 5.00%. If 20 year State of North Carolina bonds were available at 8.50%, she might well have bought some of these, despite their lower liquidity, in return for their higher yield. $100,000 worth would return her $8,500 per year, or $3,500 more than the short bond. And they would provide her with a far higher after-tax yield than the long governments—8.50% *versus* 5.25% (10.50% x .50 tax = 5.25%). And, if more long term municipals seemed suitable for her investment needs, the remaining $100,000 could buy other tax-frees, perhaps some medium-grade 10% bonds outside of North Carolina, to round out her portfolio. Naturally, these decisions involve other considerations, such as diversification, market strategy, and inflation hedging, but if the goals of suitable liquidity and maximized after-tax income are met, the investment battle is at least half won.

As we mentioned, commercial banks, insurance companies, and individuals are the largest classes of municipal bond buyers. We will be looking more closely at bank investors and how we sell them municipals in the second half of this book, and at insurance companies and individual investors in later volumes.

NOTICE OF BOND SALE

$3,855,000

Yelm School District No. 2
Thurston and Pierce Counties

Washington

General Obligation Bonds
Series 1982

Sealed bids will be received by the Thurston County Treasurer at his office in the County Courthouse, Administration Building (Building #1, Room #152) in Olympia, Washington, until 11:00 o'clock a.m., Pacific Daylight Time, on the

25TH DAY OF MAY, 1982

for the purchase of $3,855,000 of unlimited tax levy general obligation bonds of Yelm School District No. 2, Thurston and Pierce Counties, Washington.

Said bonds will be dated June 1, 1982, will be in the denomination of $5,000 each, will mature serially on the first day of June of the years 1984 through 2002, will bear interest at a net effective interest rate of not to exceed 16% per annum, payable on June 1, 1983, and semiannually thereafter on the first days of each June and December, and will be payable at the office of the Thurston County Treasurer in Olympia, Washington, or at the option of the holder, at either of the fiscal agencies of the State of Washington in the cities of Seattle, Washington, or New York, New York.

A good faith deposit of 5% of the principal amount of the bonds either in cash or by cashier's or certified check made payable unconditionally to the Thurstson County Treasurer for the credit of the school district must be submitted with each bid.

A copy of the official Notice of Sale and financial and statistical information regarding the school district and these bonds will be found in a report that will be furnished prospective bidders upon request made to Foster & Marshall/American Express Inc., 205 Columbia Street, Seattle, Washington 98104, financial consultants to the school district.

Said bonds will be sold with the opinion of Preston, Thorgrimson, Ellis & Holman, bond counsel of Seattle, Washington approving the legality of their issuance.

Treasurer of Thurston County,
Washington

Courtesy of *The Bond Buyer*

Chapter Three

The Issuers

The supply of money for buying municipal bonds comes from the investors; the demand for money comes from the borrowers, our state and local governments. Each public government unit, from states to sizable regional districts, like the San Francisco Bay Area Rapid Transit District (BARTS, we call their bonds), to cities large and small, down to tiny places such as Cromwell Fire District in Connecticut, provides its constituent citizens with varying forms of services and facilities. The board members of a school district, for instance, set policy for a staff of professionals, oversee the maintenance of their buildings, face and respond to public opinion, and determine future goals. Local governing bodies are also responsible for their own financial affairs, which fall into two distinct categories. One is the budgeting process—current accounts of income and expense, and their balance, which we will return to in later chapters. However, for now we are more concerned with the second category—the community borrowing process.

Local Government Responsibilities

Like most organizations, our local governments usually pay for this year's operating expenses from this year's income. However, when a substantial long-term improvement (such as a new junior high school) is needed, there are two reasons why it makes sense to borrow. First, taking out a loan to build a school or other project, and then repaying it year by year, spreads the cost of the facility over its expected life span, so those who benefit from it will pay for it. Second, communities rarely have enough cash on hand to cover large scale capital projects. Enter municipal bonds, which provide municipalities with cash to build now, and which are gradually repaid from future income.

Municipal Borrowing

The great majority of all new bond issues are sold by smaller communities like Oxford, Mississippi, or Yelm School District #2 in Washington. Towns and districts such as these, with populations under 25,000, and whose annual budgets run under $10 million, sell from as few as $100,000

Small, Occasional Issuers

BERKELEY HEIGHTS TOWNSHIP

P.O., Berkeley Heights. Located in Union County about 24 miles from New York City. Primarily residential. Area, 6.3 sq. miles.

School operates as Type II District.

Population: 1980, 12,549; 1970, 13,078.

Assessed Value, etc. ($000):

Yr.	Real Prop.	[1]Tot. Prop.	– Equalized – Value	Rate %	Tax per $1,000
[2]'83 ..	680,489	692,227	693,782	105.22	20.20
'82	258,314	259,033	655,690	41.53	50.20
'81	255,929	256,779	550,847	49.63	44.80

[1]Less exemptions. [2]Revaluation.

Bonded Debt, Sept. 30, 1982, $1,388,000.

Subsequent to above, Township sold $4,190,000 bonds dated Dec. 1, 1982.

Schedule of Bonded Debt:

Sewer

4.55s	'59	Ser. to 12- 1-92 J & D 1		$164,000
3½s	'64	Ser. to 6- 1-89 J & D 1		158,000
4⅞s	'72	Ser. to 12- 1-97 J & D 1		393,000
[1]9½	'82	Ser. to 12- 1-96 J & D 1		3,000,000

Park

3.35s	'65	Ser. to 1- 1-88 J & J 1		55,000

General Improvement

4.35s	'67	Ser. to 12- 1-86 J & D 1		95,000
4⅞s	'72	Ser. to 12- 1-92 J & D 1		548,000
[1]9½s	'82	Ser. to 12- 1-96 J & D 1		1,190,000

[1]Bonds are dated Dec. 1, 1982.

RATING: General obligations . . . . **Aa 1**

Interest Paid: At Summit and Elizabeth Trust Co., Summit.

BERLIN (Borough)

Located in Camden County. Area 3.7 sq. miles. Owns and operates sewer and water systems.

Schools operate as Type II District.

Population: 1980, 5,786; 1970, 4,997.

Assessed Value, etc. ($000):

Yr.	Real Prop.	[1]Tot. Prop.	– Equalized – Value	Rate %	Tax per $1,000
'83	90,328	94,203	134,214	70.39	40.46
'82	90,774	94,487	122,189	77.94	38.33
'81	90,314	93,836	110,561	86.05	34.36

[1]Less exemptions.

Bonded Debt, Dec. 31, 1982, $1,366,000. Due within one year, $115,000.

Subsequent to above, Borough sold $650,000 bonds dated Apr. 1, 1983.

Tax Collections, years ended Dec. 31 ($000):

Yr.	Taxes Levied	Current Coll. (Amt.)	%	Cur. & Del. Col. (Amt.)	%
'82	3,618	3,378	93.4	3,481	96.2
'81	3,240	3,083	95.1	3,220	99.4
'80	2,903	2,763	95.2	2,855	98.4

Accum. delinq., Dec. 31, 1982, $162,119. Tax title liens, $21,424.

Schedule of Bonded Debt, Dec. 31, 1982:

Water

3.20s	'62	Ser. to 11- 1-83 M & N 1		$5,000
4.10s	'66	Ser. to 4- 1-85 A & O 1		30,000
6s	'74	Ser. to 7- 1-94 J & J 1		498,000

Sewer

4.10s	'66	Ser. to 4- 1-96 A & O 1		833,000

Improvement

[1]8⅜s	'83	Ser. 4- 1-84-98 A & O 1a		650,000

[1]Bonds dated Apr. 1, 1983.

Issued subsequent to date of schedule.

RATING: General obligations . . . . **A**

Interest Paid: As follows:

a Paying agent not reported.

Other issues at Heritage Bank, Camden.

With thanks to Moody's Investors Service Inc.

up to $5 million worth of bonds at a time. The cost of repaving the streets of downtown Oxford, or even of buying a new pumper for the fire department, may be absorbed in the town's annual budget. However, major improvements, such as a new water or sewer treatment plant, usually have to be financed. Part of the money may be available in a surplus account, part may come from outside sources, but most of it has to be borrowed. This size issuer generally sells bonds for one substantial improvement at a time, once every few years.

Most bonds issued by small communities are general obligations. G.O.'s, as we call them for short, are backed by a community's full faith and credit, and all of its income resources are pledged to repay them. The largest single source of municipal income is the real estate tax, which is levied (charged) on land and buildings, based on the value of the property, and constituting a direct lien on it. So the owners of a $200,000 house will be billed about twice as much as will those of a $100,000 house, and if either fail to pay, the property can be taken by the community and sold. General obligation bonds, backed by an unconditional promise of a property-taxing local government, are strong securities indeed, and many conservative investors buy nothing else. In recent years, although G.O. sales have amounted to only about one-third of the dollar volume of new issues, they add up to over three-quarters of the total number of individual sales, because so many small issuers prefer this simple and effective method of financing. G.O.'s usually finance capital improvements which benefit the community as a whole (schools, libraries, roads, city halls and courthouses, and fire and police buildings, etc.), and they are usually sold at public competitive bidding. We will return shortly to the other type of municipal security, revenue bonds.

General Obligation Bonds

In the early planning stages of a capital project the community usually looks to higher governmental units for some financial help. Some states provide direct aid subsidizing municipal construction. State and federal grants are still available for specific types of municipal improvements, and local officials have become experts at securing them. For example, in 1982, the United States Environmental Protection Agency and the New Jersey Department of Environmental Protection paid $3 million toward improving the waste water treatment plant of Berkeley Heights, which raised the remaining $3 million by issuing general obligation bonds.

Grants and Subsidies

When a project nears the financing phase, bond experts (often volunteers from within the community, such as the local bankers) help with the technical and legal bond issuing requirements and secure the services of a lawyer called a bond counsel, to make sure the issue is validly designed.

CITY OF KENOSHA
KENOSHA COUNTY, WISCONSIN

RETIREMENT SCHEDULE OF OUTSTANDING DEBT ISSUES

Year Due	Less: Total School District & Gateway Technical Payments*#	Total Net Debt Service Requirements	General Obligation Bonds Proposed $3,810,000 Corporate Purpose Bonds, Series 1979		Total Estimated Debt Service**
			Principal	Estimated Interest @ 5.50%	
1979	$917,840.98	$4,839,487.77		$104,775.00	$4,944,262.77
1980	742,464.20	4,552,948.30	$ 35,000	209,550.00	4,797,498.30
1981	502,246.57	3,823,340.93	275,000	207,625.00	4,305,965.93
1982		2,792,000.00	500,000	192,500.00	3,484,500.00
1983		2,676,050.00	500,000	165,000.00	3,341,050.00
1984		2,525,887.50	500,000	137,500.00	3,163,387.50
1985		1,287,862.50	500,000	110,000.00	1,897,862.50
1986		1,232,687.50	500,000	82,500.00	1,815,187.50
1987		763,037.50	500,000	55,000.00	1,318,037.50
1988		435,625.00	500,000	27,500.00	963,125.00
1989					
1990					
1991					
Totals	$2,162,551.75	$24,928,927.00	$3,810,000	$1,291,950.00	$30,030,877.00

Revenue Debt***

Waterworks Mortgage Revenue Bonds		Sewer System Mortgage Revenue Bonds		Total Revenue Debt Outstanding
Principal	Interest	Principal	Interest	
$395,000	$284,727.50	$ 75,000	$35,438.75	$790,166.25
415,000	267,215.00	80,000	31,940.00	794,155.00
430,000	248,775.00	85,000	28,228.75	792,003.75
450,000	229,577.50	90,000	23,485.00	793,062.50
480,000	208,970.00	100,000	17,275.00	806,245.00
500,000	186,217.50	100,000	10,525.00	796,742.50
530,000	161,302.50	110,000	3,575.00	804,877.50
545,000	134,118.75			679,118.75
590,000	103,543.75			693,543.75
605,000	69,156.25			674,156.25
650,000	32,987.50			682,987.50
205,000	10,668.75			215,668.75
200,000	3,250.00			203,250.00
$5,995,000	$1,940,510.00	$640,000	$150,467.50	$8,725,977.50

The advisors may review the project cost, subtract the expected outside aid, figure the amount left to be borrowed, and estimate what will have to be paid for bond principal and interest. If the expense seems justified, the district or town government goes ahead with the political processes necessary for approving and selling the bonds.

Most states require their local communities to prepare projected future years' budgets estimating income and expenditures, including debt service (principal and interest requirements) for their bond issues. New issues can be structured to fit right into these projections, and are repaid serially (part every year) until the loans are liquidated.

Yearly Budgets and Serial Bonds

Once a bond issue is in rough form, the finance committee of the town council or other governing body comes to life and hears public comment. These days, the high cost of projects frequently draws citizen attention, leading to revised or scaled-down construction plans. When the amount needed to finance the project has been agreed upon, the results go back to the bond experts, who shape its final form. Then the proposed issue returns to the committee, which makes resolutions and motions by the dozen to authorize the official procedures.

The Political Process

At the appointed hour, the board or council meets to open the bids, and after consulting with the financial advisors, a vote is taken whether or not to accept the best proposal—that is, the one naming the lowest rate of interest. If the council votes to accept (as it does over 95% of the time), it formally awards the bonds. In the following weeks, bond counsel proceeds with the closing documents while the physical bonds are being printed up. Usually within a month the bonds are delivered to the bidder, the money is received, and the project goes on to construction. The finance committee then quiets down to normal, presumably with the gratitude of the community.

Ten states (Connecticut, Delaware, Maine, Maryland, Massachusetts, New Hampshire, New Jersey, New York, North Carolina and Rhode Island) only permit their communities to issue G.O.'s. The other states authorize either G.O. bonds, or, for certain kinds of projects, revenue bonds. What is different about revenues? They are municipal obligations, but unlike G.O.'s, the community does not back them unconditionally. Instead, revenue bonds are secured by one or more specific income sources. They may be secured by the net profits of a water system, or a municipal electric utility, or from hospital payments, to mention just a few usual types. These and other revenue-backed bonds are payable solely from their own streams of income, and no other receipts (such as state aid or property taxes) are committed. Their technical name—limited liability

Revenue Bonds

October 26, 1984

Glickenhaus & Company
84 William Street
New York, New York 10038

Attention: Municipal Bond Department

Gentlemen:

    The offer to purchase the $5,000,000 Dormitory Authority of the
State of New York Manhattan College Insured Revenue Bonds, Series
1984, contained in the Purchase Contract dated October 26, 1984, at
the purchase price of $4,950,000, plus accrued interest from
October 1, 1984 to the date of the Closing (as defined in such
Purchase Contract), and the Letter of Representation dated October 26,
1984 are hereby accepted.

                              Very truly yours,

                              Dormitory Authority of the
                              State of New York

                              By: _____
                                    Daniel J. Dugan
                              Deputy Executive Director, Finance

Receipt acknowledged:

Glickenhaus & Company

By: _____
    Title: _____

mlg/L

DORMITORY AUTHORITY — STATE OF NEW YORK — NORMANSKILL BLVD., ELSMERE, N.Y. 12054
CHRISTOPHER H. RICHMOND — EXECUTIVE DIRECTOR   GEORGE D. GOULD — CHAIRMAN

28

bonds—points out their main distinction from general obligations.

Most revenue bonds are sold to finance improvements used by some, but not all, of an issuer's citizens. Bills for the supplied services are sent to a project's users, rather than to the taxpayers as a whole. When, for instance, Augusta, Georgia, wished to improve its airport, it financed the project with bonds payable from 17% of the facility's gross revenues, and the city's general taxpayers were not charged. Revenue bonds can also be used to provide alternative financing when state debt laws restrict the issuance of G.O.'s, and can supply authorities and agencies with funds to subsidize certain quasi-public projects, such as housing, college or hospital construction.

Revenue Bonds for Special Purposes

All in all, borrowing by our smaller communities is an efficient and straightforward process, which is not surprising, since concerned citizens make the decisions and do most of the work themselves. Despite a few spectacular exceptions, in recent years well over 99% of all municipal issues have been paid as promptly as promised; on small G.O. issues the figure approaches 100%. If you call or visit local finance people at their job, or volunteers in their own offices, such as Darlene Matthews of Elberfeld, Indiana, you will come away with few doubts about their dedication and integrity.

One step up from the relatively tranquil world of the occasional borrowers are the medium-sized issuers: known, if not renowned, places such as Flint, Michigan; Trenton, New Jersey; or Kenosha, Wisconsin, whose more complex activities require continuous financial operations and regular bond sales. These municipalities, whose populations may run from 25,000 to 250,000, are substantial financial entities whose annual budgets may range from $10 million to $100 million. Generally, somewhat less than half of their income comes from property taxes, about one-quarter from local fees and charges, and the balance from state and federal payments. They often run diverse operations which call for financial coordination. Kenosha, in addition to its common council, has an independent school district with its own separate budget, taxes, and bond issues, and also a separately managed water and sewer system which is partly financed through revenue bonds. In more diversified communities, steering a bond issue to completion may not be all smooth sailing, as opposition and criticism surface. There may be extended discussions and revisions, and some governmental decisions may be contested in court. Where local law requires bond issues to be approved by public referendum, their course may be long and difficult.

Larger Communities

Cities and districts of medium size usually employ full-time officers

CITY OF KENOSHA
KENOSHA COUNTY, WISCONSIN

1978 ADOPTED BUDGET SUMMARY

REVENUES

Delinquent Taxes and Interest	$ 34,000.00
Shared and Other Taxes	7,556,000.00
Licenses and Permits	194,545.00
Fines and Forfeitures	294,200.00
Use of Money and Property	589,501.00
Gifts and Grants	1,150,100.00
Charges for Current Services	342,900.00
Contributions from Special Assessments	516,700.00
Miscellaneous Revenues	1,161,021.00
General Property Tax	
General Fund	8,759,000.00
Library	985,900.00
Museum	127,159.00
Total Revenues	$21,711,026.00

EXPENDITURES

General Government	$1,034,249.00
Community Development	116,697.00
Library	985,900.00
Museum	127,159.00
Public Safety	6,017,116.00
Public Works	2,802,523.00
Health	412,237.00
Park	1,017,444.00
Contribution to Other Funds	3,402,081.00
Reserves	1,048,000.00
Unclassified	33,200.00
Debt Service	4,714,420.00
Total Expenditures	$21,711,026.00

with titles such as Treasurer, Comptroller, or Director of Finance. They help put the policy decisions of the governmental body into practice, and their recommendations may determine whether a library gets a new $30,000 carpet this year, next year, or one of these years. These professionals, who have usually been trained in post-graduate schools of accounting or municipal finance, prepare preliminary budgets, take charge of community flows of income and expense, borrow and invest the unit's money for short periods of surplus or deficit, and collect information by the ream to meet the many financial information requirements of state and federal jurisdictions. The finance man also represents the city to the investing world. Take Gene Schulz, City Comptroller of Kenosha. If you wish information about his city or its bonds, you will find him knowledgeable about fiscal fundamentals and very much aware of the importance of good public relations.

The City Finance Director

In addition to their own staff, many larger communities employ outside paid financial consultants, who collect and distribute the current facts about the city's fiscal and economic status to potential investors, and take charge of the specialized task of setting up the bond sale itself. As a new issue approaches, the consultant meets with the city financial people and its lawyers, and starts to organize the data needed to present to underwriters and potential buyers. When the final bond amount is settled, he estimates what its interest rates will be, and submits a schedule of debt service for the governing body to consider. If they approve, the consultant readies the issue, and with the advice of bond counsel, usually writes up an offering prospectus detailing the economic and financial data needed in order to analyze the loan. He also uses this information to fill out the forms required by the two chief financial service companies in New York, and applies to one or both of them for a rating on the issue. Bidding specifications are written up in an official notice of sale, and the issue is advertised for a certain time and place. At sale time, the consultant presides over the opening of the bond bids, and his advice on whether or not to accept the winning bid usually decides the matter. Later, as settlement date nears, the advisor and the bond counsel attend to the necessary closing documents, and finally see to it that the proceeds are credited to the city's bank account for temporary investment.

The Financial Consultant

Still larger issuers seem to have most of the problems of the smaller cities, only many times over, and as their size increases the problems tend to grow more difficult. All of the usual responsibilities of providing essential services, like schools and water supplies, have to be met by a shifting combination of current income, state help, and bond issues. Often, the

The Largest Issuers

CAPITAL IMPROVEMENT PROGRAM

In connection with a comprehensive land use plan adopted in 1975 and its annual update, the Board of Supervisors annually approves a capital improvement program (the "CIP") for the ensuing five year period. The CIP is designed to balance the need for public facilities as expressed by the Countywide land use plan with the fiscal capability of the County to provide for those needs.

The CIP is an integral element of the County's budgeting process. The first year of the FY 1984-FY 1988 CIP will be adopted as the Approved Fiscal Plan for FY 1984. The remaining four years of the five-year document will be considered subsequently by the Board of Supervisors and serve as a general planning guide for the construction of general purpose, school and utility public facilities in the County. The CIP is updated and adopted each year. This annual review process prompts careful attention to the development of reliable capital expenditure and revenue estimates and the timely scheduling of bond referenda.

In connection with the CIP process, the Board of Supervisors has adopted certain policy guidelines to follow in formulating the CIP and the financing thereof. These guidelines include self-imposed restrictions on the issuance of general obligation bonds designed to keep General Fund-supported debt service expenditures to 10% of total General Fund expenditures, and to maintain the ratio of net bonded indebtedness to the market value of taxable property in the County at a level less than 3.0%. For the fiscal year ending June 30 ,1984, Fairfax County estimates debt service requirements will be 9.24% of total General Fund expenditures and net debt as a percentage of estimated market value of taxable property will be 1.52%. The policy guidelines also express the intent of the Board of Supervisors to encourage greater industrial development in the County and to minimize the issuance of underlying indebtedness by towns and districts located within the County.

The County projects its FY 1984-FY 1988 capital fund requirements as follows:

	Fiscal Year Ending June 30					
	1984	1985	1986	1987	1988	Total
General Obligation Bonds	$49,595,000	$69,255,000	$49,845,000	$55,340,000	$62,290,000	$286,325,000
General Fund	14,841,000	16,336,000	22,999,000	15,666,000	14,932,000	84,774,000
Revenue Sharing	1,168,000	1,168,000	1,168,000	1,168,000	1,168,000	5,840,000
Total New Funds	$65,604,000	$86,759,000	$74,012,000	$72,174,000	$78,390,000	$376,939,000

Of the $286.3 million proposed from the sale of general obligation bonds, $168.44 million have received voter approval at referendum. Future referenda will be required for $117.88 million which are proposed for sale but not yet approved.

39

peculiar problems of size begin to dominate capital needs. The extent of Washington, D.C.'s inner city and suburban development, for example, led to their partially successful Metro Transportation System solution. Fortunately, these larger issuers do have more options to work with. New York City is building a long-planned convention center; Chicago maintains an extensive park system; and New Orleans and Houston, among other cities, built sports-arena facilities. All of these were designed to attract and hold residents and business, and are financed with the help of specialized forms of municipal bonds.

As in smaller places, the community-wide service facilities of larger issuers are usually financed with G.O. bonds, so that the ordinary taxpayer pays off the general purpose debt. These issues usually come in $25 million to $250 million sizes. In 1983, when Fairfax Co., Va., sold $45 million in new bonds, they issued general obligations to finance school, park, road, library, transit facility, sewer, jail, and other kinds of general use facilities. However, more narrow, limited-purpose projects are logically financed by the sale of revenue bonds, and repaid from the income generated from them. For these construction projects, a $100 million issue may be only a start. For instance, from 1976 through 1982, the Texas Municipal Power Agency sold six issues of bonds, totaling $738 million, to finance the construction of generating facilities for Bryan, Garland, Greenville, and Denton. T-M-P-A's, as we call these bonds, are backed by charges on these communities, who in turn collect from their own customers according to how much power they use. Raising money for these more elaborate projects requires expert advice and professional financial consultants, either in-house or outside. Planning and development may proceed continuously, and a number of bond issues may be mapped out well into the future. Fairfax County schedules its levels of future spending for capital projects five years in advance, and presently plans to issue about $60 million in new G.O. bonds every year.

G.O.'s and Revs

The largest municipal units manage their money flexibly, and with increasing sophistication. In many cases, their top financial officials are a match for any corporate treasurer. And why not? They may be responsible for implementing budgets of from $200 million to many billions, and may often have $100 million or more in short-term money to invest or borrow. Not only can they sell bonds, but they may also use temporary financing techniques such as note sales to help them negotiate more effectively with their vendors, and to pry more aid from higher governmental units. They can sell short-term securities for another reason—to bridge the time gap between their income and expenses during the year. They may try to

The High-Powered Executive

33

DATE	CUSIP NO.	DEPT. NO.
ANALYST		

ISSUING ENTITY

1 ISSUER ....

2 CITY/COUNTY ....

3 IF NEW ISSUE — AMOUNT: .... SALE DATE: ....

4   MATURITY: .... CALL FEATURE: ....

5   SECURITY:..

6   PURPOSE: ....

7   ....

DEBT FACTORS

	DEBT STATEMENT	($'S IN 000'S)			FUTURE D/S REQUIREMENTS	FY END
8	G.O. BONDS OUTSTANDING	$		22	....	
9	G.O. BONDS SELLING	_____		23	....	
10	GROSS BONDED	$		24	....	
11	LESS: SINKING FUNDS	....		25	....	
12	SELF SUPPORTING	....		26	....	
13	....	....			% BOND MATURITIES (INCL. NEW ISSUES) RETIRED IN:	
14	....	_____		27	5 YEARS .... %	
15	DIRECT NET DEBT	$		28	10 YEARS .... %	
	OVERLAPPING DEBT					
	NAME NET DEBT	%				
16	....	....		29	DEBT LIMITS:	
17	....	....			....	
18	....	....			....	
19	....	....		30	% CURRENTLY USED:	
20	....	_____			....	
21	OVERALL NET DEBT	$				

SELECTOR CARD RATIOS

	GROSS DEBT	NET DEBT	OVERALL NET DEBT	O.N.D. P/C	O.N.D. % TRUE VALUE	S&P INDEX
31						

CAPITAL IMPROVEMENT PROGRAM

32 C.I.P. AVAILABLE ....

33 5 YEAR TOTAL PROGRAM (G.O. RELATED)........................... % TO BE BONDED ....

34 ALTERNATE FUNDING SOURCES: ....

    ....

    ....

    ....

This is one of the forms that the rating services use to assemble the information needed to rank issuers of G.O. Bonds.

outguess the market by scheduling bond sales in a favorable part of an interest rate cycle. If they succeed, they can lower their borrowing costs by millions of dollars.

In the past few years an increasing number of financing innovations have been developed by dealers and local finance officers. For instance, Los Angeles now borrows at low cost in the short-term market by issuing tax-exempt commercial paper, supplies some of its power needs from cheaper out-of-state sources financed with new kinds of bonds, and also leases instead of buying some of its equipment. Municipal finance officers from such issuers also try to influence investors, dealers, and the rating services by advertising the strong points of their community's bonds. The detailed financial and economic information they supply to back up their arguments makes for thick new issue prospectuses. They may also save on interest costs by using the zero coupon, buyer put option, or third-party credit enhancement techniques that have added a lot of spice to the old-fashioned municipal stew. We will be looking at these and other issuing operations later, but first, a chapter on the third factor in the primary market, the underwriting dealers.

Hyper-Modern Methods

$3,810,000
CITY OF KENOSHA
WISCONSIN

Corporate Purpose Bonds, Series 1979

SEALED BIDS will be received until 1:00 P.M., C.D.T., on

MAY 7, 1979,

in the Council Chambers Room in the Municipal Building in said City, at a rate not exceeding 7%. The bonds are general obligation bonds issued for the purpose of providing funds in the amounts and for the purposes as follows:

$105,000 for the purpose of constructing and equipping an engine house;

$420,000 for the purpose of constructing and equipping a library;

$1,515,000 for the purpose of improving and extending sanitary sewers system;

$1,315,000 for the purpose of improving and extending storm sewers; and

$455,000 for the purpose of providing street improvements.

The bonds are dated June 1, 1979 and will mature on December 1 as follows:

Year	Amount
1980	$ 35,000
1981	275,000
1982/1988	500,000

The City will provide at its expense the printed bonds and the unqualified approving opinion of Chapman and Cutler. The Official Statement, Notice of Sale and Bid Form may be obtained from the undersigned, or from First Wisconsin National Bank of Milwaukee, 777 East Wisconsin Avenue, Milwaukee, Wisconsin 53202, Attention: Kenneth A. Kerznar, Tel. 414-765-4171.

/s/ GAIL F. PROCARIONE
City Clerk
414/656-6130

Chapter Four

The Underwriters

Municipal bond underwriting is the process in which dealers buy whole new bond issues from state and local governments and then resell them in smaller blocks to investors. Almost all new issues are underwritten by syndicates, that is, temporary combinations of dealer firms set up for each particular sale. In these syndicate groups, the dealer members share the risk of buying and owning an issue, and then cooperate in distributing it to their customers, trying to make a profit on their mark-up. Municipal bond underwriters are required to join the N.A.S.D., and both individually and in syndicates operate under M.S.R.B. regulations.

Underwriting Municipals

Center stage of this primary market is held by approximately 50 bond dealers and dealer banks such as Paine Webber, E. F. Hutton, Merrill Lynch, Smith Barney, and the Chase Bank, who lead, or as we say, manage, most large underwritings. Another 100 or so medium-sized, and also about 250 smaller municipal bond firms, regularly bid on large new issues as syndicate members. The aim of all of them is the same: to make a profit by buying bonds from communities and then selling them to investors.

Managers and Members

As we outlined earlier, underwriting syndicates buy bonds either at competitive bidding or by negotiation. In a competitive sale, the governmental body structures the loan itself, and brings it to the market without involving dealers. Its financial officer, often assisted by an outside consultant, establishes bidding specifications, announces the time of sale, and invites interested parties to submit sealed bid proposals. What kinds of bonds are sold competitively? General obligations, and also revenue bonds with steady operating histories. In recent years an average week has seen about 20 new issues of over $5 million each come to market via competitive bidding.

Competitive Sales

As soon as managing dealers see a sale announced, they line up their syndicates, basing membership on historical patterns. For instance, in the Kenosha sale, all eight managers who had bid on the city's 1978 issue

Syndicate Marketing Work

```
*********************************************************************
URGENT PRIVATE SYNDICATE MESSAGE
ATT: MGR. MUN. BOND SYNDICATE DEPT.

TO ALL  SELLING GROUP MEMBERS:

                $75,700,000* COUNTY OF ERIE, NEW YORK
                GENERAL OBLIGATION BONDS - 1985


MOODY'S:  BA                    S&P:  AAA (AMBAC)

DATED:  1/15/85            FIRST COUPON:  6/15/85        DUE:  12/15

PRELIMINARY PRICING AS FOLLOWS:

MATURITY       AMOUNT#       COUPON       PRICE      CONC      ADD TKDWN

1985        $ 7500M        14.50%        5.50%      1/4       1/4
1986          11250M       14.50         6.25       3/8       3/8
1987           7100M        6.30         100        1/2       1/2
1988           7100M        6.80         100        1/2       1/2
1989           7100M        7.25         100        1/2       1/2
1990           7100M        7.50         100        1/2       1/2
1991           7100M        7.75         100        1/2       3/4
1992           7100M        8.00         100        1/2       3/4
1993           7100M        8.10         100        1/2       3/4
1994           7250M        8.20         100        1/2       3/4

*APPROXIMATE SUBJECT TO CHANGE.

NON-CALLABLE.

ORDER PERIOD UNTIL 12:00 NOON, E.S.T., TOMORROW, THURSDAY, JANUARY 31, 1985.

PLEASE ENTER ORDERS ON (212)607-5690.

THE COMPLIANCE ADDENDUM MSRB RULE G-11 WILL APPLY.

THE AWARD IS EXPECTED FEBRUARY 1, 1985.

THE DELIVERY IS EXPECTED ON OR ABOUT FEBRUARY 6, 1985.

EHRLICH BOBER
GOLDMAN, SACHS & CO.
CHEMICAL BANK
MANUFACTURERS HANOVER TRUST CO.
MERRILL LYNCH CAPITAL MARKETS
MORGAN GUARANTY TRUST CO. OF NEW YORK

BY:  EHRLICH BOBER

12:37:48PM 30 JANUARY
```

re-formed their groups, using most of the same members. Shortly before the sale, each group meets at its manager's office, where, without knowing what levels the competing accounts are considering, the syndicate members try to estimate the interest rates necessary to sell the bonds to investors. After discussion and compromise, each syndicate decides on the re-offering rates and prices, subtracts a profit margin, and then enters its proposals with the community. All the accounts present their bids simultaneously; we call the one which names the lowest interest cost the high bidder. The municipality usually votes to accept the bid and awards the bonds accordingly.

As soon as they hear that they are high, the winning account members go to work to sell, or, as we say, reoffer, the bonds at their fixed scale of interest rates. This temporary price fixing is permitted by securities laws in order to give a fair deal to both investors and syndicate members. At sale time, investor enthusiasm comes to a natural peak, and the buyers may or may not respond to the re-offering as the underwriters hope. Investors who decide to buy place their orders with account members, who enter them with the manager during a specified order period (often one hour). Afterward, the manager sorts through the orders received and allots bonds to members. New issue bonds are sold subject to the completion of legalities (when issued, or W.I.), but in practice almost all awarded deals go through as scheduled.

Purchases of most securities, stocks, for instance, are billed to customers at a certain price, plus commission. But not municipal new issues. Our customers usually buy bonds at the advertised price, net, and pay no commission. In order to make a profit on sales, members take down (buy) bonds from their accounts at the net customer price, less (minus) a discount called a takedown. If the net price is 100 (par), and the takedown is 2%, members take down bonds at 98, sell them at 100, and collect the 2% for themselves. If members enter enough orders to sell the whole issue, the account is closed and the underwriting profit is made. However, if some bonds are unsold, the manager releases a report called the run and balance, showing which bonds remain in the account, and the members continue their efforts. After a time, if some bonds still remain unsold, the group may have to cut price and make a smaller profit, or take a loss. When an account is closed it ceases to function and price restrictions are removed. The issue then leaves the primary and passes into the resale, or secondary, market, where bonds trade freely according to supply and demand. Eventually, the manager completes the bookkeeping and sends syndicate members profit checks (or bills, if there is a loss).

Selling the Bonds

Takedowns, Orders, Results

40

The other method of underwriting is by negotiated sale. Instead of working alone, the issuer develops a financing plan with a single underwriting group, led by one or more managers. This preliminary stage may take several months or even years, as engineering, political, and marketing problems are solved. When the issue nears final form, the manager applies to one or both rating agencies for a credit assessment. As sale time approaches, the manager mails out papers describing the issue's credit provisions and may conduct information meetings to further describe the issue to potential investors and to hear their reactions. When all is ready, the manager, with the issuer's permission, prices the issue, that is, sets a tentative scale of interest rates to test actual investor demand. If buyers enter orders for enough of the bonds, the manager returns to the issuer to set the final terms. If, however, the first rates fail to attract enough business, they may have to be raised in a second, or even a third, try until enough of the issue is spoken for to make underwriting it seem a good risk. Then the manager and issuer settle any remaining details, and the underwriters take on the commitment. If all goes well, the bonds are all sold to investors and the syndicate makes its profit.

Negotiated Sales

In the past few years well over half of the new issue volume has been negotiated, including almost all the big revenue bond deals. For instance, after a unique oil-handling facility—the Louisiana Offshore Oil Project— was first proposed, a new state authority was created to finance it. LOOPs (as we call the bonds), because of the elaborate contract provisions with the corporations who guarantee them, would have been impossible to sell at public bidding. However, after many months of negotiations, a First Boston Corp. group brought the deal to market and the $450 million underwriting went smoothly.

Trends

For municipal issuers, bond flotations are the cheapest source of one of the supplies they regularly need—money to build public facilities. From the saver-investor's point of view, they are a major source of high after-tax income. Dealers have an entirely different perspective—the new issue market is one field on which their battle for profits can be won. How much gross profit do underwriters make? Overall, about 2% of the principal amount, of which something like 90% goes to pay expenses, leaving about $2 as their net profit for each $1,000 underwritten. So if a company underwrites $1 million on an average business day, giving it a gross margin of $20,000, and if 10% remains after expenses, its underwriting department will produce a yearly profit of half a million dollars. Where do all the expenses come from? Commissions to sales people, salaries to staff, operating overhead, service fees, and communications, among other items.

The Dealers and Their Sales Forces

CHEMICAL BANK

†●   20 Pine Street, 15th Floor 10005
MUNICIPAL DEALER DEPARTMENT
Ronald E. Curvin, V.Pres., D.H., 212-820-6148; Paula Shoneman, Secretary, 212-820-5801
BOND TRADING, 212-820-6145; Thomas J. Lynch Jr., V.Pres.-Long Bonds; David W. Frank, Asst.V.Pres.-General Market; James S. Wilson, Asst.V.Pres.-General Market; Christopher J. Gaertner, Asst. V.Pres.-NY State; Nancy Tuttle, NY State
NOTE TRADING AND UNDERWRITING: Elaine M. Brennan, V.Pres.; Kyle B. Pulling, A.S.; Kathleen Cominskey; J. Patrick Dean
UNDERWRITING, 212-820-6155; John B. Esau, V.Pres. & Mgr.; J. Alex Kerr, Asst.V.Pres.; Arthur DiLegge, Asst.V. Pres.; Jo-Ann Gallerstein, A.M.; Helen Maloney
MONEY CENTER INSTITUTIONAL SALES; Peter Duffy, V.Pres. & Mgr., 212-820-6171
REGIONAL INSTITUTIONAL SALES: Douglas A. Schmitt, V. Pres. & Mgr., 212-820-6169
DEALER SALES: Michael M. Zee, V.Pres. & Mgr.; Valerie Okon; Dudley MacFarlane, A.M., 212-820-6171
RETAIL SALES: George Kotsonis, V.P. & Mgr., 212-820-6191
RETAIL SALES LIAISON: Jean M. Bougades, 212-820-5066
COMPLIANCE: John T. Hudson, A.S., 212-820-5701
PUBLIC FINANCE: Herman R. Charbonneau, V.Pres., 212-770-2311
John F. Wallace III, Asst.V.Pres.; Edward L. Prince, Asst.V.Pres.; Steven J. Chilton, Asst.V.Pres.; Michael A. McKinnon, Asst.V.Pres.; Jerome A. Kalmus, A.S.; William R. Lacy; Hunter Holding, 212-820-5850
PUBLIC FINANCE ADMINISTRATIVE SUPPORT: Margareth Caballero, O.A., 212-820-5851
MUNICIPAL CREDIT ANALYSIS: Elsie T. Smith, A.V.P., 212-770-1182; Edward A. Rabson, A.V.P., 212-770-1829; Joseph M. Donatacci, A.S., 212-770-3077; Joseph L. Lebenson, A.S., 212-770-3078; James M. Beck, A.M., 212-770-3417; Martha E. Staudt, A.M., 212-770-1892; William R. Fasciano, M.A., 212-770-

Continued on page 288

Continued from page 286
3033; James L. McGrane, M.A., 212-770-1596
DEALER ADMINISTRATIVE SUPPORT: Adele Pilch, A.V.P., 212-820-5800; Lorri J. Yackley, A.S., 212-820-5801; Joe Torres, 212-820-5802
Fails: Aida Reyes, 212-820-5804
BOND CLEARANCE DEPARTMENT: Joseph A. Horvath, A.V.P., 212-820-5789
CONFIRMATIONS & COMPARISONS: P&S Department, 212-820-5798, Room 428, 55 Water Street, N.Y., N.Y. 10041
Tax I.D. No.: 13-6208535

CITIBANK, N.A., CAPITAL MARKETS GROUP

●   55 Water Street 10043
MONEY MARKET DIVISION: Mark F. Keesenich, Jr., Sr.V.Pres., 212-668-3851; Richard Kezer, Sr.V.Pres., 212-668-3719; Richard W. Stuart, V.Pres., 212-668-3778
TAX-EXEMPT SECURITIES
Trading & Underwriting: Peter M. Sughrue, V.Pres., 212-668-3616
Note Trading & Underwriting: Michele L. Smith, V.Pres., 212-668-3615; William P. Connelly, Jr., Asst.V.Pres., 212-668-3618; Deborah A. King, Mgr., 212-668-3617; Ann Carlston, Asst. Mgr., 212-668-3625
Bond Trading: Joseph J. Petrelli, V.Pres., 212-668-3614
Peter C. Barnes, Mgr., 212-668-3625; Timothy H. Thornton, Mgr., 212-668-3620; Brian Austin, 212-668-3613; Charles White, 212-668-3624
Bond Underwriting: John W. Young, II, V.Pres., 212-668-3619; William Ludolph, V.Pres., 212-668-3611
Syndicate Support: Margaret H. McAuliffe, Asst.V.Pres., 212-668-3621; Wanda Peri, Asst.V.Pres., 212-668-3622; Kenneth T. Stiers, Asst.V.Pres., 212-668-3873
TAX-EXEMPT SECURITIES SALES: Vincent A. Matrone, V. Pres., 212-668-3737
Financial Institutions: Anthony X. Morell, V.Pres., 212-668-3680; James H. Allen, V.Pres., 212-668-3701; John F. McCormack, V.Pres., 212-668-3678; Angela P. Policriti, V.Pres., 212-668-3713
Money Managers: N. Anthony Werner, V.Pres., 212-668-3705; Jon H. Hammond, V.Pres., 212-668-3692; Maria L. Reynolds, Asst.V.Pres., 212-668-3685; Roger Quinn, Asst.V.Pres., 212-668-

In 1984, about 5,000 people worked in municipal underwriting, about one half of them in sales. As in most businesses, we pay salesmen by actual production, so that the more bonds they sell, the more they earn. Beginners now start at about $20,000 a year, and if successful, within a few years may reach the annual level that is often considered the mark of a good salesman—$100,000. However, it's not an easy life.

As we noted, there are around 400 investment dealers who regularly underwrite municipal bond issues. The new issue departments of the largest managing firms (located mostly in New York) each have 100 or more employees and as many as ten committing underwriters who actually decide which and how many bonds their firms will buy and sell, and at what prices. Committers' annual salaries averaged about $60,000 in 1984, lower among less experienced people, and sometimes much higher with the most successful. Salary accounts for most of their income; but additional compensation such as bonuses may, in a good year, add considerably to the salary base. A beginner who started after college at $15,000 to $20,000 might be earning $30,000 within three years, and expect to be making around $100,000 per year, if she, or he, after five to ten years, comes to head a reasonably successful department. *Personnel-Underwriters*

Each underwriter is backed by other people who provide needed support. They keep the syndicate files up-to-date, compile a detailed list of the week's calendar of new issues, record new issue scale prices and distribute them to the sales force, enter and confirm orders, and attend preliminary syndicate meetings. A starting salary for this assisting position may be quite low—around $15,000, or even less, when, for example, a promising office temp is hired permanently. Syndicate departments also have their clerical and secretarial staffs, whose salaries match those in similar Wall Street positions. *Support Staff*

Although many underwriters work almost exclusively in competitive new issues, many others, like Tom Metallo of Glickenhaus & Co., also work in municipal finance, helping to market negotiated issues. Some also operate in the secondary markets, trading new issue bonds recently released from syndicates. All in all, underwriting is a varied and challenging job, and offers multiple possibilities for profit and satisfaction. And it's not small, either. $100 billion worth of new issues a year amounts to over 2½% of the whole gross national product, provides about half the funds needed for municipal construction, and sends almost $2 billion of gross income our way. *The Underwriter's Career*

DESCRIPTION

The City of Kenosha is located in south-eastern Wisconsin on the western shores of Lake Michigan. Kenosha is approximately 35 miles south of Milwaukee and 55 miles north of Chicago. Kenosha encompasses 14 square miles in Kenosha County which has approximately 273 square miles. Kenosha is the County Seat.

Kenosha has diversified industry and much of the success of Kenosha's industrial development may be attributed to the City's ideal position between the Milwaukee and Chicago areas. Although Kenosha was founded on the shores of Lake Michigan, the lake itself has played a relatively minor role in Kenosha's short-lived industrialization. Kenosha made a swift transition from a small town to a major industrial establishment in less than fifty years. The following firms employ the largest number of employees in the City of Kenosha: American Motors Corporation, Anaconda Company – Brass Division, Eaton Corporation – Dynamatic Division, C & H Products, Inc., Jockey International, Inc., Kenosha Auto Transit Corp., Kohler Co., LeBlanc Corporation, Macwhyte Wire Rope Company, Montgomery Ward & Co., Inc., Ocean Spray Cranberries, Inc., Piggly Wiggly, Sears Roebuck & Co., and Snap-On Tools Corporation.

Some of the largest employers located within the City and their 1977 Equalized Valuations are: American Motors Corporation–$59,467,597; Anaconda Company–Brass Division–$12,997; Snap-On Tools Corporation–$11,899; Eaton Corporation–$11,991,878; Ocean Spray Cranberries, Inc.–$8,486,966; Jockey International, Inc.–$7,664,785; Macwhyte Wire Rope Company–$7,413,955; Frand J Newell & W.–$7,247,564; Vlad Building Company–$5,655,899; C. LeBlanc Corporation–$5,604,764; Charles Vaurus–$4,987,209.

Interstate Highway 94 connects Kenosha with the four corners of the United States by bus, truck, automobile and air. Transportation is also provided by major airlines and Kenosha is only 40 miles from Chicago's O'Hare International, the busiest airport in the world.

TAX RECORD		(FISCAL YEAR					)
COLLECTION YEAR	TAX LEVY	END OF YEAR OF LEVY	%	COLLECTED OR UNCOLLECTED AT	1/1/1979	%	
1975	$ 21,608,524.66	$ 389,010.57	1.80%	$ 30,005.76	0.14%		
1976	25,210,773.96	445,068.64	1.77%	63,127.53	0.29%		
1977	28,119,484.24	536,635.96	1.91%	115,074.42	0.41%		
1978	28,213,806.94	445,286.97	1.58%	206,321.92	0.73%		
1979	29,140,220.26	2,883,781.79	9.90%	In Process of Collection			

NOTE: The City of Kenosha collects its own taxes until July 31 and then turns them over to Kenosha County for collection. The taxes can be paid in three installments (1/3 due January 30, 1/3 due April 30 and 1/3 due July 31). The County reimburses the City 100% after July 31 of each year for uncollected real estate and special assessment taxes. The bonded special assessment taxes are held in trust and reimbursed as they are paid. The City of Kenosha collects its own personal property taxes.

FINANCIAL STATEMENT AS OF April 1 19 79 POP 19 70 PER CENSUS 78,817 EST 80,889 (1976)

EQUALIZED ASSESSED VALUATION (ESTIMATED) (1976)		$ 1,106,253,320.00
ASSESSED VALUATION, 1978	108.33 % OF EQUALIZED ASSESSED	$ 1,145,117,957.00
REAL PROPERTY	$	
PERSONAL PROPERTY		
SPEC. FRANCHISES, ETC.		
TOTAL FUNDED DEBT INCLUDING THIS ISSUE		$ 23,122,613.72
LESS SINKING FUNDS 400,000.00 (See Note Below) SINKING FUND (WATER EXCLUDED) $ 2,396,000.00		2,796,000.00
NET FUNDED DEBT (1.77 % OF ASSESSED; $ 251.27 PER CAPITA)		$ 20,326,613.72
FLOATING DEBT (TAX ANTIC. NOTES, ETC.) (NOT INCL. ABOVE)		$ –0–
OVERLAPPING DEBT		$ 14,855,428.16
COMBINED NET DEBT ($ 434.92 PER CAPITA) (3.17 % OF EQUALIZED ASSESSED)		$ 35,180,041.88

REMARKS:

NOTE: On February 12, 1979 the City of Kenosha borrowed $400,000 for the benefit of the Kenosha Water Utility. This loan will be repaid from proceeds of the Waterworks Revenue Issue selling June 18, 1979.

Courtesy of *The Bond Buyer*

Chapter Five

G.O. Bond Credit Analysis
Part 1—General and Legal

Now that we have an idea how municipal investors, issuers, and underwriters operate, let's take a closer look at bonds themselves. In Chapter Three we discussed how municipalities issue general obligations backed by their full faith and credit—as unconditional promises to repay, with no ifs, ands, or buts. However, since G.O. issuers come in widely different sizes and degrees of financial power, their bonds vary sharply in credit quality. The job of bond analysis is to distinguish between stronger and weaker credits, estimating the probability that a particular bond will return principal and pay interest as promised. Before delving into a G.O. issuer's assets and liabilities, we have to take two preliminary steps. First, we must determine that the bond in question represents a legal, enforceable debt, payable from all the issuer's resources, including taxes on real property. Second, we must determine that its interest is exempt from federal income tax. After these criteria are satisfied, we then go on to examine the issuer's assets—economic, social, political, and financial—in order to arrive at an overall asset judgment. Next, we look at the liability side, especially the amount of debt the municipality has outstanding. Finally, we weigh assets against liabilities. If the assets seem substantially greater, we give the bonds a high ranking. If the liabilities appear heavier, for example if the community has an especially high debt load, we give them a lower ranking. *The First Steps*

Who actually does all this research? Municipal bond analysts employed by investors, dealers, and financial service companies. Large investors like Citibank, the Fidelity Fund, and the St. Paul Insurance Companies maintain their own municipal research departments to approve or disapprove bonds their investment people may buy. Many dealers also employ research staffs to develop individual credit opinions and make appraisals of classes of bonds (like public power or housing bonds) in order to help their sales forces influence customers. Finally, two proprietary financial service organizations, Moody's Investors Service, Inc. and Standard & Poor's Cor- *The Searchers*

MUNICIPAL BOND ATTORNEYS
OF THE
UNITED STATES

This list of attorneys is published for the convenience of municipal bond dealers, investors and other interested parties. To be eligible for listing, a bond counsel firm must have rendered, according to The Bond Buyer records, a sole legal opinion in connection with the sale of state and municipal bonds (short-term issues excluded) during the two-year period preceding publication of this directory. The legal opinion rendered may be on either publicly offered or privately placed bond issues. Attorneys acting as counsel to the underwriter do not qualify. No other representation is expressed or implied by The Bond Buyer. The following list of attorneys should not necessarily be presumed to be a complete list at the time of publication.

ALABAMA

Birmingham, AL

BALCH, BINGHAM, BAKER, HAWTHORNE, WILLIAMS & WARD
(Formerly Martin Balch Bingham Hawthorne & Williams)
(S Eason Balch, John Bingham, Schuyler A Baker, William J Ward, A Key Foster, Jr, Edward S Allen, Walter M Beale Jr, J Foster Clark, Frank H Hawthorne, Montgomery Office, Richard L Pearson)
600 North 18th St
Tel 205-251-8100
Birmingham, AL 35203

BRADLEY, ARANT, ROSE & WHITE
(Formerly White Bradley, Arant, All & Rose)
(Ellene Winn, John P Adams, John T Andrews Jr, John G Harrell, P Nicholas Greenwood, Alan K Zeigler, John K Molen)
1400 Park Place Tower
Tel 205-252-4500
Birmingham, AL 35203

CABANISS, JOHNSTON, GARDNER, DUMAS & O'NEAL
(Formerly Dumas O'Neal & Hayes)
(Lawrence Dumas, Jr, M Camper O'Neal, Robert H Walston, Charles L Hayes, Lawrence Dumas III, James L Birchall, J Hobson Presley Jr, J M Breckenridge)
1900 First National-Southern Natural Bldg
Tel 205-252-8800
Birmingham AL 35203

JOHNSON & THORINGTON
(Also see Johnson & Thorington Montgomery AL)
(Joseph H Johnson, Jr, David W Spurlock)
920 First Alabama Bank Building
Tel 205-326-0990
Birmingham, AL 35203

LANGE, SIMPSON, ROBINSON & SOMERVILLE
(John E Grenier, C John Holditch, Samuel E Upchurch, Jr)
1700 First Alabama Bank Building
Tel 205-252-7000
Birmingham, AL 35203

NORTH HASKELL SLAUGHTER YOUNG & LEWIS PROFESSIONAL ASSOCIATION
(James L North, Wyatt R Haskell, William M 'Slaughter, J Brooke Johnston Jr, Meade Whitaker Jr, Robert E L Garner, A Lee Martin Jr, E Alston Ray, Mark E Ezell)
1710 First National-Southern Natural Build~g
Tel 205-252-8847
Birmingham AL 35203

SIROTE, PERMUTT, FRIEND, FRIEDMAN, HELD & APOLINSKY, P.A.
(Donald B Henderson, Jr.)
2222 Arlington Avenue South
Tel 205-933-7111
Birmingham, AL 35255

THOMAS, TALIAFERRO, FORMAN, BURR & MURRAY
(Joseph G Stewart, Eric L Carlton, George M Taylor III)
1600 Bank for Savings Bldg
Tel 205-251-3000
Birmingham, AL 35203

Huntsville, AL

CLEARY, LEE, EVANS, ROWE & BAILEY
(James R Cleary)
P O Box 65 300 Clinton Ave West
Tel 205-533-9025
Huntsville AL 35804

JACK GILES, ATTORNEY AT LAW
(Jack Giles)
211 Randolph Avenue
Huntsville AL 25801

Mobile, AL

WILKINS & DRUHAN
(J Michael Druhan, Jr, Robert B Wilkins)
Hannah Houses, 157-159 North Conception St, P O Box 154
Tel 205-432-0738
Mobile AL 36601

poration, grade thousands of municipal and other bonds, and also publish their conclusions on a wide range of credit topics. There are presently about 500 people working full-time in the analytical end of our business. Starting salaries range from $20,000 to $30,000 a year, and an experienced person can earn well over $50,000, so you can see that we take research seriously.

However, don't jump to the conclusion that credit analysis sets bond prices. Bond prices and interest rates are determined by investor demand interacting with current supply; analytic work is one of the factors that make up the demand. The detailed tools available to measure revenue bonds often make judging their quality seem quite scientific. However, although research can help influence investors' views on a G.O., its effects appear more slowly and uncertainly. G.O.'s are inherently harder to evaluate than revs, and the demand for them is largely governed by existing attitudes. In other words, the ranking of G.O.'s is formed chiefly through experience, while revenue bonds are subject to more rational review.

Prices and Quality

As noted, the first step of research is to make sure that the bond in question is validly issued. Back in the dim days of the 1800's many carelessly designed local bonds for speculative real estate ventures were sold to the public. Later, when times turned rough, some municipalities repudiated these debts, leaving their owners holding worthless pieces of paper. Investors soon learned to demand legally sound obligations for their money, and municipal bonds are now issued in accordance with specific state bond laws, the enabling legislation. When the city of Kenosha, Wisconsin, was planning the 1979 issue we mentioned earlier, it followed Article XI, Section 3, of the Wisconsin constitution, which authorizes municipalities to issue G.O. bonds. Under this Article, the Wisconsin State Legislature, in 1971, passed section .05, "Bond Issues: Procedures" of Chapter 67 ("Municipal Borrowing and Municipal Bonds") to establish the exact procedures for localities in that state to follow when issuing bonds. So the State Constitution (Article XI) authorized its communities to borrow, the enabling legislation (Chapter 67) spelled out the issuing rules, and Kenosha sold the bonds accordingly. In practice, Kenosha employed a specialized lawyer, called a bond counsel, to see that its issue was designed correctly. We will return to see how the city, its financial advisor, and its bond counsel put that issue together.

Binding Obligations

Few analysts take the trouble to examine the underlying documents authorizing an issue, and for most purposes, a recognized bond attorney's approval, summarized by the issuance of a formal Legal Opinion, is good enough. The usual opinion describes the issue exactly, identifying its purpose, maturities, and call features. It briefly describes the bond's security,

The L.O.

47

LEGAL OPINION

regarding
$3,810,000
CORPORATE PURPOSE BONDS, SERIES 1979
of the
CITY OF KENOSHA, KENOSHA COUNTY, WISCONSIN

The bonds are dated June 1, 1979; are of $5,000 denomination; are numbered 1 to 762, inclusive; mature serially without option of prior redemption on December 1 of each year and bear interest payable December 1, 1979 and semiannually thereafter at rates per annum, as follows:

Year	Amount	Interest Rate
1980	$ 35,000	6.75%
1981	275,000	6.75%
1982	500,000	6.40%
1983	500,000	5.30%
1984	500,000	5.40%
1985	500,000	5.40%
1986	500,000	5.40%
1987	500,000	5.40%
1988	500,000	5.50%

We have examined the documents which we deem pertinent to the validity of said bonds, including the certified record evidencing the authorization of said bonds by the Common Council of said city. On the basis of such examination we are of the opinion that said bonds have been lawfully authorized and issued under the laws of the State of Wisconsin; that they are the lawful and enforceable obligations of said city in accordance with their terms; that they are payable from taxes to be levied on all taxable property in said city, without limitation as to rate or amount; and that executed bond number one of said issue, which we have examined, is in proper form.

It is also our opinion, based on existing laws, regulations, decisions and interpretations, that interest on said bonds is exempt from present Federal Income Taxes.

CHAPMAN AND CUTLER

It is hereby certified that the foregoing is a correct and complete copy of the text of the legal opinion of Chapman and Cutler, Chicago, Illinois, regarding the issue of which the within bond is one, the original of which opinion was manually executed, dated and issued as of the date of the delivery of and payment for said bonds.

Geo. F. Pressine

City Clerk

whether general obligation or revenue, from what source it is payable, and with what limitations. This description is followed by two central statements. The approving law firm puts its weight behind its opinion that the bonds are 1.) Valid and binding enforceable obligations of the issuer, and that 2.) The interest to be paid is exempt from U.S. income tax. One member of the law firm signs the opinion and a copy is printed on the back of each bond. Up to 1960, copies of legals were simply stapled to the physical bonds, but attached or printed, a legal opinion must accompany a bond to qualify it for good delivery.

The legal side of municipal issuance meets high standards—only the notorious Washington Public Power Supply System bonds come to mind as an example of investors being harmed by buying invalidly issued bonds, and that is a continuing revenue bond story all its own. Facing presents a copy of the Kenosha L.O. No doubt this sight would have pleased Will Rogers, who said, "It's not the return *on* my principal that concerns me, it's the return *of* my principal." As you see, the decision on a bond's legality is a yes/no, go/no-go matter. When we are sure that an issue is a valid, tax-exempt obligation, it can undergo further research and then proceed to market.

City of Kenosha
Kenosha County, Wisconsin

1978 ASSESSMENT REPORT

Real Estate:	Assessed Value	Equalized Value	Ratio
Residential	$743,047,500	$710,505,700	
Mercantile	183,663,900	183,963,100	
Manufacturing	84,003,900	82,181,300	
Agricultural			
Swamp and Wasteland			
Forest Land			
Total Real Estate	1,010,715,300	976,650,100	103.49%
Personal Property:			
Merchants' Stock	15,760,920	15,764,980	
Manufacturers' Stock	80,607,037	78,154,210	
Machinery, Tools and Patterns	8,800,820	8,725,900	
Furniture, Fixtures and Equipment	25,403,930	25,177,340	
Steamboats and Other Watercraft	40,590	40,400	
All Other Personal Property	3,789,860	3,740,390	
Total Personal Property	134,402,257	131,603,220	102.87%
Total Real Estate and Personal Property	1,145,117,557	1,108,253,320	103.33%

Breakdown of Equalized Valuation

Category	Valuation	Percent of Total
Residential	$710,505,700	64.11%
Mercantile	199,728,080	18.02%
Manufacturing	194,238,750	17.53%
Agricultural		
Other	3,780,790	.34%
	$1,108,253,320	100.00%

Chapter Six

G.O. Bond Credit Analysis
Part 2—Real Estate Values

There are two distinct parts to analyzing the economic side of a G.O. issuer: weighing its real estate values; and investigating its overall economic health, that is, the levels of income and wealth of its citizens and businesses. This division ties into the main sources of local governments' income: real estate and personal property taxes; and fees, income, and other taxes. First let's spend some time on real estate, and then go on to broader municipal economics.

Property and Economics

The job of local governments is to provide the services and facilities which we, the people, need but cannot supply ourselves, such as schooling children or constructing a sewer system. Some small governmental units, the Montecito County Water District, California, for example, supply limited services to people in certain areas. But general purpose government bodies like the city of Kenosha meet a wider range of needs, from maintaining streets and sidewalks to operating hospitals and community colleges. One level higher are our state governments, which concentrate on regional services, like providing higher education facilities, protecting the environment, and running comprehensive health and social programs. Nationwide matters, such as regulating commerce and communications and conducting foreign affairs, are the Federal Government's business, and lie outside state and local government spheres.

Local Government Function

Towns and cities have one ready source of income to pay for the services they supply, the real estate tax, which provides about half of all their income. Through it, property owners are charged an annual tax based on their real estate assets. Most municipalities have a tax assessor, who assesses, or estimates, the dollar value of individual parcels of land and buildings. Then each year the governing body votes one or more tax rates against the assessments. Bond lawyers call this an *ad valorem* (according to the value) tax. For example, in 1978 Kenosha had assessed every house, store, and factory in the city. Then the city, and several overlapping districts,

Tax Assessments

City of Kenosha
Kenosha County, Wisconsin

Year	Assessed Valuation	Equalized Valuation
1978	$1,145,117,557	1,108,253,320
1977	1,115,850,620*	1,048,203,800
1976	497,358,580	941,713,900
1975	498,141,190	871,006,680
1974	493,168,035	748,356,670
1973	513,858,938	676,603,000
1972	503,012,000	600,868,000
1971	503,146,600	571,997,000
1970	497,851,900	553,234,400
1969	482,998,400	524,695,550
1968	483,819,000	535,113,300

* Re-assessment

applied a combined tax rate of 2.152% to each assessment, and bills were sent out to the property owners, due in equal installments in January, April, and July. So if in one block there were four houses assessed at $40,000, $50,000, $60,000 and $70,000, and one store on the corner assessed at $100,000, they would each owe 2.152% of their assessments, or $860.80, $1,076.00, $1,291.20, $1,506.40, and $2,152.00, respectively.

Assessed valuation (A.V.) is the figure municipalities use to determine tax bills. However, A.V. is not the same as market value; in practice, it is usually lower. The assessed value of a home which just sold for $100,000 might range from $20,000 to $75,000 in different states, with something like $50,000 being the national mean. So if a $100,000 house is assessed at 35% of its worth, its A.V. would be $35,000. (Facing shows that Kenosha's yearly increase in A.V. averaged about 8.5% per year, a strong and healthy rate.) Back in 1978, Kenosha's total assessed valuation was $1.145 billion. This produced a levy (total billing) of $28 million, or 38% of the city's income that year. The old statistic most often used to compare communities' relative debt loads was B.D./A.V., or bonded debt divided by assessed valuation. In 1978, Kenosha's figure was 2% ($23 million debt divided by $1.145 billion A.V.), quite a low number. By comparison, Aaa rated Milwaukee's number was 1.9% and Aa rated Chicago's 5.7%. One related statistic—about 66% of Kenoshaites owned their own homes, considerably above the U.S. average.

Assessed Valuation

Assessed value is mentioned in most G.O. bond analyses, but since its basis varies from place to place, municipal researchers prefer a different standard, estimated true value, or the actual market worth of the property. So, the E.T.V. of a house which recently sold for $100,000 would be about $100,000. In Kenosha, the assessments were very close to actual market value, and so we use its A.V. as the E.T.V., a relatively rare exception to the general rule. Notice that estimated true value is strictly an analytical tool; using it does not change assessments or the tax rates. E.T.V. is one part of our single most useful G.O. bond statistic: the ratio of the community's bonded debt to its estimated true value, B.D/E.T.V. Dividing what is owed by what is owned provides a clear basis for measuring the debt load of a community, and for comparing it with others. The lower the percentage, the better the bond should be.[1]

Estimated True Value

You can see on page 54 that after the $3.810 million issue was sold,

---

(1) Equalized valuation is a variant of true valuation. Most states provide financial aid to their communities according to political realities, and one factor in calculating the amounts of aid is a formula which converts true value to E.V. In Kenosha's case, A.V. was 103% of equalized valuation.

Kenosha County Debt In Process of Issuance (dated 4-1-79, date of sale 4-3-79)	$10,000,000.00	
City of Kenosha Share of Debt		$5,406,400.00
Kenosha Unified School District No. 1 Debt	$12,992,941.96 (See Note 2)	
Less: 1979 Sinking Funds	459,000.00	
	$12,533,941.96	
City of Kenosha Share of Debt		$9,295,171.36
Gateway VTAE District Debt	$785,000.00 (See Note 3)	
Less: 1979 Sinking Funds	160,000.00	
	$625,000.00	
City of Kenosha Share of Debt		$105,875.00
Total Overlapping Debt		$14,855,428.16
Net Direct and Overlapping Debt After Issuance of Bonds		$35,180,041.88
Net Direct and Overlapping Debt Per Capita		$434.92
Ratio of Net Direct and Overlapping Debt to Equalized Valuation		3.17%
Debt Limit Remaining After This Issue		$35,088,052.28
Percent of Debt Limit Remaining		63.32%

General Obligation Debt: As of April 1, 1979

Gross General Obligation Debt Outstanding

Promissory Note	$ 400,000.00 (See Note 1)	
Notes	10,500.00	
Bonds	20,955,000.00	
	$21,365,500.00	
Less: 1979 Sinking Funds	$ 2,398,000.00	
Promissory Note to be repaid by Water Utility with proceeds of Water Revenue Issue	400,000.00 (See Note 1)	
School District Portion of Debt	1,417,886.28 (See Note 2)	
Gateway Technical Portion of Debt	635,000.00 (See Note 3)	
Net Direct Debt		$16,514,613.72
Estimated Population, 1978		80,889
Net Direct Debt Per Capita		$204.16
Ratio of Net Direct Debt to Equalized Valuation		1.49%
Mortgage Revenue Debt	$6,165,000.00 (See Note 4)	
Authorized New Issue		$3,810,000.00
Total Net Direct Debt After Issuance of Bonds		$20,324,613.72
Net Direct Debt Per Capita		$251.27
Ratio of Net Direct Debt to Equalized Valuation		1.83%

Kenosha's net direct debt would be $20.324 million. This figure divided by the E.T.V. gives a ratio of bonded debt (B.D.) to E.T.V. of under 2.0%, a relatively low figure. However, this statistic does not tell the whole story, any more than merely listing one's mortgage debts provides sufficient credit information for a bank loan. The people of Kenosha were also responsible for 74% of Kenosha's independent school districts' debt and for 54.1% of Kenosha County's debt. When these debts, which also had a claim on the real estate tax base of the city, were added in, Kenosha's total bonded debt, including its share of their overlapping bonds, amounted to $35 million. This total bonded debt divided by the E.T.V. came to about 3.2%. In the same year, the average figure in Wisconsin was about 4.5%, and for the U.S. as a whole about the same, so Kenosha's ratio was significantly lower, and therefore better, than that of most American cities.

To measure the debt burden of an issuer in another way, we often use the per capita bonded debt, or B.D./Population. Kenosha's number in 1979 was somewhat lower than the national average of about $500. We sometimes use another measure to compare the per capita property value. This per-person value is calculated by dividing true value by population. Kenosha's A.V. of $1.145 billion divided by its 1978 estimated 80,889 population came to $14,155. Wisconsin's per capita property value was $15,500, and the U.S. average about $17,000. How would you summarize Kenosha's real property assets at that time? If you said they showed a steady growth pattern, at a level near the middle range of all American cities, I would agree.

Per Capita Values

Over 80% of all houses and apartment buildings in the U.S.A. are mortgaged, and real estate taxes are usually included in the monthly payments. For both positive and negative reasons, people tend to feel strongly about their mortgage liabilities. On the one hand, paying for one's home is a natural source of pride. On the other hand, failure to meet the required payments has serious consequences. If a home or apartment building owner fails to pay his real estate taxes, the municipality automatically acquires a lien on the property. After a specified time, the municipality can seize the property and sell it to satisfy its claim of unpaid taxes, evicting the owner in the process. Real estate taxes are not easy to avoid or evade, and collecting them is a straightforward process, with the property a hostage asset. So it is no wonder that bonds backed by the real estate of healthy communities warm the hearts of conservative local investors, the chief buyers of G.O. bonds. That finishes property values for the moment, and now on to municipal economics.

Pay the Mortgage, Sam

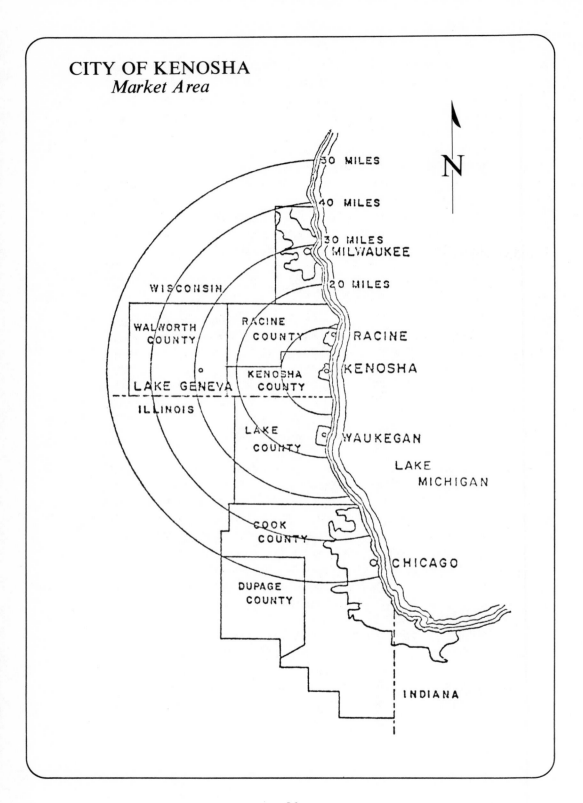

CITY OF KENOSHA
Market Area

N

50 MILES
40 MILES
30 MILES MILWAUKEE
20 MILES

WISCONSIN

WALWORTH COUNTY

RACINE COUNTY

RACINE

LAKE GENEVA

KENOSHA COUNTY

KENOSHA

ILLINOIS

LAKE COUNTY

WAUKEGAN

LAKE MICHIGAN

COOK COUNTY

CHICAGO

DUPAGE COUNTY

INDIANA

Chapter Seven

G.O. Bond Credit Analysis
Part 3—Economics

Individual communities located in the same state, like Kenosha, LaCrosse, and Madeline Island, Wisconsin, though very different in character and finances, are in many ways politically and financially cross-connected. So, understanding Kenosha involves understanding Wisconsin and its distinctive economic patterns. Dealers and investors make these connections all the time. For instance, when we think of Lansing, it may go: Lansing—excellent, but it's in Michigan, a problem state. And when Baltimore comes up: Baltimore—may be questionable, but it's in Maryland, which is strong, and so forth.

The State Context

Back in 1979, Wisconsin was our sixteenth largest state in population, with over 4.5 million souls (one-third living near Milwaukee) and was growing at about the average national rate. Its median family income was $7,555, or 4% below the U.S. average. About 30% of its work force was engaged in manufacturing, 25% in commercial services, 20% in trade, and 20% in governmental and other services. The 5% in agriculture, mostly dairy farming, made Wisconsin's farm income #9 in the U.S. This balanced diversity and steady growth pattern appeals to many analysts, with good reason, and in fact during the recession years of 1974 and 1975 the state's economy outperformed that of the U.S. as a whole.

The State—Wisconsin

As for Kenosha itself, you can get there by driving north from Chicago on Interstate 94, gradually leaving that urban world behind. Only 45 minutes later, after crossing the Wisconsin border, the next exit leads east toward Lake Michigan, where commercial and suburban development thickens in the five remaining miles to Kenosha. If you take Sheridan to 56th Street, then turn west, you will soon run smack into two American Motors assembly plants, 6 million square feet total and among the largest in the country. These and other smokestacked plants spread for dozens of long blocks piled high with supplies, crossed by railroad sidings, and circled by tall wire fences, the evidences of a mighty industry. After the shock of

Kenosha

EMPLOYMENT

	Male	Female
Manufacturing	10,647	2,614
Non-manufacturing	8,345	8,639
Commercial	3,132	2,787

Percent Mfg. Workers in Unions 80%

Unemployment 7.3% 1977 labor force.

Strikes (past 5 yrs.) affecting 1% or more of the labor force.

1970 Census (U.S.)   825 (1.32%) October, 1977- April, 1978

AGE BREAKDOWN *

Age Group	SMSA	City (% total population)
0 - 17	18.0	30.2%
18 - 24	25.5	13.1%
25 - 34	15.9	15.8%
35 - 49	16.0	15.6%
50 and Older	24.6	25.3%

	SMSA	City
Total Effective Buying Income	$740,169,000	$ 496,182,000
Per Capita Effective Buying Income	$ 5,907	5,844
Median Household Effective Buying Income	16,997	16,464

*Sales Management - Survey of Buying Power - July 1977

58

finding such a giant in town wears off, you begin to see that, despite its Gulliver, Kenosha is not a bad looking place at all. Modest, well-maintained homes come right up to the factory gates. Its downtown district is busy and tidy, and the municipal and commercial buildings are modern and pleasant. Impressions of this sort are useful up to a point, and can be added profitably to the hard economic data which usually fill up official statements.

But Kenosha is a one-industry manufacturing city, no doubt about it, and because of the sharp ups and downs such cyclical businesses have experienced in recent years, investors treat issuers dominated by them with caution. If you mention Kenosha in the bond world, the first response, particularly when the auto business is bad, is always "American Motors." I know; partly because of such feelings, I recently sold a nice block of Kenosha County bonds at a substantial loss. Renault of France now owns almost half of American Motors, and in 1978 had invested $350 million to modernize and improve their plants there, increasing their replacement cost to over $1 billion. In 1978 40% of the people employed in the city were engaged in making durable items (cars and car parts, metal goods, and tools) compared to a national average of under 15%. Two-thirds, or about 9,700 people, worked for American Motors, and most of the rest for Anaconda and Snap-On Tools. A total of 86 individual plants produced added value of about $350 million, and provided a payroll of about $400 million. Bank deposits in Kenosha were high—over $300 million. Retail sales were average—about $3,000 *per capita*, and the value of building permits in 1978 reached $34.2 million, a five-year increase of 65%.

The City

Facing shows how these and other economic data appear in standard forms. Most of these figures indicated fairly steady growth since the early 1960's. Through the 1960's and early 1970's, Kenosha's unemployment rate was consistently under 4%—lower than both the Wisconsin and U.S. rates. But in 1976-78, it jumped to 7.5%, higher than average, partly because of weak auto sales. In 1976, its citizens, not counting the corporations, reported a gross income of $420 million. The property tax levy on everything, factories and all, was $28.1 million. So the average citizen paid only $350 a year to run the local government, including debt service on all its bonds. Compared to the U.S. as a whole, Kenosha appeared to be growing, but quietly, and typified a healthy small industrial city. Up to this point a careful bond analyst might have looked at these numbers and said to herself, "What is good for American Motors is good for Kenosha."

Facts & Figures

Moving from numbers to words, what economic picture emerges from these figures, strokes, and dots? In 1978, Kenosha, predominantly indus-

Asset Summary

March 26, 1979

The following information was supplied to me by Mr. Clyde Fredrickson, Chief City of Kenosha Inspection Department:

YEAR	NO. BUILDING PERMITS ISSUED	VALUE OF BUILDINGS
1974	3,709	$20,649,317.00
1975	3,399	$15,969,747.00
1976	3,794	$25,572,126.00
1977	3,857	$33,379,270.00
1978	3,791	$34,170,847.00

Gail F. Procarione, City Clerk-Treasurer
Kenosha, Wisconsin

trial, had an unusually stable, blue collar population, and a steady, if low-level, growth pattern. Although other painter-analysts might interpret it differently, they would probably produce a somewhat similar Kenosha scene (unless they were into non-objective art). Thinking ahead, if its other assets proved to be of medium strength, and if it had a heavy debt load (in the $100 million range, or 10% of Estimated True Value), we might guess that a medium—low quality ranking would be appropriate, perhaps a Baa. On the other hand, if Kenosha had a light debt burden (2 or 3% of E.T.V.), we might lean toward ranking its bonds more generously, A, or even Aa. But first, on to the city's socio-political and financial assets, and then to its bonded liabilities, finally arriving at our overall credit opinion.

Local 72 News

Chapter Eight

G.O. Bond Credit Analysis
Part 4—Social, Political, Financial

The phrase *ability and willingness to pay* is often used to summarize an issuer's credit qualities. We looked at local economics, which corresponds to the ability to pay, in the last chapter. Now we turn to the social and political side, where we will see more about the willingness. Professional researchers, perhaps leary of seeming prejudiced, have in the past largely ignored the social factors; however, the market does not, and in fact most recent municipal problems have stemmed from social causes, not economic ones. For example, Propositions 13 in California and 2½ in Massachusetts, both protesting movements of one group of citizens against others, wreaked havoc on many bonds. Traders and salesmen can afford to be more pragmatic about such matters, perhaps saying of Kenosha, "Well, you may say it's all cars, but if you were there, you wouldn't think you were in Detroit."

Social Factors

However, we should be realistic enough to acknowledge that personal factors strongly affect bond prices. In the 1940's and '50's, for example, most investors refused to buy bonds located much south of Pennsylvania. Houston, and Fairfax County, Virginia, were considered to be medium- or low-grade credits, partly because many buyers didn't trust those old Confederates, odd though that may sound now. Economic factors were weighted too, but for whatever reasons, salesmen would hear the phrase "No southern bonds" over and over again. Now the term "southern" has disappeared from our jargon. Instead, it's the Sunbelt and we often hear "nothing in the Northeast."

We can assess social factors in two ways: one, directly, by observing particular patterns of living, and the other, indirectly, by studying a community's bond and other borrowing trends. Let's take a closer look at Kenosha, starting with its demographics—the population trends and the breakdowns into age, education, and employment groups. Kenosha's population grew rapidly after 1950, then declined slightly and leveled off. More homogeneous than most urban communities, it is predominantly white,

The People

Kenosha Labor
opinion page

City Jeeps-- right move

MAYOR PAUL SAFTIG, the City Council and the city administration must be commended for backing the purchase of the AMC Jeep vehicles for city administration use.

The city officials have had excellent comments about the practicality and comfort of the Jeep vehicles. We feel that it is necessary for our local tax dollars to be spent providing employment locally. City officials are well pleased with the nine Jeeps that have been on the road for the last three to four months.

It's hard to believe skeptics of such sound practices actually exist but they do. People will actually criticize the City of Kenosha for purchasing American Motors vehicles. Strange but true.

high in factory workers, and lower than average in education. If you suspect that it is ethnic, you are right, with people of German and Polish descent predominating, and not assimilated as fully as in most other cities. There are few rich families, and few poor. Kenosha is a working town (the parents complain about their kids' attitudes) not a spending town (the shopkeepers say Kenoshaites are just plain cheap) and proud of it. But if you happened to be driving through Kennedy Park on a certain Sunday in June, you might see how enthusiastically the annual city-sponsored fishing tournament, the Coho-Rama, is enjoyed by the citizens. A harmonious community such as this is quite easy to distinguish from one in which civic business always seems to be conducted in conflict, signaling trouble for its creditors.

The kinds of dissent, and the nature of the opposition parties and their complaints, can reveal where social pressure bears heavily on politics. For example, in Kenosha in the late 1970's, the environmentalists were scarcely visible, which was just as well for the city, considering its industrial base. The tone of the dominant Democratic organization was, and still is, cooperation between the city and the industrial companies, and no liberal reform group commanded any substantial following. However, Kenoshaites are fierce watchdogs on city taxation, and budget meetings there are heavily attended by citizens making sure their money doesn't go for unnecessary extras. We won't be far off base if we summarize this city's sociological background like this: homogeneous, dedicated, blue collar, steady and conservative, with almost no dissent; the sort of community to which many investors feel comfortable lending money.

The Opposition

Now to indirect social measuring, which centers on attitudes toward debt. One measure is a community's clear record of payment on its bonds, and some investors' rules prohibit them from buying obligations of a community which has ever defaulted. However, since so few communities ever have (mostly in the 1930's depression, when things were far different) this isn't very helpful today. A more useful willingness-to-pay indicator is the attitude toward temporary debt. If a community only rarely borrows against future tax proceeds in the short-term market, and then, when the receipts come in as scheduled, retires the debt and returns to a balance of income and expense, we may be confident that its borrowing practices are responsible. On the other hand, if short-term obligations steadily increase, and old notes are rolled over with new ones, we may easily conclude that the issuer is not facing the funding of its debt, putting its willingness to pay in question. Kenosha's practice and policy was to keep its books balanced and to avoid short-term borrowing. Why pay interest if you don't have to?

Temporary Financing

CITY OF KENOSHA
KENOSHA COUNTY, WISCONSIN

TAX COLLECTION RECORD

Collection Year	Tax Year	Tax Levy	Uncollected Taxes as of January 1, 1979		Percent Collected
			Real Estate and Special Assessment Taxes	Personal Property Taxes	
1979	1978	$29,140,220.26	In Process	of Collection	
1978	1977	28,213,886.94	$196,009.37	$10,312.55	99.27%
1977	1976	28,119,484.24	103,519.24	11,555.18	99.59
1976	1975	25,210,773.96	56,089.53	7,038.00	99.75
1975	1974	21,603,824.66	23,947.04	6,058.72	99.86

Another indirect indicator of willingness to repay is the maturity schedule of the outstanding bonded debt. For instance, an exceptionally long bond maturity pattern means postponement of repayment, while short maturities evidence a real desire for debt reduction. And in dollars and cents, this shows up in lower interest charges, because long bonds usually carry higher rates. In 1979, Kenosha's debt averaged only 4½ years and its average interest cost under 5%. Although Kenosha can, under Wisconsin law, sell 20-year maturity bonds, its aggressive debt retirement plan concretely demonstrated a strong will to repay. One word comes to mind to describe Kenosha's debt schedule: appropriate. Although American Motors might indeed falter some day, most of this city's debts would be paid off before it did. Can you feel a pattern growing stronger as we go along? *Maturity Shape*

One final index in this somewhat non-numerical subject: the percentage of levied taxes actually collected. Facing shows how tax-collection figures are usually presented: one column for the total real estate tax levied, one for the amount as yet uncollected, and a percent column. A 95% collection rate achieved on a current basis is usually considered acceptable. As we might expect, Kenosha's numbers were far higher. How do you read these social factors? If you said strong throughout and consistent with its economics, I would agree with you. *Tax Collections*

The conventional American opinion about politics is scornful: the word politician often carries a soiled connotation. And this is not all bad—distrusting our leaders and being suspicious of their motives reflects participatory democracy at work. Though eternal vigilance is certainly the price of liberty, we in the bond world don't have to take the usual clichés about politicos too seriously. In fact, our municipal governments' people are dedicated, effective, honest men and women; the rare exceptions persist where corrupt behavior is tolerated by the citizenry. *Political Factors*

In theory, G.O. bondholders get repaid from municipal cash flow, but in practice this flow is regulated by politicians, who represent the society, which in turn rests on its economic base. When the people of a prospering economy interact peacefully within a sound political structure, things eventually fall into place, sometimes quietly, sometimes after a struggle between differing opinions. But when parties harden into groups pressing their own interests with small regard for the other side, discord dominates and purely selfish activities prevail. And if the conflict is not soon settled, the bonds of the community often begin to suffer declines in market value, as investors demand higher return for accepting their higher risk.

Coming back to Wisconsin, if you talk to people in Kenosha about politics, in one sense, you'd think you were down in Chicago. It's Demo- *The Politicians*

	General Fund
ASSETS	
Cash and Investments - Pooled Account Total of $9,248,735.66	$ 2,656,800.67
Accounts Receivable - Net of Allowance $42,391.80	877,437.22
Taxes Receivable	
Personal Property - Delinquent	57,933.55
Special Assessments	
Delinquent	180,336.56
Special Charges Receivable	52,566.87
Inventories	113,310.00
Deferred Expenditures	101,091.61
	$ 4,039,476.48
LIABILITIES, RESERVES AND FUND BALANCE	
Vouchers Payable	$ 688,625.28
Advance Tax Collections	1,934,864.00
Deferred Income	1,400.00
	2,624,889.28
Restricted Reserves	
Encumbrances	97,717.48
Subsequent Year's Budget	200,000.00
Delinquent Taxes	216,722.64
Inventories	84,800.00
Claims and Losses	37,444.02
	636,684.14
Unrestricted	
Fund Balance	777,903.06
	$ 4,039,476.48

crats all the way. In 1980 56% of them even voted for Jimmy Carter. Les Aspin had been Kenosha's representative to Congress since 1970, succeeding Kastenmeier, who had served since 1958. Their state senator: John J. DeMaurer; Assemblymen: Joseph Andrea, a former cable splicer and president of the L.W.U. local, and Eugene Doff, a sheet-metal worker. Talking about unions, the United Auto Workers, especially Local 72, soon comes into any conversation about Kenosha. Closely connected to the right wing of the Democratic Party, it supports the city's decisions, and *vice versa*. Wildly progressive, workers for the Revolution? Not at all, no more than the rest of our labor movement—conservative to the core; at least as long as we thrive so remarkably.

By financial assets we mean the levels of a community's flow of income and expense, and the quality of its reporting these facts. It was quite clear that throughout the seventies Kenosha's books were balanced, if sometimes narrowly, and that no substantial deficits had ever been carried over year's end. However, the plain truth is that no one, however expert, can look at the books and records of governmental units the size of Kenosha and tell you what is really going on there. The irregular nature of municipal income and expenditures, the complexities of intergovernmental transfers, the lack of businesslike standards for such things as depreciation, and the absence of the kinds of controls corporations use to determine profit or loss, cumulatively produce degrees of vagueness and departures from accurate financial reporting which make local government financial statements practically meaningless.

Financial Factors

It's true that we have what are called generally accepted accounting principles (G.A.A.P.), and that every year each community's own auditor, or a certified public accountant (it doesn't matter which, very much), swears that everything in the parades of numbers had been reported according to those rules. And we also have a carefully defined set of accounting procedures especially designed and revised by the Government Finance Officers Association, called the Governmental Accounting, Auditing and Financial Reporting Standards (G.A.A.F.R.). But even when a municipality follows them as scrupulously as Kenosha does, the individual variants of each factor, and the imprecision of defining the dozens of accounts, makes it impossible to get any true meaning from them. It's not that the numbers are falsified in any way; it's that their balances at any one moment are reported in invalid form. No doubt to try to help us out of the situation, the C.P.A. Association came up with their own approach: Audit Guidelines for State and Local Governmental Units (A.S.L.G.U.), which has done little except to standardize confusion.

Municipal Credit Report

KENOSHA, WISCONSIN
                                                        April 30, 1979
                                                                    G

Sale: $3,810,000 bonds for bids May 7. Please see last page for details.

                            Rating: A 1

Opinion: While debt burden is moderate and financial operations satisfactory, the economic dependence on the cyclical automobile industry makes the economy vulnerable.

Summary: Kenosha is located in Southeastern Wisconsin on the western shores of Lake Michigan, approximately 35 miles south of Milwaukee and 55 miles north of Chicago. Kenosha is the county seat. The economy, although having diversified somewhat in recent years, is still heavily dependent upon American Motors, and is therefore vulnerable to economic fluctuations. The City maintains a moderate debt burden with payout rapid. Financial operations appear stable with margins narrow. City is a frequent issuer with a continuing capital improvements program.

Type unit	: City	Debt burden	: 3.4%	Med. fam. inc. :$10,191
Incorporated	: 1850			
Area, sq. mi.:	14	Debt per cap.	: $469.56	F.V. per capita:$13,701
Pop. density	: 5,778 per sq.mi.			
County	: Kenosha	% due in 10 yrs.:	100.00%	
SMSA	: Kenosha			

	Assessed Value			Population			
						% Change	
Year	Value (000)	% Ch.	Year	City	City	State	U.S.
1974	$ 493,168,035	-4.0	1950	54,368	11.5	9.5	14.5
1975	498,141,190	1.0	1960	67,889	24.9	15.1	18.5
1976	497,358,580	-2.0	1970	78,805	16.1	11.8	13.3
1977	1,115,850,620	124.4[a]	1978 est.[a]	80,889	2.6	–	–
1978	1,145,117,557	2.6	a. Source: City.				

a. Reassessed at full value.

Equalization rate: 103.33%   Full Value: $1,108,253,320

DEBT FACTORS: City is frequent issuer with bond proceeds for specific projects as well as an ongoing Capital improvements program. Debt burden is moderate with payout rapid, all bonds maturing within nine years. Due to political reorganization in 1967, outstanding debt of both the Kenosha City School District (now part of the Kenosha Unified School District) and the Gateway Technical Institute (now part of the Gateway Vocational, Technical and Adult Education district) are now shown as overlapping debt with payments made by unified districts for City G.O. debt outstanding for those purposes.

With thanks to Moody's Investors Service Inc.

In short, a bond person who thinks he or she can discern significant facts from municipal audits is barking up the wrong tree, and fortunately, not too much time is wasted there. Much better to look for municipal financial truth in other indicators, such as short-term borrowing patterns, in the sunshine of the real world.

THE WHOLE PICTURE

Now that we have collected all five of Kenosha's asset ingredients called for in our bond credit cake recipe—legal, economic, social, political, and financial—it's time to blend them together properly, trying to produce a reasonably smooth batter. Before we start, let's note that these ingredients are often combinations of each other—for instance, our political observations started on the social side, and extended well over into the financial section, and so how we define each one influences the results. *The Assets*

On the legal points, we relied on a recognized bond attorney, and concluded that Kenosha's bonds were validly issued, and that their interest was tax exempt; so asset number one was prime. *Legal*

Then we looked at Kenosha's real estate, and found that it was composed of high-value industrial facilities, chiefly American Motors, and also of slightly below-average value but well-maintained single-family homes. The tax collections averaged 99.6%, far above the national average. The overall economy was heavily dependent on the auto business, but Renault and A.M.C. seemed to be there to stay, investing large amounts on new production facilities. The aggregate levels of citizen income, employment, and savings seemed adequate and unusually stable, and their trends positive, characterized by slow growth. The summary of the economic assets: strong, if not robust, and steady, but in the shadow of a single, reasonably healthy industrial giant. *Economic*

We found Kenosha's social pattern quite distinctive. It is a city of workers, slightly below average in education, and pervaded by tradition-minded families. The citizens, if not exactly on the companies' side, are pro-industrial, and support the union which represents many of them. Not an upscale dynamic gentrified sort of place at all, but deeply conservative, responsible, and orderly. And they elect politicians who reflect their views. Their representatives come from old-line Kenosha, all Democrats, and run the city in a predictable, tight-fisted way, spending what they must, but wasting little of their hard-earned money. *Social-Political*

The city's financing habits were consistent with this view of its sociology: it rarely borrowed by selling notes. The bond maturity schedule was unusually short, saving on interest costs. And in 1979 Kenosha's financial *Financial*

71

Debt Statement (as of 4/1/79 in 000)   Defaults: None reported. Last sale
Bonded debt outstanding $27,120 $4,055,000 4/17/78.
Current offering (5/7/79)   3,810
Gross bonded debt $30,930   Security: G.O., U.L.T.
Unfunded debt-Notes   11
          Promissory note[a]   400   Trend: City has been a consistent
Gross direct debt $31,341   issuer. Last sale 4/17/78.
Less: Water & Sewer rev. bds.   6,165
School District debt[b]   1,418   Structure: Full payment of outstdg.
Gateway Tech. Inst. debt[c]   635   G.O. debt in nine years with payout
Direct net debt $23,123   peak in 1979 steadily declining
Overlapping debt   Amt.   %   until 1988.
Kenosha County (4/3/79) $10,088 54.1 5,458
Kenosha U.S.D.   12,534 74   9,295   Principal Maturities-including new
Gateway Tech.Inst.   625 17   106   issue (000): Calendar fiscal year
Overall net debt $37,982 1979 $3,864   1984 $2,800
a. City anticipates payment from Revenue   1980   3,796   1985   2,000
    bond issuance in mid-1979.   1981   3,482   1986   2,000
b. Due to reorganization of School District   1982   2,825   1987   1,225
    in 1967, Debt assumed by Unified School   1983   2,825   1988   925
    district which makes payment of Principal/Interest to pay City's G.O. debt
    originally borrowed for School purposes. Principal payments are therefore
    included in overlapping debt.
c. Due to reorganization, City's debt originally issued for the Gateway Institute
    has been assumed by the Gateway UTAE district, and is included in overlapping debt.

	Debt Ratios				Rate of Retirement		
Net Debt	Per Capita	Median*	% F.V.	Median*	Bonds Due	Amt.(000)	% of Total
Direct	$285.86	$279.90	2.1%	2.6%	In 5 yrs.	$15,728	71.9%
Overall	469.56	460.06	3.4	4.4	In 10 yrs.	21,878	100%

* Cities 50-100,000 population.

Bonds authorized but unissued: City anticipates issuance of $2,900,000 in Waterworks
Revenue bonds in mid-1979, and will continue ongoing capital improvement program
with annual issuance of approximately $4 million per year. Issuance for sewer
plant in near future is also reported.

Short term borrowing: City utilizes short-term borrowing.

Debt limits: 5% of Equalized valuation.

Interest rate limits: 7%   Use of proceeds: Various capital improvements.

GOVERNMENT FACTORS: Kenosha has a Mayor-Aldermanic form of government with the
Mayor elected for 4-year term and 18 alderman elected for two-year terms on a
ward basis.

Service Provision: Full Service City

Welfare: County   Schools: Unified School District # 1

Enterprises/Utilities: Sewer and water systems.

Public employees: City employs 715 people.

Pensions: The unfunded accrued liability for the City of Kenosha for its coverage
under the State-administered. Wisconsin Retirement fund totalled $3,968,632 at 1/1/79.
City contributions in 1978 amounted to $1,258,601. City is currently paying
81-100% of employee's required contribution depending on category of employment.

With thanks to Moody's Investors Service Inc.

situation was sound, and it was operating firmly in the black. Overall, Kenosha's assets were not spectacular, but convincingly consistent, providing the element of predictability which careful investors welcome.

Against its assets, the city's liabilities were few and relatively simple, boiling down to what it owed its bondholders. Its total debt, including the overlapping districts, was $35 million, or 3.2% of the E.T.V. This compared to Milwaukee (then Aaa rated) at 3.5%, Chicago (Aa) at 5.7%, New Orleans (A) at 4%, and a U.S. average of about 5%. What about other obligations? Short-term or postponed borrowing: negligible. The somewhat nagging problem of unfunded pension liabilities? A total of $4 million, a relatively low level. Another question: in what shape was the city's physical plant? According to best estimates, well above average, partly because their growth rate had been moderate. So there was no reason to anticipate large future borrowing. How about the utilities? The water and sewer systems were funded by revenue bonds, and in sound financial condition. Any other problems on the horizon? Not really. Kenosha stood out as a place of few surprises, a welcome change from many of our decaying industrial centers.

The Liabilities

So it comes down to a debt of $35 million, against a real estate value of $1.1 billion. On these figures alone, a high-grade rating would almost certainly have been in order. But property does not pay off bonds; income does. And there was Kenosha's weak point. Although the city's debt burden was low in relation to its real estate values, the income from which residents repaid it chiefly came from hourly manufacturing wages. In addition, a properly skeptical analyst would have looked at A.M.C's dominance in town, and even if Kenosha's economic and social assets seemed adequate to support a top bond ranking, its lack of diversification would have influenced him, or her, to grade it medium to upper medium in quality. And who could fault that decision? Not I—how about you?

A Verdict

BOND DENOMINATIONS

Number of Pieces

Principal	$5,000 Denominations	$1,000 Denominations
$ 1,000	—	1
5,000	1	5
50,000	10	50
100,000	20	100
900,000	180	900
1,000,000	200	1,000
5,000,000	1,000	5,000

Bond Principal Amounts

Principal	Spoken	Price	Total Dollar Value
$1,000	one bond (or a bond)	100 (Par)	$1,000
5,000	five bonds	100 (Par)	5,000
50,000	fifty bonds	100 (Par)	50,000
100,000	one hundred bonds	100 (Par)	100,000
900,000	nine hundred bonds	100 (Par)	900,000
1,000,000	one million bonds	100 (Par)	1,000,000
5,000,000	five million bonds	100 (Par)	5,000,000

Notice that we say one hundred bonds for $100,000, nine hundred for $900,000, but jump it to one million for $1,000,000 principal amount. Why? Just custom, but a million it is.

Chapter Nine

Dollar Pricing

So far we have studied the municipal market by examining the operations of its participants—the investors, the issuers, and the underwriters— and by looking at the strengths and weaknesses of bonds themselves. If, instead, the subject were baseball, we might have begun by discussing the fans, the leagues, and the players, and later looked at bats and balls. But bond people in action don't think in these terms, any more than third basemen ponder theories of physics. Municipal underwriters buy and sell bonds one issue at a time, attacking their dollars and cents aspect, using words and money instead of gloves and pine tar. Now, for two chapters, let's look at the language that dealers use, so we can see what it's like to be at the underwriting plate.

Bonds Qualitatively and Bonds Quantitatively

First, a few words about denominations. Since the nineteen-sixties, almost all municipal bonds have been printed on pieces of paper standing for $5,000 principal each. We call them $5,000 denominations, or fives, for short. Before then, bonds were usually printed in $1,000 denominations (ones) and municipal jargon originally developed using that amount. Since both fives and ones trade in the secondary market, to avoid confusion our figuring unit has remained $1,000. One bond still means $1,000 in principal amount, five bonds means $5,000, fifty bonds means $50,000, one hundred, $100,000, and so on. When an underwriter in a State of New Jersey syndicate meeting says, "We can do one hundred of the '94's," he means that his firm can sell $100,000 worth of the issue's 1994 maturity. The New Jersey bonds will be printed as fives, but it would be immaterial if for some reason they were ones. So don't worry about denominations: it's like eggs, where two half-cartons of six contain the same number as one of a dozen; 100 bonds means $100,000 will be repaid, whether evidenced by 20, or 100, pieces of paper. And if sometime in the future the standard bond denomination changed again, no doubt we would continue to use the same old $1,000 figuring base.

Denominations: Ones Then, Fives Now

DOLLAR PRICE PER $1,000

	hundreds of points	tens of points	points	.	dollars	dimes	cents
We use this six space form to convert $1,000 units onto a 100% scale	___	___	___	•	___	___	___
This stands for $1,000	1	0	0	•	0	0	0
Every space has its own fixed meaning	hundreds of points	tens of points	points	•	dollars	dimes	cents
Each one unit is valued so	$1,000	$100	$10		$1	$.10	$.01
101.234% of principal reads	1	0	1	•	2	3	4
	1	0	1	•	2	3	4
	x	x	x		x	x	x
Per $1,000 bond	$1,000	$100	$10		$1	$.10	$.01
	‖	‖	‖		‖	‖	‖
	$1,000	$0	$10		$2	30¢	4¢

$1,010

$2.34

$1,012.34

We figure the value of a particular bond using two different systems. The first system, dollar pricing, quantifies its principal, and the second, yield to maturity, quantifies its income. We will stick to dollar prices in this chapter, then continue on to yield in the next. In dollar pricing, 100 stands for the full principal amount, the amount the holder will collect when the bond is paid off. We measure a bond's worth by applying straightforward percentages to its principal, like 100, 99, 98, 96%, etc., which in decimals would be 1.00, .99, .98, .96, etc. Bonds priced in dollars are easy to understand and sell, and we offer them at the simplest price of all, 100 (par), as often as possible. For instance, when a $76 million issue of the Wisconsin State Housing Finance Authority was negotiated on March 18, 1982, the bonds due in 2002 were offered to investors at 100. An investor who bought 5 bonds paid $5,000, a 500 bond buyer paid $500,000, and so on, in each case 100% of the principal amount.

Dollar Price— Principal Percentages

Amount (M)	Description	Coupon	Maturity	Price
#1 100	Wis. HFA	14	11/1/02	100

This shows how dealers describe bonds in shortened form. Here $100,000 principal amount of Wisconsin State Housing Finance Agency Bonds, which will pay 14% per year interest, and are due November 1, 2002, are offered at their face value, 100. (The M after amount is the Latin 1,000.) If a dealer actually sold these bonds at 100, he would send his customer a bill figured by multiplying the principal by the decimal equivalent of the dollar price ($100,000 x 1.00 = $100,000).

After bonds are distributed, their values go up or down, changing with the market. We use dollar prices to measure these changes, splitting principal into units of 1%. Since $1,000 is our figuring base, each 1% is $10 per bond ($1,000 x .01 = $10). These 1%'s are called *points.* One point is $10, two points $20, and so forth. To repeat, 100 means 100% of the $1,000 face amount; 99 is our way of saying 1% (or 1 point, or $10) per bond below 100, 98 is 2% below 100, 97 is 3% below, 101 means 1 point above 100, 102 is 2 points above 100, and so forth.[1]

The Units of Dollar Price

Let's go back to the Wisconsin HFA example. By late March, 1982, prices in the tax-exempt market had risen, and the few dealers who still owned some Whiskeys were no longer willing to sell them at 100. Some of

1 Point = $10

(1) We write 100, but we say "par," and anyone who says, "The bonds are offered at one hundred" sounds odd. It goes 95, 96, 99, 100, 102, etc., said "ninety-five," "ninety-six," "ninety-nine," "par," "one-oh-two," and so on. So say "one hundred miles," or "one hundred and a half degrees," but say "par" or "par and a half," when you mean dollar prices.

DOLLAR PRICING—EVEN POINTS

Principal	(Spoken)	Dollar Price	Decimals	Total
$ 1,000	one bond	100 (par)	1.00	$ 1,000
1,000	one bond	99	.99	990
5,000	five bonds	100	1.00	5,000
5,000	five bonds	99	.99	4,950
25,000	twenty-five bonds	100	1.00	25,000
25,000	twenty-five bonds	99	.99	24,750
100,000	one hundred bonds	99	.99	99,000
1,000	one bond	98	.98	980
5,000	five bonds	98	.98	4,900
25,000	twenty-five bonds	97	.97	24,250
100,000	one hundred bonds	96	.96	96,000
100,000	one hundred bonds	91	.91	91,000
100,000	one hundred bonds	75	.75	75,000
100,000	one hundred bonds	100	1.00	100,000
100,000	one hundred bonds	101	1.01	101,000
100,000	one hundred bonds	102	1.02	102,000
500,000	five hundred (or half a million) bonds	102	1.02	510,000
1,000,000	a million bonds	113	1.13	1,130,000

them raised their offering by one point, to 101, and later by another, to 102. If a customer wanted to buy 100 bonds then, he would have had to pay 102% of their principal amount, or $102,000 ($100,000 x 1.02 = $102,000), and 500 would have cost him $510,000 ($500,000 x 1.02), etc. As the market goes up, or down, dollar price changes continue to be expressed like this, in percents of full principal amount. So if bonds formerly for sale at 67 are now offered at 68, we say that they have gone up a point, even though that particular $10 move is more than 1% of market value (1 divided by 67 = 1½%).

Although points are precise enough for many purposes, competitive pressures often compel us to divide them into eighths (⅛ of 1%), and this creates two problems. Problem one comes from machines. Since computers do not accept them, fractions like ⅜ or ½ must first be converted into decimals. Problem two comes from people. Although the math may sound elementary, most people now entering the bond business can't turn fractions into decimals readily. I interview a lot, and not one applicant in three knows the decimal equivalent of ⅜ right off. So let's review fractions.

A
Fraction
Review

Fractions of Points	(Spoken)	Decimals
⅛	an eighth (of a point)	.125
¼	a quarter	.250
⅜	three-eighths	.375
½	a half	.500
⅝	five-eighths	.625
¾	three-quarters	.75
⅞	seven-eighths	.875
1	one point (or a point)	1.00
1⅛	a point and an eighth	1.125
1¼	a point and a quarter	1.25
1⅜	a point and three-eighths	1.375
1½	a point and a half	1.5
1⅝	a point and five-eighths	1.625
1¾	a point and three-quarters	1.75
1⅞	a point and seven-eighths	1.875
2	two points	2.000

DOLLAR PRICING—FRACTIONS AND TOTALS

Fractions	Decimals		1 Point		Dollar Amt.		Number of 1,000 Bonds		Total
⅛	.125	×	$10	=	$1.25	×	1	=	$1.25
¼	.25	×	$10	=	2.50	×	1	=	2.50
⅜	.375	×	$10	=	3.75	×	1	=	3.75
½	.5	×	$10	=	5.00	×	1	=	5.00
⅝	.625	×	$10	=	6.25	×	1	=	6.25
¾	.75	×	$10	=	7.50	×	1	=	7.50
⅞	.875	×	$10	=	8.75	×	1	=	8.75
1	1.00	×	$10	=	10.00	×	1	=	10.00

One eighth of a point is $1.25 per bond, a quarter of a point is $2.50, three-eighths is $3.75, etc.

$7	.7	×	$10	=	7.00	×	10	=	$70.00
1⅛	1.125	×	$10	=	11.25	×	10	=	112.50
$12.40	1.24	×	$10	=	12.40	×	10	=	124.00
1¼	1.25	×	$10	=	12.50	×	100	=	1,250.00
1½	1.50	×	$10	=	15.00	×	100	=	1,500.00
2½	2.5	×	$10	=	25.00	×	500	=	12,500.00
½	.5	×	$10	=	5.00	×	1,000	=	5,000.00

Seven dollars a bond on 10 bonds is $70, a point and a quarter on 100 is $1,250, etc.

COMPOUND DOLLAR PRICES

Dollar Prices	Spoken	Decimals		Principal	Total for 1 Bond	Total for 100 Bonds
81¼	eighty-one and a quarter	.8125	×	$1,000	$812.50	$81,250
99⅜	ninety-nine and three-eighths	.99375	×	1,000	993.75	99,375
101.234	one-oh-one two-three-four	1.01234	×	1,000	1,012.34	101,234
102.234	one-oh-two two-three-four	1.02234	×	1,000	1,022.34	102,234

Eighty-one and a quarter on 100 bonds is $81,250, etc.

Notice that these fractions come between whole 1% points. Since 1 point is $10 a bond, ½ of a point is $5 per bond, and ¼ of a point is $2.50 per bond ($10 x .25). And ⅛ of a point is $1.25 per bond ($10 x .125); ⅜ is $3.75 per bond; ⅝ is $6.25; ¾ is $7.50; and ⅞ is $8.75. Then 1⅛ points is $11.25 ($10 x 1.125), 1¼ points is $12.50, and so on, as shown across the way. Even eighths do not satisfy all competitors; sometimes we work more finely, in dollars, dimes, and sometimes even in cents per bond. Since we often think in terms of fractional profit margins, knowing their dollar equivalents comes in very handy. If you sell 100 bonds for ⅜ point profit, you could find the total by multiplying $100,000 by .00375, but it's a lot easier to think 100 times $3.75 is $375; and $4 on 200 bonds is $800; $7, $1,400, etc.

Dollars, Dimes and Cents

Dollars can be used to compare and evaluate different bond offerings. When a bond is offered at a lower price than another one just like it, it stands out immediately as the better buy. If you can buy the same brand of butter in two equally convenient stores, it's price that counts. So, if in early April, 1982, two offerings had looked like this:

Offerings in Dollars

	Amount (M)	Description	Coupon	Maturity	Price	Total
#2	100	Wis. HFA	14	11/1/02	102	$102,000
#2A	100	Wis. HFA	14	11/1/02	102½	102,500

picking the better value would have been simple.

Municipal issues are often designed so that many of their bonds come due on one maturity date (term bonds); these are usually priced in dollars (and are often called dollar bonds when they reach the secondary market). Using easily comparable percentage-based dollar prices greatly simplifies trading in them; most U.S. Treasury and corporate bonds usually trade in somewhat different forms of dollars, too.

Dollar Bonds

Dollar prices are also handy as a constant between bonds carrying different interest rates. When two similar bonds are offered at the same price, it is easy to see that the one with the higher coupon is the better investment.

Comparing Coupons

	Amount (M)	Description	Coupon	Maturity	Price	Current Yield
#3	250	Hawaii	11½	8/1/93	100	11.50%
#4	250	Hawaii	12	11/1/93	100	12.00%

CURRENT YIELD

1. To find a bond's current yield, divide its coupon by its dollar price.

$$\frac{\text{Coupon}}{\text{Dollar Price}} = ? \text{ Current Yield}$$

					Price	Current Yield
#4A	100	Hawaii	12	11/1/93	101	?

Divide 12 by 1.01

$$\frac{12}{1.01} = 11.88\% = \text{Current Yield}$$

---

2. To find at what dollar price a bond gives a certain current yield, divide its coupon by that current.

$$\frac{\text{Coupon}}{\text{Current Yield}} = ? \text{ Price}$$

					Price	Current Yield
#4C	100	Hawaii	12	11/1/93	?	11.59

Divide 12 by 11.59

$$\frac{12}{11.59} = 103\frac{1}{2} = \text{Price}$$

On line #3, the coupon rate is 11.50% and on #4, 12.00%. Since both are priced at 100, the 12% bond is the better buy (bigger pineapples at the same price). On the other side of the fence, if Hawaii's finance director were able to issue 7% bonds at the same price as 8% bonds, he would surely do that, for the same reason, reversed.

Current Yield, Stock Yield

The Hawaii example contains one additional column, for current yield. When a 12% bond is bought at 100 and is eventually redeemed at 100, it returns 12.00% every year, or $12 for every $100 invested. This return rate is called its current yield. When bought at 100 in 1985, a 12.00% bond due in 1993 returns its holder $120 annually for each $1,000 invested. That is 12.00% in 1985, 12.00% in 1986, and every year up to maturity. On $5,000 this would be $600 ($5,000 x .12), on $100,000, $12,000, on $250,000, $30,000, etc. Current yield is sometimes used to calculate the return on municipals, but more often it is applied to common stocks and other investments which, unlike bonds, have no maturity.

Coupon Divided by Dollar Price

How is current yield figured? By dividing coupon by dollar price. At 100 (the whole thing, or 1.00) it's easy; 11½% divided by 1.00 is 11.50%, and 12.00% divided by 1.00 is 12.00%. Dividing any number by one results in the same number, and the current yield of a bond at 100 is the same as its coupon rate. 12's at 100 have a current yield of 12.00%, the current on 7½'s at 100 is a 7.50%, and so on.

What happens to the current yield at prices over 100, on what we call premium bonds? Suppose that the Hawaii 12's were bought at 101.

	Amount (M)	Description	Coupon	Maturity	Price	Current Yield
#4A	250	Hawaii	12	11/1/93	101	11.88%
#4B	250	Hawaii	12	11/1/93	102	11.76%
#4C	250	Hawaii	12	11/1/93	103½	11.59%

Premiums

Dividing the 12% coupon by the 101 dollar price gives a current yield of 11.88% (12.00% divided by 1.01 = 11.88%). 250 bonds bought at 101 would still provide an income of $30,000 a year, because neither the coupon rate nor the amount of bonds changed. However, since the amount invested is higher ($252,500) the current return is lower ($30,000 divided by $252,500 = 11.88%). This makes common sense—if the bonds return 12% at 100, they should return less at 101. And at 102, the current yield is lower still, 11.76%, and so on. Since dividing a number by a number higher than one results in a lower number, the current yield of a premium bond is always lower than its coupon. As the dollar price goes up, the current yield goes down.

TUESDAY
APRIL 9, 1985

YIELD CORNER

						OUR MARKETS	CURRENT YIELD
Ba/BB	100	Mass Muni Wholesale El	6 1/8	7/1/17 ca		50-2	11.78
Ba/BB	100	Mass Muni Wholesale El	6 3/8	7/1/15 ca		51-3	12.03
Ba/BB	100	Mass Muni Wholesale El	6.80	7/1/18 ca		55-7	11.93
Ba/BB	100	Mass Muni Wholesale El	7.20	7/1/08 ca		57-9	12.20
Ba/BB	100	Mass Muni Wholesale El	7 1/4	7/1/14 ca		57-9	12.28
Ba/BB	100	Mass Muni Wholesale El	10 1/8	7/1/17 ca		78-80	12.66
Ba/BB	100	Mass Muni Wholesale El	10 1/4	7/1/08 ca		78-81	12.65
Ba/BB	100	Mass Muni Wholesale El	12 1/8	7/1/06 ca		93-5	12.76
Ba/BB	100	Mass Muni Wholesale El	12 1/8	7/1/18 ca		92-4	12.90
Ba/BB	100	Mass Muni Wholesale El	12 1/4	7/1/17 ca		93-5	12.89
Ba/BB	100	Mass Muni Wholesale El (Series B '81)	13 3/8	7/1/17 ca		99-100	13.38
Ba/BB	100	Mass Muni Wholesale El (Series A '82)	13 3/8	7/1/17 ca		99-100	13.38

PLEASE SHOW US YOUR SECONDARY MARKET
ITEMS FOR THE BID

Wilson White   Pat Finnegan
Nancy Lane   John Murphy
Dean Plithides   Alicia Soukup
Jim Sexton   Emily Nolan

	Amount (M)	Description	Coupon	Maturity	Price	Current Yield
#4D	250	Hawaii	12	11/1/93	99	12.12%
#4E	250	Hawaii	12	11/1/93	97	12.37%
#5	250	Hawaii	12	11/1/99	97	12.37%

Discounts

And to finish the picture, the current yield of a discount (priced under 100) bond is always higher than its coupon. To find how much higher, again divide the coupon by the dollar price. Hawaii 12% bonds at 99 provide a current yield of 12.12% (12 divided by .99 = 12.12%); at 97, 12.37%, etc. As the dollar price goes down, the current yield goes up.

The Limitations of C.Y.

Where do gains up to 100 at maturity, and losses down to 100, enter the current yield equation? They don't. Current yield is just the now yield. It tells the whole income story at 100, and only at 100. For a more complete gauge of income we must go beyond dollar prices and current return, and go on to the second half of our bond pricing language double-header, yield to maturity.

**Price and yield calculations on coupon securities
scheduled to pay one or more coupons before maturity,
i.e., on securities paying *periodic* interest**

Case I: Price given yield to maturity: Let

$y =$ yield to maturity
$c =$ coupon rate
$a_i =$ accrued interest per dollar of face value
$P =$ price per dollar of face value
$N =$ number of remaining coupons
$t_{sc} =$ days from settlement to next coupon
$B =$ basis (number of days) in the coupon
period in which settlement occurs

Then

$$P = \left[\frac{1}{\left(1+\frac{y}{2}\right)^{N-1+(t_{sc}/B)}} \right] + \left[\sum_{k=1}^{N} \frac{c/2}{\left(1+\frac{y}{2}\right)^{N-1+(t_{sc}/B)}} \right] - a_i$$

Case II: Yield to maturity given price:

$y = y$ in the above equation for P
$P =$ known price
$y_1 = $ *first* estimate of yield to maturity
$Y =$ security's current maturity in years

$$y_1 = \frac{cY + 1 - P}{Y - (1 - P)\left(\frac{2Y + 1}{4}\right)}$$

courtesy of:
Money Market Calculations: Yield, Break-Evens, and Arbitrage
by Marcia Stigman in collab. with John Mann
Dow Jones–Irwin, Homewood, IL 60430. 1981 p. 112,136

Chapter Ten

Yield Pricing

We saw in the last chapter how dollars are used to quantify bond principal, and how current yield is figured by dividing coupon by dollar price. Our second pricing system, yield to maturity, quantifies total bond income using the first formula on the facing page. This yield formula, in addition to coupon and dollar price, weighs in the effect of gain or loss and also the length of time to maturity, thus giving a more accurate picture of bond return. Yield to maturity, or as we shorten it, yield, is expressed in one annual percentage rate, like 6.00%, 8.20%, 11.11%, etc. So a bond priced at a 6.00% yield to maturity will provide its holder an average annual 6% return; $6 for every $100 invested, $60 per $1,000, $6,000 per $100,000, etc. And that's just the way we say it, priced to yield. Why? Because every bond offered at a certain yield has an exact dollar price equivalent, as we will be seeing shortly.[1]

Yield to Maturity

These days, bank certificates of deposit are heavily promoted. Someone who buys a one year $100,000 8% C.D. expects to get his $100,000 back and to receive $8,000 in interest. However, if the same C.D. had been bought for $98,000, its return would be higher than 8%; or if bought at $102,000 its return would be lower, since in addition to receiving interest, the holder would realize a profit or loss. Figuring the total income of discount and premium bonds works similarly. If $100,000 of one year 8% bonds were bought at a 2 point discount, at 98, they would return more than 8%; if bought at a premium, say 102, they would return less, and yield to maturity shows us exactly how much. Memorize the price-to-yield and yield-to-price formulas, and you will probably be unique in the bond business; fortunately, we have machines which calculate yield automatically. By using one, we can easily figure that a one year 8% bond bought at

Gain and Loss Effect

(1) When bond people say *yield*, that's yield to maturity; when, on occasion, current yield does come up, they will specify it, for instance, "At a nine forty-five (meaning a 9.45% yield to maturity) their current is only eight (8.00%)."

UNITS OF YIELD—BASIS POINTS

This four space form
expresses yield,
or average annual
return

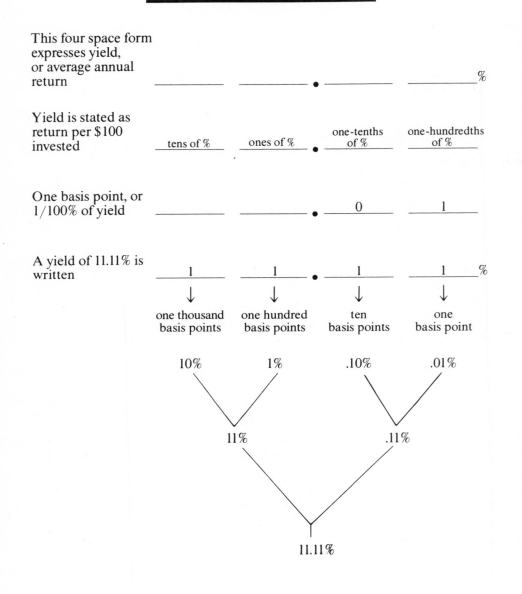

tens of %	ones of %	one-tenths of %	one-hundredths of %

Yield is stated as
return per $100
invested

One basis point, or
1/100% of yield

A yield of 11.11% is
written

one thousand basis points   one hundred basis points   ten basis points   one basis point

10%   1%   .10%   .01%

11%   .11%

11.11%

88

98 yields a 10.15%; and if bought at 102, returns 5.91%. What, again, does a 10.15% yield mean? A 10.15% average annual return.

We saw how dollar prices measure bonds in percentages of principal amount, and how dealers use units of $10 points to mark changes in value. How do we measure price changes in yield? By percents, each expressing 1% of annual *income*. The difference between a bond at a 6.00% yield and one at a 7.00% yield is 1% in annualized return. And moving from 10.00% to 9.00% is also a change of 1% in yield. We then divide each of these one percents of yield into 100 parts. These .01%'s are called basis points. From a 11.00% to an 11.01%, and from a 11.11% to an 11.10%, is a distance of one basis point, or 1/100 of 1% of average annual return. Basis points, or .01's, (spoken oh-ones), and their multiples are among the most frequently used terms in the municipal business. *The Units of Yield*

Before we go on, let's recognize that the similarity of two of our terms, points and basis points, is potentially confusing. We had it cold that one point is 1% of principal, or $10 per bond. Now *basis* points? 1/100 of 1% of yield? To help distinguish them, remember that points are big, but basis points are little. Points are percents of the whole principal, each one always $10 a bond; but a basis point is just a measly 1/100 of one percent of income. When we say "the bonds are up a point" we mean their dollar price has risen $10, perhaps from 92% to 93% of principal, a fairly hefty amount. But when we mean basis points we say, "The second bid was just one basis point away, a 7.96% and a 7.97%!," which in most new issues works out to be something like 75¢ a bond. *Points, Basis Points*

Again, one basis point is 1/100 of 1% in yield. Five of them make up one .05%, or 1/20 of 1%. This .05 (oh-five) is our single most common municipal bond yield pricing increment. Why? One percent in yield represents one whole percent in annual interest return, as from a 9.50% to a 10.50%. In practice, bond yields usually rise or fall less drastically, quite often in steps of five basis points. So the .05, like the five-minute marks on a clock face, has proven to be a handy division of bond value changes. Now let's look at how lowering a bond's dollar price raises its yield. *The .05*

Settlement Date 10/1/84

	Amount (M)	Description	Coupon	Maturity	Price	Current Yield	Yield
#1	100	Hull, MA	8	10/1/85	100	8.00	8.00
#1A	100	Hull, MA	8	10/1/85	98	8.16	10.15
					Difference	.16%	2.15%

BASIS LANGUAGE

Yield	Spoken	Change	Spoken
6.00	A six (or a six basis)		
7.00	A seven (or a seven basis)	1.00	one hundred basis points
9.00	A nine (or a nine basis)	2.00	two hundred basis points
9.50	A nine-fifty	.50	fifty basis points
9.70	A nine-seventy	.20	twenty basis points
9.80	A nine-eighty	.10	ten basis points
9.85	A nine-eighty-five	.05	an oh-five (or five basis points)
9.90	A nine-ninety	.05	an oh-five
9.95	A nine-ninety-five	.05	an oh-five
10.00	A ten	.05	an oh-five
11.00	An eleven	1.00	one hundred basis points
11.01	An eleven oh-one	.01	an oh-one
11.10	An eleven-ten	.09	nine basis points
11.11	An eleven-eleven	.01	an oh-one
11.111	An eleven one-one-one	.001	an oh-oh-one (one tenth of a basis point)

In #1, the Hulls are priced at 100, where, because there will be neither gain nor loss at maturity, they yield their coupon, 8.00%. Change their price to 98, and their yield becomes 10.15%, because in addition to interest, the holder will receive a $2,000 gain in just one year. The price is down and the yield is up, or as they say officially, price and yield move inversely. This is similar to the way we saw current yield work, except that yield to maturity shows the change better; notice that the current yield barely moves. Now let's take two bonds at the same dollar price, but with different maturities, to see how yield figures in time.

S.D. 10/1/84

	Amount (M)	Description	Coupon	Maturity	Price	Current Yield	Yield
# 1A	100	Hull, MA	8	10/1/85	98	8.16	10.15
# 2	100	Hull, MA	8	10/1/92	98	8.16	8.35
					Difference	.00	1.80%

We see the same coupon and the same dollar price, but two vastly different yields to maturity. What causes the difference? The time differential. The one year buyer gets a 10.15% total return, while the eight year buyer only gets an 8.35%. Although the coupon and the gain are the same, one holder gets his $2,000 profit much sooner, and yield to maturity shows the results of this advantage clearly. To sum it up in mathematical terms, yield to maturity is a function of coupon, price, and time.

Time Effect

In weather forecasting, it's degrees and barometer inches, and in the sterling market, it's pounds and pence, but in bonds it's "yield, yield, yield" and "oh-five, oh-five, oh-five" all day long. One fine point about basis language before we move on: when we say, "a nine-fifty," we mean a (yield of) 9.50%; yield to maturity is understood, but not stated. So to say it right, it's "*a* nine fifty," or "*a* nine eighty-five," with "a" standing for "a yield of." If you said "the Cal's are at ten" you would sound unprofessional, because "ten" spoken without an "a" means a dollar price of 10. When we mean at a dollar price of 10, or 75, we say just "at ten," or "at seventy-five," with no "a." "*A* seventy-five" would be a 75.00% yield to maturity, quite a different proposition. Sometimes, to avoid misunderstandings, we say "a fifteen basis" to emphasize that we mean yield, not dollars. This would mean at a 15.00% yield (which might, for instance, figure to a dollar price of 85¼), and not at a dollar price of 15.

At a Ten Basis Vs. at Ten

Not only does yield describe a bond's return accurately, it also serves as an excellent gauge for comparing the values of bonds with different

YEARS and MONTHS 5½%

Yield	8-3	8-6	8-9	9-0	9-3	9-6	9-9	10-0
5.00	103.34	103.43	103.50	103.59	103.66	103.74	103.81	103.90
5.10	102.66	102.73	102.79	102.86	102.91	102.98	103.03	103.10
5.20	101.98	102.04	102.08	102.13	102.17	102.23	102.26	102.32
5.30	101.31	101.35	101.38	101.42	101.44	101.48	101.50	101.54
5.40	100.65	100.67	100.68	100.71	100.71	100.74	100.74	100.76
5.50	99.99	100.00	99.99	100.00	99.99	100.00	99.99	100.00
5.60	99.34	99.33	99.31	99.30	99.28	99.27	99.25	99.24
5.70	98.69	98.67	98.63	98.61	98.57	98.55	98.51	98.49
5.80	98.05	98.01	97.95	97.92	97.87	97.83	97.78	97.75
5.90	97.41	97.36	97.29	97.24	97.17	97.12	97.06	97.01
6.00	96.77	96.71	96.62	96.56	96.48	96.42	96.34	96.28
6.10	96.15	96.07	95.97	95.89	95.80	95.72	95.63	95.56
6.20	95.52	95.43	95.32	95.23	95.12	95.03	94.92	94.84
6.30	94.90	94.80	94.67	94.57	94.45	94.35	94.23	94.13
6.40	94.29	94.17	94.03	93.91	93.78	93.67	93.54	93.43
6.50	93.68	93.55	93.39	93.27	93.12	92.99	92.85	92.73
6.60	93.08	92.93	92.76	92.62	92.46	92.33	92.17	92.04
6.70	92.48	92.32	92.14	91.99	91.81	91.67	91.50	91.36
6.80	91.88	91.71	91.52	91.36	91.17	91.01	90.83	90.68
6.90	91.29	91.11	90.91	90.73	90.53	90.36	90.17	90.01
7.00	90.71	90.51	90.30	90.11	89.90	89.72	89.52	89.34
7.10	90.13	89.92	89.69	89.49	89.27	89.08	88.87	88.68
7.20	89.55	89.33	89.09	88.88	88.65	88.45	88.22	88.03
7.30	88.98	88.75	88.50	88.28	88.03	87.82	87.59	87.38
7.40	88.41	88.17	87.91	87.68	87.42	87.20	86.95	86.74
7.50	87.85	87.60	87.32	87.08	86.82	86.58	86.33	86.10
7.60	87.29	87.03	86.74	86.49	86.22	85.97	85.71	85.47
7.70	86.73	86.46	86.17	85.90	85.62	85.37	85.09	84.85
7.80	86.18	85.90	85.60	85.32	85.03	84.77	84.48	84.23
7.90	85.64	85.34	85.03	84.75	84.44	84.17	83.88	83.62

coupon rates and prices. Although it is obviously better to buy 10% bonds at 100 than to buy the same ones at 101, and better to buy 9½'s at 95 than to buy otherwise comparable 9's at the same price, choosing between two offerings of bonds, one of which carries both a lower coupon and also a lower dollar price, may not be easy.

S.D. 2/1/84						
	Amount (M)	Description	Coupon	Maturity	Price	Yield
#3	250	Vermont	6.80	2/1/94	100.	6.80
#4	250	Vermont	5½	2/1/94	87.703	?

Here we have two hypothetical Vermont offerings both due in 10 years. Comparing them by yield is the sort of job we do every bond market hour. Which one is the better buy, the 6.80's at 100, or the 5½'s at under 88? You might answer, the one with the higher yield to maturity, and that's right. But which one is it? The 6.80's have a higher coupon, but what about the 5½'s' lower price? Will the 12 point (100-88 = 12) gain to be made in 10 years give the buyer a better overall return? To decide, we figure the yield to maturity on the 5½'s and see if it is higher than the known 6.80%. It's like the unit pricing on supermarket shelves. Just as it is pretty hard to guess whether you are paying more per pound for a dozen and a half oranges at $2.69 or for a three pound bag at $1.17, it would take some good guessing, even for a bond expert, to figure which of the two Vermont offerings provides the higher yield to maturity.

How is this done? In the old days, we would have looked up 10 year 5½'s in a basis book to see if 87.703 produced a yield higher or lower than 6.80%. Basis books, which contained page after page of cumbersome columns of figured-out prices, coupons, maturities and yields, are obsolete because we now have $1200 desk-top minicomputers which do much faster and better work. The yield equations are hard-wired right into them, and they certainly have made life easier for bond people.

To find the yield equivalent of a known dollar price using a minicomputer, after entering the settlement (cash due) date (here, 2/1/84), you simply enter the bond's coupon, maturity, and price, then push the TO YIELD button; out comes the answer in about five seconds. So, for 5½'s due 2/1/95, you enter 5.5, push the COUPON button; 2.01.95, push the MATURITY button; 87.703 and push the TO YIELD button. Answer? 7.25%. A 5½% bond due in ten years at a dollar price of 87.703 yields a 7.25% to maturity. In goes coupon, time, and price; out comes yield. The 6.80's yield a 6.80% and the 5½'s yield a 7.25%, or 45 basis points more.

The Blue List
of Current Municipal Offerings

(A Division of Standard & Poor's Corporation)

Published every weekday except Saturdays and Holidays by
The Blue List Publishing Company, 25 Broadway, New York, N. Y. 10004
Telephone 212 208-8200

Reg U S Patent Office • Printed in U S A

The bonds set forth in this list were offered at the close of business on the day before the date of this issue by the houses whose offerings are shown in The Blue List. Every effort is made by The Blue List Publishing Company and the houses mentioned, subject to prior sale and change in price. The Blue List to avoid mistakes and inaccuracies, but due to the fact that many offerings come in by wire and that the list is published after the offering houses have closed for the day, occasional errors are unavoidable. Neither The Blue List Publishing Company nor the offering houses take responsibility for the accuracy of the offerings listed herein.

+ Items so marked did not appear in the previous issue of The Blue List.
• Prices so marked are changed from previous issue.
c Items so marked are reported to have call or option features. Consult offering house for full details.

ANNUAL SUBSCRIPTION RATE (approximately 250 issues): Hand Delivery (Wall Street Area) $440.00; First Class Mail $570.00

ALABAMA

AMT. M	SECURITY	PURPOSE	RATE	MATURITY	YIELD OR OFFERED PRICE	OFFERED BY
265	ALABAMA		4.60	3/ 1/88	6.75	FBC
250	ALABAMA		11.90	12/ 1/92	7.90	ROTHCHLD
200	ALABAMA		4.90	5/ 1/93	8.25	FBC
+ 35	ALABAMA		7.90	9/ 1/94	100	HARRISCH
+ 50	ALABAMA		8.10	3/ 1/96	100	HARRISCH
400	ALABAMA	P/R @ 103	11.50	9/ 1/96 C92	7.80	POLLOCKW
325	ALABAMA		8.25	3/ 1/98	8.60	OPCONY
100	ALABAMA		8.25	3/ 1/98	8.60	OPCONY
150	ALABAMA HIGHWAY AUTH.ETM	P/R @ 103	11.875	3/ 1/01 C92 *	7.75	HARRISBK
			6.70	11/ 1/86	5.00	BANKBOST
+ 250	ALABAMA HIGHWAY AUTH.		8.25	9/ 1/87	6.00	FIRBIRMS
200	ALABAMA HIGHWAY AUTH.ETM		5	11/ 1/87	6.00	PRUBAATL
100	ALA.HSG.FIN.AU.		9.25	10/ 1/92	8.65	PORTER
+ 250	ALA.HSG.FIN.AU.		10	10/ 1/98	102 3/4	MOOSEACO
250	ALA.HSG.FIN.AU.		10	10/ 1/98	9.60	PORTER

ALABAMA—CONTINUED

AMT. M	SECURITY	PURPOSE	RATE	MATURITY	YIELD OR OFFERED PRICE	OFFERED BY
20	ALA.HSG.FIN.AU.	*H&G*	8.125	12/ 1/07	100	THUMSNSY
75	ALA.HSG.FIN.AU.		13.875	12/ 1/11	12.00	CHEMICBK
25	ALA.HSG.FIN.AU.	SNGL.FAM.	6	6/ 1/13	9.60	CENTBKNM
+ 100	ALA.PUB.SCH.&COL.AU.		10.60	12/ 1/89	7.00	LISSTENN
+ 100	ALA.PUB.SCH.&COL.AU.		10.60	12/ 1/89	7.25	LISSTENN
+ 130	BESSEMER MED.CL.BD. (BESSEMER CARHANAY)	ETM	6.55	10/ 1/89	100	ASHOWNBA
20	BIRMINGHAM MED.CL.BD.(BAPTIST)		9.25	4/ 1/08	9.50	BURNAMPCU
150	BIRMINGHAM P.H.A.		5	1/ 1/87	6.25	PRUBAATL
30	COOSA RVR.WTW.SK&FINE AU.		9	11/15/95	27 1/8	STERLING
50	COURTLAND I.D.R.	(CHAMP.INTL)	5.75	11/ 1/97	75	BAHRBRUS
50	COURTLAND I.D.R. (CHAMPION INTL.)	SER.67	5.75	11/ 1/97	75	BEARSTER
25	COURTLAND I.D.R. (US PLYWOOD)	SERIES 67	5.75	11/ 1/97	74	MABONIDB

THE BLUE LIST
OF CURRENT MUNICIPAL OFFERINGS

April 15 1985 Monday

Volume 199 Number 10

S.D. 2/1/84

	Amount (M)	Description	Coupon	Maturity	Price	Yield
#3	250	Vermont	6.80	2/1/94	100.	6.80
#4	250	Vermont	5½	2/1/94	87.703	7.25
					Difference	.45%

From Yield to Price

Suppose you start with a yield; how do you find the dollar price? Do the calculation in reverse. Enter the coupon, maturity, and yield; then push the TO PRICE button. For the same 5½% bond due 2/1/94 at a 7.25% yield, enter 5.5, 2.01.94, and 7.25; push TO PRICE, and out comes 87.703.

Discounts

We saw in the last chapter that the current yield of a bond priced at 100 is the same as its coupon, and that the current of a discount bond is higher than its coupon. The same goes for yield to maturity. Bonds at 100 yield their coupon, and discounts yield more. Or, saying it the other way around, bonds yielding more than their coupon sell under 100. Why? A combination of two factors. 1.) A discount bond buyer puts up less than the face amount and so gets a current return higher than the coupon. 2.) Since he will be paid 100 percent at maturity, he will realize a gain equaling the amount of the discount.

Low Coupon, Low Price

Why are some bonds worth less than 100? Supply and demand. If a new issue of Kenosha 10½% bonds were available at 100 in a certain maturity, older Kenosha 4¼% bonds due in the same year would have to be worth less than 100. The market adjusts their price down below 100, until they provide a yield competitive with the new, higher interest rates. For instance, on March 22, 1982, my trading position included 250 Kenosha 4¼% bonds due 4/1/86, which I was trying to sell at a yield of 11.00%, then a dollar price of 78.584. That big a discount was necessary to sell them, because, among other things, competing dealers were offering quite comparable high coupon West Allis, Wisconsin, bonds at a 10.50% yield.

Premiums

Premium bonds, priced above 100, carry a lower yield to maturity than their coupon rate. The reasons? 1.) Their current yield is lower than the coupon. 2.) There will be a loss down to 100 at maturity.

S.D. 2/1/84

	Amount (M)	Description	Coupon	Maturity	Yield	Price
#3	250	Vermont	6.80	2/1/94	6.80	100
#5	250	Vermont	7½	2/1/94	6.80	?

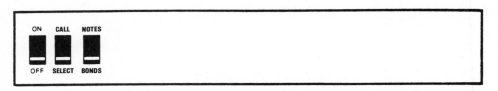
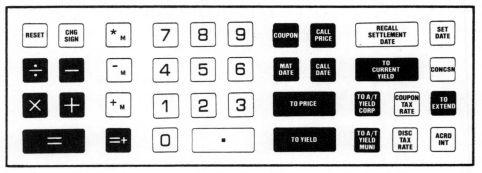

The keyboard of a Compucorp dollar price calculator.

Suppose some older 7½% Vermont bonds due in 1994, which had sold earlier when interest rates were higher, had come into the secondary market in early 1984, at the same time that 6.80% Vermont bonds were worth 100. To find their price at a 6.80% yield, enter these numbers.

#5			
	1.) Coupon	—	7.50%
	2.) Maturity	—	2/1/94
	3.) Yield	—	6.80%

Looking at these figures, we can expect a premium price because the yield is lower than the coupon. Answer?

4.) TO PRICE = 105.019

And starting with a dollar price of 105.019, finding yield is just the same process in reverse.

#5			
	1.) Coupon	—	7.50%
	2.) Maturity	—	2/1/94
	3.) Price	—	105.019
	4.) TO YIELD	=	**6.80**

High Coupon, High Price

Why would anyone pay a premium for a bond? On the demand side, because its coupon is higher than that currently available on similar bonds. If the Vermont 6.80's due in 1994 were worth 100, then someone would be willing to pay more than 100 for 7½'s. Naturally, it is better to get $75 per year than to get $68, and if Vermont 6.80's are worth 100, the 7½'s are worth more and will sell higher. On the supply side, the same logic shows—an investor owning 7½'s wouldn't sell them at the same price he saw holders of 6.80's receiving; he would want more. Bonds are worth premium prices after interest rates fall; they are also used, for technical reasons, in the early maturities of many new issues, as we will be seeing later.

Yield Equates to Price

Another use of yield involves tracking price changes. Example #3 shows a 6.80 at 100. What happens in dollars if the dealer originally offering these bonds at 100 marked them up to a 6.75%?

S.D. 2/1/84

	Amount (M)	Description	Coupon	Maturity	Yield	Price
#3	250	Vermont	6.80	2/1/94	6.80	100.000
#3A	250	Vermont	6.80	2/1/94	6.75	100.359
				Difference	.05%	.359

DOLLAR VALUE OF THE .05

S.D. 2/1/85

Coupon	Maturity		Yield		Dollar Prices	Value of .05	Years to Maturity
6.80	2/1/86	@	6.75	=	100.047		
		@	6.80	=	100.000	47¢	1
					.047		
6.80	2/1/87	@	6.75	=	100.092		
		@	6.80	=	100.000	92¢	2
					.092		
6.80	2/1/88	@	6.75	=	100.133		
		@	6.80	=	100.000	$1.33	3
					.133		
6.80	2/1/89	@	6.75	=	100.172		
		@	6.80	=	100.000	$1.72	4
					.172		
6.80	2/1/90	@	6.75	=	100.209		
		@	6.80	=	100.000	$2.09	5
					.209		
6.80	2/1/91	@	6.75	=	100.243		
		@	6.80	=	100.000	$2.43	6
					.243		
6.80	2/1/95	@	6.75	=	100.359		
		@	6.80	=	100.000	$3.59	10
					.359		
6.80	2/1/95	@	8.95	=	85.986		
		@	9.00	=	85.691	$2.95	10
					.295		
6.80	2/1/05	@	6.75	=	100.544		
		@	6.80	=	100.000	$5.44	20
					.544		
8	2/1/05	@	7.95	=	100.496		
		@	8.00	=	100.000	$4.96	20
					.496		

The price of a one year 6.80 at an .05 premium (6.75) is 100.047. Subtract 100 (6.80), and we get 47¢, or roughly 50¢ as the value of a one year .05.

With coupon and maturity constant, the yield has been changed from a 6.80% to a 6.75%, a difference of one .05. Result? An increase of $3.59 per bond in dollar price. Starting at a 6.80% on the yield scale and at 100 on the dollar price scale, we move to a 6.75% yield, and so to a new place on the dollar scale, 100.359. In our everyday way of speaking, this .05 is worth $3.59. And if the dealer succeeded in selling the bonds at a 6.75%, he would get 100.359 ($250,897.50) for them, instead of his original price of 100. Although the bonds were priced in yield both times, these figures have to be converted into the real world of dollars and cents. After all, you can spend $900, but where can you spend an .05?

In dollar pricing, one point is always $10. Is the value of the .05 always the same—$3.59, for instance? Let's change one factor, maturity, and see.

S.D. 2/1/84

	Amount (M)	Description	Coupon	Maturity	Yield	Price
#6	125	Vermont	6.80	2/1/85	6.80	100.000
#6A	125	Vermont	6.80	2/1/85	6.75	100.047
			Difference		.05%	.047

We saw that the value of the .05 of a ten year 6.80 at 100 is $3.59. But here, in this one year bond the value of an .05 is only 47¢, less than one seventh as great. Why? Its maturity is much shorter. Length of time to maturity is by far the most important variable affecting the value of the .05. Short bonds have smaller .05's, and long bonds larger .05's. In round numbers, near 100, a one year .05 is usually about 50¢, a two year .05 about $1.00, a seven year .05 about a quarter of a point, and out to about a half a point for long bonds. Our discussion of liquidity in Chapter Two ties in here. Since a one year .05 is worth 50¢, a change of twenty of them (from an 8.00% to a 9.00% yield, for example) amounts to 1 point (20 x 50¢ = $10). But if a long term bond whose .05 is worth $5 changes by the same 1.00%, its value declines by ten points (20 x $5 = $100), a ten times greater loss.

The Value of the .05

As you see, learning about municipals is something like learning English—its oddities make it tough to get to know, but once you have it, it's special. Now that we have fully mastered both prices and yields, let's get some practice in a real-life underwriting.

Kenosha's New Issue
Chapters 11-14

$5000 $5000 $5000

№   №

UNITED STATES OF AMERICA
STATE OF WISCONSIN
COUNTY OF KENOSHA

CITY OF KENOSHA

CORPORATE PURPOSE BOND, SERIES 1979

Statement of the value of all the taxable property in the City of Kenosha according to the last preceding assessment thereof for state and county taxes, as equalized by the State of Wisconsin Department of Revenue, being for the year 19_____ $1,108,253,320

Aggregate amount of existing bonded indebtedness of said city, including this issue

KNOW ALL MEN BY THESE PRESENTS: That the City of Kenosha, (the "City") in the County of Kenosha and State of Wisconsin, hereby acknowledges itself to owe, and for value received promises to pay to bearer, or if this bond be registered, to the registered holder of this bond then shall then be registered as to principal, the principal sum of

FIVE THOUSAND DOLLARS ($5000)

on the FIRST DAY OF DECEMBER, _____ 1980 _____

with interest at the rate of _____ per cent (_____ %) per annum

from the date hereof until the principal amount shall have been fully paid, such interest being payable December 1, 1979, and semiannually thereafter on June 1 and December 1 of each year, interest to maturity being payable only upon presentation and surrender of the interest coupons attached hereto as they severally mature. Both principal and interest hereon are hereby made payable in lawful money of the United States of America at the principal office of The Chase Manhattan Bank, National Association, New York, New York. For the prompt payment of this bond with interest hereon as aforesaid and for the levy of taxes sufficient for that purpose, the full faith, credit and resources of the City are hereby irrevocably pledged.

This bond is one of an issue of $3,810,000 issued for the purpose of providing funds in the amounts and for the purposes as follows:

$105,000 for the purpose of constructing and equipping an engine house;
$420,000 for the purpose of constructing and equipping a library;
$1,515,000 for the purpose of improving and extending the sanitary sewer system;
$1,315,000 for the purpose of improving and extending the storm sewer system;
$455,000 for the purpose of providing street improvements.

pursuant to and in all respects in compliance with Chapter 67 of the Wisconsin Statutes and acts supplemental thereto, and a resolution duly adopted by the Common Council of the City on April 2, 1979.

This bond is registrable as to principal in accordance with the provisions endorsed on the reverse side hereof.

It is hereby certified and recited that all conditions, things and acts required by law to exist, to be or be done, precedent to and in the issuance of this bond and the issue of which it is a part, have existed, have existed, and have been performed in due form and time as required by law, that the indebtedness of the City, including this bond, does not exceed any limitation imposed by law, and that the City has levied a direct annual irrepealable tax sufficient to pay the interest hereon when it falls due and also to pay and discharge the principal hereof at maturity.

IN WITNESS WHEREOF the City of Kenosha, by its Common Council, has caused this bond to be signed by its Mayor with his facsimile signature, and by its City Clerk, and its corporate seal to be impressed hereon, and the coupons hereto attached to be signed by said Mayor and City Clerk with their respective facsimile signatures, and said officers, by the execution of this bond, do adopt as and for their own official signatures their respective facsimile signatures appearing on said coupons, as of the first day of June, 1979.

_____
Mayor

_____
City Clerk

UNITED STATES OF AMERICA
STATE OF WISCONSIN
COUNTY OF KENOSHA

CITY OF
KENOSHA

CUSIP 489414 KG 5 *

$5000

%
CORPORATE PURPOSE BOND,
SERIES 1979

DATED JUNE 1, 1979
DUE DECEMBER 1,
_____ 1980 _____

INTEREST PAYABLE
DECEMBER 1, 1979 AND
SEMIANNUALLY THEREAFTER ON
JUNE 1 AND DECEMBER 1

PRINCIPAL AND INTEREST
PAYABLE AT THE PRINCIPAL OFFICE OF
THE CHASE MANHATTAN BANK,
NATIONAL ASSOCIATION
NEW YORK, NEW YORK

CUSIP 489414 KH 6
CUSIP 489414 KJ 2
CUSIP 489414 KK 9
CUSIP 489414 KL 7
CUSIP 489414 KM 5
CUSIP 489414 KN 3
CUSIP 489414 KP 8
CUSIP 489414 KQ 6

CHANGE PER SCHEDULE

SUBMITTED MAY 8 1979 BY _____
NORTHERN BANK NOTE COMPANY
P.O. BOX 406
LA GRANGE, ILLINOIS 60525
TELEPHONE 402 3900 AREA CODE 312

PROOF APPROVED
BY: _____
DATE: _____

PLEASE REFER TO ATTACHED SCHEDULE OF SERIAL MATURITIES FOR CHANGES IN BOND MATURITIES, INTEREST DATES, NUMBER, AND COUPONS.

ON DEC. 1, 1979
$ _____
No. 1

TO BE APPROPRIATELY REDUCED

The CITY OF KENOSHA, Wisconsin,
will pay to bearer the amount shown hereon in lawful money of THE UNITED STATES of America at the principal office of THE CHASE MANHATTAN BANK, NATIONAL ASSOCIATION, New York, New York, upon presentation and surrender of this coupon for interest due that day on its CORPORATE PURPOSE BOND, SERIES 1979, dated June 1, 1979, NO. _____

FACSIMILE SIGNATURE OF
Gail F. Procanione   Paul Saftig
City Clerk   FACSIMILE SIGNATURE   Mayor

Chapter Eleven

Interest and Principal Payment

Over the years, investors have become accustomed to receiving their municipal bond interest and principal payments in certain sensible ways. Now for a few pages we will trace these processes, continuing to use Kenosha as our example. We will see that Kenosha was scheduled to make the first interest payment on its 1979 issue that December 1, or as we say it, its first coupon was 12/1/79. Most municipal issuers pay interest twice a year (semi-annually) and this was no exception. One interest coupon is usually paid on the same month and day that the principal is due (most often on the first of the month, but sometimes on other days, such as the fifteenth). The other coupon is paid six months later. This issuer's principal due date was December 1, and its interest paying dates were June 1 and December 1.[1]

Semi-Annual Interest Payments

How did Kenosha provide for actually paying the interest it owed? By printing paper coupons attached to the physical bonds. Each coupon (pronounced dove-like, coo-pon) states the amount owed, its due date, and the paying agent (here Chase Manhattan Bank in N.Y.C.). When a coupon comes due, the holder cuts (or clips, as they say) it apart from the mother bond and either sends it directly to the paying agent, or, like a check made out to cash, deposits it into a checking account, instructing the bank to send the coupon on to the paying agent for collection. Meanwhile, the issuer keeps track of each interest amount coming due and shortly in advance sends the necessary funds to the paying agent, who later credits it to whoever presents the coupons. (This system was in effect back in 1979, and bonds issued that way remain payable by coupon. We call them coupon bonds, or bearer bonds. However, Congress changed the rules in 1983, and so new issues now come in registered form, to which we will return later.)

Interest Coupons

(1) For interest figuring purposes, we call these bonds J and D 1. Bonds with interest payable January 1 and July 1 are called J and J 1, and then comes F and A 1, M and S 1, A and O 1, and M and N 1, and J and D 1.

MONTHLY ACCRUED INTEREST ON $1,000 AT 3.60%

Settlement Date	Accrued Interest	Interest Day	Settlement Date
Jan. 1	$ .00	0	July 1
2	.10	1	2
3	.20	2	3
4	.30	3	4
5	.40	4	5
6	.50	5	6
7	.60	6	7
8	.70	7	8
9	.80	8	9
10	.90	9	10
11	1.00	10	11
12	1.10	11	12
13	1.20	12	13
14	1.30	13	14
15	1.40	14	15
16	1.50	15	16
17	1.60	16	17
18	1.70	17	18
19	1.80	18	19
20	1.90	19	20
21	2.00	20	21
22	2.10	21	22
23	2.20	22	23
24	2.30	23	24
25	2.40	24	25
26	2.50	25	26
27	2.60	26	27
28	2.70	27	28
29	2.80	28	29
30	2.90	29	30
31	3.00	30	31
Feb. 1	3.00	30	Aug. 1

Why a 3.60% coupon for this table?

Because it works out to 10¢ a day per bond, tying evenly into the 360 day year.

Settlement Date 7/16/86

100 California   3.60%   7/01/06   @50

Principal: $50,000   Interest Days: 15

Interest: $150   Total: $50,150

Now a purely technical term: dated date, which is sort of the official birth date of a bond issue (roughly coinciding with its day of sale) by which it is officially identified. This issue is known in the trade as Kenosha, Wisconsin G.O.'s dated 6/1/79. In over 90% of all cases, the municipality starts owing interest from its dated date. Interest on these bonds was regular; it would start to accrue from 6/1/79.

However, bonds are rarely delivered to underwriters exactly on their interest date. Following standard practice, an interest accrual is made so that the winning group starts drawing interest only from the actual delivery date, that is, the day it put its money up. As the Notice of Sale stated, the high bidder would pay the bid price, plus accrued interest. How is accrued interest figured? By prorating the interest amount between the issuer and the buyer proportionally to the time each holds the bonds. So for every day after the set interest accrual date, one-thirtieth (1/30, or 1 day's worth) of one month's interest would be paid by the underwriters to the city, splitting the amount fairly.[2]

This system of accrued interest continues into the future and is calculated every time a bond changes hands. So, unless a bond trades on an exact interest date, there will be two amounts due on the purchase: the principal and the accrued interest. The principal due is calculated by multiplying the number of bonds by the dollar price. For example, if 100 bonds are bought at 98, the principal comes to $98,000. The interest due is calculated by multiplying the number of bonds by the accrued interest on one bond. So if the interest rate is 12% (accruing at $10 a bond per month) and the purchase occurs exactly half way through the first month, the accrued interest would be $5 per bond. On the 100 bonds this would be $500, making the total price $98,500.

Another technical term: 360-day year. The municipal bond year has the usual 12 months in it, but with one neat twist. Every municipal month, even February, is assigned exactly 30 days, and interest accrues on a uniform 360 day calendar, leap years and common years alike. The first day of every month is a zero interest day. The second day of the month is the number 1 interest accrual day; the third day of the month is number 2, and so forth up to the thirty-first, which is interest day number 30. What happens to the shorter months? Enough interest days are assigned to them to bring their total up to 31 before the next month starts. Thus, every month has exactly 30 interest days, 360 per year.

As we saw earlier, most bonds come in $5,000 denominations. There-

(2) One more complication: issuers often choose irregular interest accrual or first payment dates. In these cases we have to adjust the figures for either a short, or a long, first coupon.

YEARLY ACCRUED INTEREST ON $1,000 AT 3.60%

	Accrued Interest	Interest Day	
Jan. 1	0	0	July 1
2	.10	1	2
3	.20	2	3
28	2.70	27	28
29	2.80	28	29
30	2.90	29	30
31	3.00	30	31
Feb. 1	3.00	30	Aug. 1
2	3.10	31	2
28	5.70	57	28
(29)	5.80	58	29
x	5.90	59	30
x	6.00	60	31
Mar. 1	6.00	60	Sept. 1
2	6.10	61	2
30	8.90	89	30
x	9.00	90	x
Apr. 1	9.00	90	Oct. 1
2	9.10	91	2
30	11.90	119	30
x	12.00	120	31
May 1	12.00	120	Nov. 1
2	12.10	121	2
30	14.90	149	30
31	15.00	150	x
Jun. 1	15.00	150	Dec. 1
2	15.10	151	2
30	17.90	179	30
x	18.00	180	31

	365
We take away the first day of every month:	− 12
	353
We then add 7 non-days	+ 7
The result is a 360 day year	360

106

fore, if the winning bidder named a 6% coupon, Kenosha would owe $300 interest on each $5,000 bond every year ($5,000 x .06 = $300). This $300 would be paid out semi-annually, so every $5,000 bondholder would collect $150 twice a year. And if the coupon rate were 5½%, each coupon would read $137.50 ($5,000 x .055 = $275.00 divided by 2 = $137.50), etc. At 5½%, this would add up to $209,550 ($3,810,000 x .055). The city would plan to send $104,775 to Chase every J & D 1 until the first principal is paid off, and declining amounts thereafter, until the whole loan is retired.[3]

Kenosha, like most communities, pays some principal on its serial loans once a year (annual principal). So the city budgets debt service payments twice a year for each loan outstanding, one for interest only and one for principal and interest. During 1978, for example, Kenosha paid over $4 million principal and $1 million interest on 19 separate G.O. loans, some every month of the year. To keep up with all these payments, the city Clerk/Treasurer maintained a separate debt service ledger; after the 1979 issue was delivered Mr. Gail Procarione entered a new set of principal payments—$35,000 on 12/1/80, $275,000 on 12/1/81, right on to the last maturity of the loan, 12/1/88.

How were Kenosha's bondholders to get their principal back at maturity? Since the bonds were issued in bearer form, they could either send them directly to the paying agent, or deposit them, like coupons, into their checking accounts. Bearer bonds state that the issuer will pay the principal due to the bearer, that is, the actual possessor and presenter of the physical bonds. In this respect bearer bonds are something like a check made out to cash. Although there are ways to stop payment if they are lost or stolen, the paying bank simply pays the person, or bank, presenting them. So, as the 12/1/80 maturity date approached, Kenosha sent Chase $35,000 and Chase credited their bearers; later the paper bonds were cancelled and eventually destroyed. Again on 12/1/81, $275,000 was paid off, and this process of serial redemption will continue through 12/1/88, when the loan will quietly expire. No report is made to the taxing authorities on either interest or principal, so undoubtedly bearer bonds help people to evade capital gains and make other tax cheating easier.

Investors used to have a choice of buying new issue bonds in either bearer or registered form. However, in 1983 Congress passed a law, which took full effect July 1, 1984, requiring municipal bonds issued after that date to be registered. What happened to outstanding coupon bonds? They

(3) Some relatively minor distortions occur using this system, and some short-term securities are figured on a more precise 365 day calendar; but in the long-term market, our 360 day year evens out almost perfectly.

COUPON
AND
REGISTERED BONDS

	Coupon	Registered As to Principal Only	Fully Registered
Interest Paid to:	Bearer	Bearer	Registered Owner
Principal Paid to:	Bearer	Registered Owner	Registered Owner

were left unchanged and still trade, often at premium prices, in the secondary market. What is a registered bond? One which is made out to a specific owner, like a check made out to one designated payee. Instead of each bond stating that the principal will be paid to the bearer, there is a column of blank spaces on its back where the owner's name is entered by a designated agent. Registered bonds are transferable, but each time they change hands the seller must sign them over to the buyer, whose name is recorded on the agent's books as the new registered holder.

How are interest payments made on registered bonds? The paying agent simply mails checks to the address of the owner. No coupons are needed, and the process is simpler, easier, and probably cheaper for all concerned. Repayment of principal is handled similarly. Checks for the face amount are mailed in time to arrive on the due date. Now that we understand all these technical matters perfectly, on to a real bond issue and its designers.

Payments to Registered Holders

1979 - 1983

CAPITAL IMPROVEMENT PLAN

As Recommended by:

Committees

City Plan Commission 9/21/78

Administration/Mayor 9/29/78

Finance Committee 10/11/78

Common Council 10/24/78

Chapter Twelve

Designing A Bond

We mentioned earlier how small communities rely on volunteers for advising them on their financial operations and how the largest issuers employ staffs of experts to do the job. Kenosha fell into a mid-range of bond issuers—too big to rely on informal financing advice, but not quite active enough in the borrowing world to need a full-time specialist. So, like many other medium-sized cities, it employed a paid outside consultant to design its bond issues. For many years it had used Paul Speer, in 1976 switched to the First Wisconsin National Bank, and presently employs Clayton Brown. Financial consultants perform three main functions: helping their clients develop long range capital spending plans; implementing them through bond sales; and representing the community to the investing public. As Ken Kerznar said, "The financial consultant is the bridge between political reality and the underwriters' concept of a desirable market instrument."

Public Finance

In practice, the work on Kenosha's bond issue was performed by a three-person team composed of the City Comptroller (Mr. Eugene Schulz), the financial advisor (Mr. Kenneth Kerznar), and a bond counsel (Richard Goss, Esq.). Gene Schulz, with a degree in accounting from Western Michigan University, was the city's chief financial person. He is a C.P.A. and a member of the Government Finance Officers Association. Among his duties are managing Kenosha's cash flow, investing its short-term money, and preparing the many necessary financial statements for the state and other bodies, in addition to assembling the figures needed to float bond issues. He works with the City Clerk/Treasurer and the City Council all year long, and with the financial consultant, especially in the periods before bond sales. A busy man indeed.

The Comptroller

Like most local governments, Kenosha is required by state law to prepare future capital improvement plans, in this case on a five-year basis. In accordance with the priorities determined through political processes, Kenosha's plan allocated $22 million for sewer improvements, $9 million

Long Range Finance

	Date of Issue	Outstanding Dec.31,1977	1978 Maturities	Final Date of Maturity
Corporate Purpose Bonds				
Series 1958	11-1-58	$ 20,000	$ 20,000	1978
Series 1959	11-1-59	95,000	45,000	1979
Series 1960	10-1-60	500,000	150,000	1980
Series 1961	10-1-61	930,000	235,000	1981
Series 1963	5-1-63	245,000	245,000	1978
Series 1964	5-1-64	720,000	365,000	1979
Series 1965	10-1-65	1,395,000	465,000	1980
Series 1966	8-1-66	2,220,000	450,000	1981
Series 1968	7-1-68	340,000	340,000	1978
Series 1969	8-1-69	600,000	275,000	1979
Series 1970	8-1-70	1,200,000	300,000	1981
Series 1971	6-1-71	475,000	175,000	1980
Series 1972	8-1-72	1,040,000	300,000	1981
Series 1973	4-1-73	1,650,000	275,000	1983
Series 1974	5-1-74	3,250,000	250,000	1984
Series 1975	4-1-75	3,250,000	250,000	1984
Series 1976	3-1-76	3,350,000	225,000	1986
Series 1977	4-1-77	2,545,000	245,000	1987
Board of Education		22,500	7,500	1980
		----------	----------	
		$23,847,500	$ 4,617,500	

for streets, $8 million for the Park Department, and smaller amounts for the airport, the library system, and other projects. Of the $48 million total, 15.8% would be paid from current income, and the balance funded through bonds, starting with the 1979 issue. A total of $11 million had been formally requested for that year by various city departments, an amount far larger than the city's usual bond issues, and it would be up to the Council to determine which projects would go to the head of the line.

Gene Schulz called Kerznar early in 1979 about tentative plans for the bond sale, tacitly confirming the Council's intentions to continue using *The Financial* First Wisconsin as their financial advisor. Ken Kerznar, a graduate of the *Advisor* University of Wisconsin Business School, was an associate member of the Wisconsin affiliate of the M.F.O.A. He asked Schulz to send him the latest update on the financial projections, and the rest of the data needed for preparing the issue. His work fell into three categories:

1. Shaping the issue and fitting it into the city's financial situation.
2. Preparing an Official Statement.
3. Bringing the issue to market.

At this point the question of whether to sell privately, through negotiation, or publicly, at competitive bid, often comes up. Most states require that G.O.'s be sold competitively, but a growing minority of issues, particularly the larger ones, are, in 1985, being negotiated. Kenosha had no choice, since Wisconsin law compels public sale for G.O.'s.

Kerznar started projecting a schedule of debt service payments, and noted that the city was to receive 86% of its state revenue sharing payment *Scheduling* on November 1. Seeing that December was a relatively light month for *Interest* principal and interest, he put down that month as a possible principal date for this new issue. Then he began to think what interest rate the city would have to pay, and after checking with the experts, made an estimate of from 5½ to 6%. So he put down 6%— as a matter of sound practice, and also of salesmanship, it is usually better to be a little conservative (that is, on the high side) when presenting possible rates, so that any surprises will be pleasant ones. $114,000 would be paid out that D1, the next J & D1, and so on, gradually decreasing as the principal was repaid. He checked Schulz's estimates of cash flow and saw that the city could handle those amounts quite easily.

Then Kerznar went to work on the principal amounts, which presented several problems. On the one hand, the city fathers had indicated that they *Scheduling* wanted the annual debt service on this issue to be less than $750,000, and *Principal* with only a token amount to be paid out before 1981. On the other hand, with Schulz's concurrence, they were sticking to a long-standing policy of

OFFICIAL PUBLICATION
Initial Resolutions

The following initial resolutions were introduced and read at the March 5, 1979 regular meeting of the Common Council of the City of Kenosha and will be considered for adoption at the regular meeting of April 2, 1979.

INITIAL RESOLUTION authorizing not exceeding $105,000 bonds of the City of Kenosha.

BE IT RESOLVED by the Common Council of the City of Kenosha, Wisconsin, that there shall be issued the general obligation bonds of said City in the principal amount of not exceeding $105,000 for the purpose of constructing and equipping an engine house of said City. For the purpose of paying the various installments of principal and interest on said bonds as they severally mature, there is hereby levied on all taxable property in said City a direct annual irrepealable tax sufficient for that purpose.

INITIAL RESOLUTION authorizing not exceeding $420,000 bonds of the City of Kenosha.

BE IT RESOLVED by the Common Council of the City of Kenosha, Wisconsin, that there shall be issued the general obligation bonds of said City in the principal amount of not exceeding $420,000 for the purpose of constructing and equipping a library of said City. For the purpose of paying the various installments of principal and interest on said bonds, as they severally mature, there is hereby levied on all taxable property in said City a direct annual irrepealable tax sufficient for the purpose.

INITIAL RESOLUTION authorizing not exceeding $1,515,000 bonds of the City of Kenosha.

BE IT RESOLVED by the Common Council of the City of Kenosha, Wisconsin, that there shall be issued the general obligation bonds of said City in the principal amount of not exceeding $1,515,000 for the purpose of improving and extending the sanitary sewer system of said City. For the purpose of paying the various installments of principal and interest on said bonds as they severally mature, there is hereby levied on all taxable property in said City a direct annual irrepealable tax sufficient for that purpose.

INITIAL RESOLUTION authorizing not exceeding $1,315,000 bonds of the City of Kenosha.

BE IT RESOLVED by the Common Council of the City of Kenosha, Wisconsin, that there shall be issued the general obligation bonds of said City in the principal amount of not exceeding $1,315,000 for the purpose of improving and extending the storm sewer system of said City. For the purpose of paying the various installments of principal and interest on said bonds as they severally mature, there is hereby levied on all taxable property in said City a direct annual irrepealable tax sufficient for the purpose.

INITIAL RESOLUTION authorizing not exceeding $455,000 bonds of the City of Kenosha.

BE IT RESOLVED by the Common Council of the City of Kenosha, Wisconsin, that there shall be issued the general obligation bonds of said City in the principal amount of not exceeding $455,000 for the purpose of providing street improvements of said City. For the purpose of paying the various installments of principal and interest on said bonds as they severally mature, there is hereby levied on all taxable property in said City a direct annual irrepealable tax sufficient for the purpose.

/s/
GAIL PROCARIONE,
City Clerk
Publish:
March 8, 1979
March 15, 1979
 Note: Letter authorizing this legal dated March 5, 1979 from City Clerk.

limiting bond maturities to a maximum of 10 years. So there was no sense trying to persuade them to reduce current debt service by extending their maturities into the future; it was just not Kenosha's style. Most G.O. issuers see it differently, and tailor their bond maturities to the expected useful life of a financed facility, so that the taxpayers who benefit from it will pay for it. A school bus issue may be paid off in five years, a municipal building loan in 20, and bonds sold to construct a water system may run out to 30 or 40 years. As consumers we borrow similarly, using credit cards for clothes and vacations, taking out three year loans for cars, and arranging long-term mortgages for homes, matching the financing with the life of the purchase. But not Kenosha. They just didn't like paying all that interest, and that was that. So Kerznar roughed out a combined schedule of P & I, assuming a 6% rate, and sent it to Schulz in March for his comments. It looked fine to the Comptroller, and soon Kerznar heard that the Council had informally approved his plan, and that the sale was on for June. This was his signal to complete and print up the Official Statement.

In the meanwhile, bond counsel Goss, after hearing from Schulz that the issue was on its way, put it on his forward work calendar. Richard Goss, a graduate of Clark University, had received his law degree from Northwestern. He was a member of the Illinois and Wisconsin bars, and was active on a number of their local government committees. By the end of March he had reviewed the Wisconsin bond statutes for any recent changes, thus updating his long checklist for issuing bonds in that state. As we discussed in Chapter 5, after a local government body decides to sell bonds, the bond counsel's job is to make certain that their intentions are translated correctly into the processes mandated by the enabling legislation. The Kenosha Council proceeded promptly, and Goss drafted five resolutions for them to pass, one for each of the several purposes of the issue, including one for the library we spoke of earlier. He then sent them, along with a letter outlining all of the documents he would need to render his legal opinion, to Schulz for submission to the Council, and to Mr. James Conway, the city's own attorney. On March 5, 1979, they were read on the Council floor, and notice was published in *The Kenosha Labor* on March 8 and 15, complying with that provision of the state statutes. On April 2 these resolutions were adopted by a 15 to 1 vote, and were subsequently printed in the local paper, too.

The Legalities

Kerznar was by then well into his most comprehensive project—preparing the Official Statement, a fact-filled booklet which underwriters and investors refer to for data on an issuer's social, economic, political, and financial situations. Gene Schulz had provided him with last year's final

The O.S.

OFFICIAL STATEMENT CHECK LIST

Name of Issue: *City of Kenosha*
Amount: *$ 3,810,000*
Sale Date: *May 7, 1979*
Covers To Internal Service: *April 9, 1979*
Official Statement To Internal Service: *April 9, 1979*
Mail Official Statement: *April 23, 1979*

Done	Typed	
		Cover to Internal Service
		Table of Contents
✓		Official Notice of Sale
✓		New Issue Summary
✓		City Government
✓		Map
✓		Value of Taxable Property, Legal Debt Limits and Debt
✓		Outstanding Debt Issues
✓		Anticipated Financing
✓		Debt Administration
✓		Retirement Schedule of Outstanding Debt Issues
✓		General Obligation Debt Trend
✓		General Obligation Debt and Projected Equalized Valuation
✓		Property Valuations and Tax Levies
✓		Assessed Tax Rates
✓		Tax Collection Record
✓		Assessment Reports (5 Years)
✓		Retirement Plan
✓		Introduction to Financial Statements
✓		Financial Statements (5 Years)
✓✓		Budget Summary
✓		General Information (Location, Historical, Government, Education, Schools, Enrollments, Utility, Litigation)
✓		Demographic Information (Population, Per Capita Income, Unemployment Rate, Median Age, Building Permits, Bank Deposits, Postal Receipts)
		Economic Information (Principal Industries & Commercial Entities, 20 Significant Taxpayers)
✓		Financial Consultant
✓		Representations of the City
✓		Work Sheet
✓		Bid Forms

figures, estimates for that fiscal year, and projections for the following years, both for balance sheets and income statements, and also the current list of the outstanding bond issues, plus the tax collection numbers for 1978-79. Kerznar also consulted with Earl Hammill and Company, the city's accountants, who had already been asked to begin the auditing procedures on the city's financial statements, including the revenue, expenditures, and fund balance numbers, so that Hammill could later render a letter of opinion that the city's financial condition had been presented fairly, and in conformity with generally accepted accounting principles.

After the O.S. and the bond mechanics were under way, Kerznar turned to the dealers and the potential investors in the issue, hoping to impress them favorably. We saw earlier that credit quality comes into focus when a bond issue is submitted for rating to Moody's and/or Standard & Poor's, the independent financial service companies who act as research proxies for most dealers and investors. Since their ratings strongly affect buyers' opinions of credit quality, and therefore the interest rates the dealers finally name, a financial consultant does well to make his best pitch to them. Ken Kerznar did just that in February 1979, applying only to Moody's, who had previously rated Kenosha A1, or upper medium grade. He informed them of the coming sale, provided them with the necessary legal proofs, and sent them the latest financial and economic numbers. Moody's started their review process and sent an analyst to the city to add some first hand impressions to the bare figures. We can imagine that during the visit Schulz and Kerznar tried some polite arm twisting to obtain a higher rating. While Moody's digested the statistics and sights, Kerznar sent all the pertinent information for the printing of the physical bonds to the Northern Banknote Co. in LaGrange, Illinois. The actual engraving was postponed until after the bond sale, when the coupon rates would be set by the winning bidder.

Applying for a Rating

By late March the loan had been drawn up in nearly final form, and Goss gave First Wisconsin the legal go-ahead. Kerznar consulted with his own marketing experts and picked May 7, 1979, for the date of the sale. Since state law required that at least 30 days notice be given for bond sales, Kerznar picked April 5 to advertise in *The Daily Bond Buyer, The Wall Street Journal,* and *The Kenosha Labor.* (Theoretically, anyone reading one of those notices can submit a bid, but over 99% of all proposals come from bond houses.) On May 1, Moody's notified First Wisconsin that their A1 rating had been reviewed and retained—apparently there was too much American Motors there for them to raise it to Aa. However, an A1 rating is perfectly respectable, and it's not impossible that Schulz and Kerznar were

To Market, To Market

MOODY'S INVESTORS SERVICE, INC.
99 CHURCH STREET, NEW YORK, N.Y. 10007 (212) 553-0300

May 1, 1979

Mr. Ken Kerzner
First Wisconsin National Bank
 of Milwaukee
777 East Wisconsin Avenue
Milwaukee, Wisconsin 53262

Dear Mr. Kerzner:

We wish to inform you that our Rating Committee has
assigned the rating of A 1 to the $3,810,000 Kenosha,
Wisconsin General Obligation ULT Bonds scheduled for sale
on May 7, 1979.

In order that we may maintain the currency of this
rating over the period of the loan, we will require current
financial and other updating information. We will appreciate
your continued cooperation in the future.

Sincerely yours,

Freda Stern Ackerman
Senior Vice President

RG/cm
cc: Ms. Gail F. Procarione
     City Treasurer
     City of Kenosha
     Council Chambers of Municipal Building
     Kenosha, Wisconsin 53140

relieved to have kept it.

When sale time approached, Goss reviewed the resolutions as actually voted, collected affidavits of proof that the bond issuing resolutions had been properly advertised (a frequent cause of faulty issuing), checked these and other documents, some properly notarized, and provided the council with the correct form of resolution for accepting the winning bid. Kerznar saw that all was ready, and the sale we will be monitoring in the next two chapters went forward.

This, like most competitive new issues, was to be actually delivered and paid for about a month after the sale date. In early June, after the sale had come and gone, since no one had filed a petition in court to threaten the issue, Goss prepared a certificate of non-litigation. As the actual delivery date approached, when bonds and money would change hands, he saw to it that the necessary closing documents (including arbitrage and disclosure certificates) were signed, and personally inspected one of the printed bonds. By delivery date, Goss had organized all the documents into a thick bundle called the Transcript of Proceedings, headed by his firm's legal opinion that the bonds were validly issued G.O.'s, and that their interest was exempt from federal income taxes. He sent a copy to the underwriters, the city, and the financial consultant, in case some question about the legal aspects ever arose.

Calendar of
Sealed Bid Opening

		$	Ratings Moody's	S&P's	Bidding Details
5/ 4	Milan, Tenn.	1,655,000	t	x	4/17
5/ 7	Corbin, Ky.	1,800,000	t	x	5/3
5/ 7	Duluth, Minn.	5,275,000	A1	x	4/24, 30
5/ 7	Emmet Co., Mich.	1,400,000	t	x	4/26
5/ 7	Flowing Wells Unif. Sch. Dist. No. 8, Ariz.	2,200,000	s	x	4/26
5/ 7	Kenosha, Wisc.	3,810,000	A1	x	4/4, 5, 27
5/ 7	King Co., Wash.	38,831,000	Aa	AA	4/25; 5/2
5/ 7	Lewisville, Tex.	1,250,000	A	A	4/25
5/ 7	Marana Elem. Sch. Dist. No. 6, Ariz.	2,440,000	A	x	4/10
5/ 7	Marana High. Sch. Dist. No. 106, Ariz.	1,700,000	A	x	4/10
5/ 7	Mount Belvieu, Tex.	3,500,000	A	x	4/25; 5/1
5/ 7	South St. Paul, Minn.	2,615,000	A	x	4/16, 24
5/ 7	West Fargo, N. D.	785,000	t	x	5/4
5/ 8	Anchorage, Alaska	11,350,000	A	A	4/27; 5/3
5/ 8	Anchorage, Alaska (MBIA Qual.)	11,350,000	t	AAA	4/27; 5/3
5/ 8	Hillsboro Sch. Dist. No. 7, Ore.	3,375,000	A	x	4/16; 17, 26
5/ 8	Long Beach Redev. Agency, Calif.				
	Parking Lease Rev.	6,830,000	cA1	Ap	4/25
	Tax Allocation	4,860,000	s	x	4/25
5/ 8	Navarro Ind. Sch. Dist., Tex.	850,000	Baa1	x	4/25
5/ 8	Ormond Beach, Fla. (Water & Sewer Rev.)	2,500,000	A	A	4/20, 24; 5/1
5/ 8	Ormond Beach, Fla. (Water & Sewer Rev.) (MBIA Qual.)	2,500,000	t	AAA	4/20, 24; 5/1
5/ 8	Owatonna, Minn.	3,925,000	s	x	4/24
5/ 8	Paducah, Ky. (Sch. Bldg. Rev.)	1,790,000	t	Ap	4/26, 27, 30
5/ 8	Port of Bellingham, Wash.	5,750,000	A1	A	4/26, 5/2
5/ 8	Rolling Fort Public Util. Dist., Tex.	930,000	t	x	5/2
5/ 8	South Pittsburgh, Tenn.	950,000	s	x	4/24; 5/1
5/ 8	Spartanburg Sanitary Sewer Dist., S.C.	2,520,000	A	A	4/25, 26
5/ 8	Stewartville Ind. Sch. Dist. No 534, Minn.	1,650,000	A	x	4/25, 27
5/ 8	Wentzville Sch. Dist. R-IV, Mo.	1,985,000	A	x	4/23
5/ 8	Wilton, Conn.	2,200,000	s	AA	4/18, 23
5/ 8	Wilton, Conn. (MBIA Qual.)	2,200,000	t	AAA	4/18, 23
5/ 8	Wisconsin Rapids, Wisc.	2,040,000	A	x	4/24, 5/1
5/ 9	Chesterfield Co. Sch. Dist., S.C.	1,000,000	A	A	4/26, 27; 5/2
5/ 9	Dayton Ind. Sch. Dist., Tex.	2,880,000	A1	x	4/25, 5/1
5/ 9	East Hampton, N.Y.	1,277,500	A1	s	4/27, 5/2
5/ 9	East Hampton, N.Y. (MBIA Qual.)	1,277,500	t	AAA	4/27; 5/2
5/ 9	New Hampshire	40,500,000	Aaa	x	4/5, 23
5/ 9	Northwest Harris Co. Pub. Util. Dist. No. 1, Tex.	1,885,000	t	x	4/26
5/ 9	Pickerington Local Sch. Dist., Ohio	2,115,000	A	x	4/25; 5/1
5/ 9	Shelby Eastern High Sch. Bldg. Corp. Ind. (First Mtg. Rev.)	5,800,000	t	x	5/4
5/ 9	Sumner Sch. Dist. No. 320, Wash.	1,860,000	A	x	3/26, 4/24
5/ 9	Tri-City Water Dist., Ore.	1,350,000	t	x	4/24
5/ 9	Williston, N. D. (Ref. Impr. Water & Sewer Rev.)	2,735,000	t	x	5/4
5/10	Clute, Tex.	1,800,000	Baa1	x	4/25
5/10	Evergreen Sch. Dist. No. 114, Wash.	8,735,000	A	x	3/28, 4/30
5/10	Evergreen Sch. Dist. No. 114, Wash. (MBIA Qual.)	8,735,000	t	AAA	3/28, 4/30
5/10	Little Rock Sch. Dist., Ark.	6,000,000	A1	x	5/1
5/10	Macomb Co., Md.	15,000,000	s	x	5/3
5/10	Michigan State Building Authority (Bldg. Rev.)	89,450,000	s	s	5/2
5/10	Minneapolis, Minn.	18,175,000	s	s	4/27
5/10	Norwood-Norfolk Central Sch. Dist., N.Y.	2,183,296	s	x	5/3
5/10	South Windsor, Conn.	3,515,000	s	x	4/19, 30
5/10	Warrick Co. Elem. Sch. Bldg. Corp. Ind. (First Mtg. Rev.)	5,650,000	cA	x	4/18

Chapter Thirteen

Underwriting an Issue

As anxious as Kenosha's finance people were to receive favorable bids on their bonds, this sale comprised only one small part of the tax-exempt world, where in May, 1978, investors had 100 or more new issues to choose among. Positioned between the City's financial team and the potential buyers was another group that cared—the dealers who regularly bid on this and other municipal bond new issues. What is the dealers' aim? To buy bonds at the lowest possible price (the highest interest rate) and resell them at the highest possible price (the lowest interest rate). Let's assume for a moment that an average yield of 5.50% would be just sufficient to persuade investors to buy Kenosha's bonds that day. If an underwriting group were to bid too cheaply, planning to offer a 5.70% yield to investors, for example, it would probably miss the issue and a chance for profit. On the other hand, if a group were to price it too high, at, say, a 5.30% yield, investors would refuse to buy the bonds and the syndicate would probably lose money. So each competing syndicate tries to bid higher than all its competitors while maintaining a price low enough to attract buyers.

As we saw in Chapter 2, some investors need short-term bonds to match certain liability dates, while others prefer long-term bonds for more permanent investment. In most markets the prevailing level of supply and demand produces what we call an ascending yield curve, that is, a pattern of interest rates which increase with length of maturity. So Kenosha's one year bonds might yield 5.25%, its five year bonds 5.50%, and its last year, 5.75%. The primary job of underwriting is to set the yields on the various maturities of an issue so they will attract enough investors to buy each one. In the U.S. Treasury market, where bonds are identical in credit, and where plenty in every maturity trade all day long, pricing is a comparatively simple process. But in municipals, where bonds vary widely in credit quality, and where only a few dozen different names are in the market in a given week, pricing is more complex, and more subjective. The best guidelines are the

WISCONSIN

Kenosha, Wisc. — $3,810,000 — Sealed bids May 7, at 1 pm CST, for purchase of corporate purpose unlimited tax bonds.

Dated June 1, 1979. Due Dec. 1, 1980 to 1988. L.O.: Chapman & Cutler, Chicago.

GAIL F. PROCARIONE,
City Clerk.

Last Comparable Sale

$4,055,000 — Corporate purpose Series 1978 bonds were sold on April 17, 1978 to a group headed by First Wisconsin National Bank, Milwaukee in association with a group headed by Blyth Eastman Dillon & Co., Incorporated, **NIC 4.876%.**

Reoffered at 4.10% in 1979 to 5.00% in 1988.

The Bond Buyer Index 5.74%.
Other bidders were:

First National Bank of Chicago and associates, **NIC 4.8861%.**

Continental Illinois National Bank & Trust Co., Chicago and Bache Halsey Stuart Shields Inc. (Co-managers) and associates, **NIC 4.8909%.**

Northern Trust Co., Chicago and associates, **NIC 4.89106%.**

John Nuveen & Co. Inc., Marine National Exchange Bank, Milwaukee and LaSalle National Bank, Chicago (Co-managers) and associates, **NIC 4.9296%.**

Harris Trust & Savings Bank, Chicago and associates, **NIC 4.9508%.**

Morgan Guaranty Trust Co., and Citibank, NA, both ofNew York (Co-managers) and associates, **NIC 4.9789%.**

First National Bank, Minneapolis and associates, **NIC 4.9978%.**

prices and yields currently available on similar tax-exempt bonds. Let's take Kenosha's first substantial maturity year, 1981. In one way or another the yields on other two-year A-rated bonds were going through the minds of every underwriter bidding on Kenosha. Some might have remembered the 5.10% that the State of Wisconsin carried the week before in its 1981 maturity. Since Wisconsin, a high grade state name, came at 5.10%, the Kenosha bond had to be worth less, perhaps a 5.30%. Several others might have referred to Baltimore, a medium grade but somewhat weaker selling bond than Kenosha, which was priced at a 5.40% in 1981. So a range of reoffering yields from a 5.20% to a 5.35% would have seemed reasonable for Kenosha in 1981, and very probably such thoughts were expressed in all the syndicates bidding on it, with the same line of reasoning continuing for all the years of the loan.

Once the offering yields have been agreed on, the group sets the potential profit it wants to bid for. If a group bids too low a profit margin, there may be nothing worthwhile left. But if a syndicate tries for too large a spread, the issue may be lost to another group willing to work for a smaller margin. What considerations influence this judgment? The length of maturity, the credit risks involved, and comparisons with actual profits on other deals. In 1979, the probable range for an issue like this would have been from $7.50 to $12.50 per bond. In other times the profit margins would be smaller or larger, depending on market conditions. *The Profit Margin*

In the bidding process, each member of a syndicate has a set of internal factors to consider, including the ability of its sales force, the number of actual or potential orders for bonds, and the level of its inventory of other bond issues. There are also external factors to evaluate—the worth of that particular bond, the current tone of the market, the future direction of interest rates, among others. Weighing these factors is up to the individual dealer, since each has the right to withdraw from the group. The decision usually comes at the final meeting, where members review all the information, then make up their minds to stay or to drop. *The Bidding*

Now let's go back to 1979 and see if we can read the mind of an imaginary underwriter, let's say the V.P. in charge of the municipal syndicate department of a medium-sized Chicago dealer. For most underwriters the winter and spring of 1979 had been quiet, with average volume and steady interest rates—a welcome change from the financial tumults of the middle seventies. Yields on high grade tax-exempts due in 10 years had ranged from about 5% to 5.5%, and the forward calendar of new issues promised more of the same. Although Kenosha had been working on its issue for some months, our underwriter first saw it on April 4 in a little *The Syndication*

Undivided Account

$4,000,000 Des Moines, Iowa General Obligations
        Selling: April 16, 1985

MEMBERS AND PARTICIPATIONS

Manager A	$1,000,000
Manager B	1,000,000
Major A	600,000
Major B	600,000
Minor A	400,000
Minor B	400,000
Total	4,000,000

Preliminary Meeting: April 15, 3:00 p.m.
Conference Room D
Final Meeting: April 16, 11:00 a.m.

notice in *The Bond Buyer*. He called the Chicago bank with whom his firm had always bid on Kenosha, and sure enough, they planned to function again. Meanwhile, other syndicates which had bid on the 1978 and earlier issues also re-formed for this sale. The next time Kenosha crossed his mind was on April 26, when he saw one of First Whiskey's green and orange Official Statements in his in-box. Then on the following day he received a standard undivided account syndicate letter from his manager formally inviting his firm and the other members to bid. The syndicate letter also established the due legalities among the underwriters and announced the time and place of the price meeting. He was glad to see that his firm was third in the lineup, with a participation of 500 bonds.

What is a participation? Each member's individual share of the account's liability, for profit or loss. Municipal underwriting firms come in all sizes, and syndicate managers assign different participations to their members to enable large and small to bid together equitably. So, on a six-member, $4 million bond issue, the two largest firms might have participations of $1 million each; the next two firms might have 600 bonds each, and the last two, 400. We would say that the account has three brackets of liability: a $1 million bracket for the joint managers, a 600 bond bracket for the majors, and a 400 bond bracket for the minors, which works out to 25, 15, and 10%, respectively. When all bonds have been sold each member receives its percentage of participation of the total profit. So, in this example, if the underwriting profit came to $10,000, two checks for $2,500, two for $1,500, and two for $1,000 would go out to the members. The same goes for losses, each firm sharing in proportion to its participation.

Participation

This issue, like most competitive syndicates, was organized as what we call an undivided, or Eastern, account. In an undivided account, takedowns by any member reduce the liability of all members in accordance with their percentage participations. So, even if one member firm sells 50% of a new issue all by itself, while none of the other members sells any, that firm, and all the others, remain responsible for 50% of its original participation. Undivided accounts assume a cooperative member sales effort, and are suitable for short term and high grade bond issues like Kenosha and Vermont. We will be looking at divided syndicate accounts in the next volume.

The Undivided Account

On Monday morning, May 7, 1979, our underwriter had, of course, arrived at his desk bright and early, and soon started organizing his work. He saw that he was bidding on 12 competitive deals that week, with King Co., Washington, Michigan Building Authority, and New Hampshire the largest, and among the smallest, the $3.810 million Kenosha G.O. deal.

The Kenosha Set-Up

$3,810,000
CITY OF KENOSHA
KENOSHA COUNTY, WISCONSIN

CORPORATE PURPOSE BONDS, SEREIS 1979
(Non-Callable General Obligations)

Date and Time of Sale:	Monday, May 7, 1979, 1:00 P.M., C.D.T.
Good Faith Check:	$76,200 payable to the City Treasurer.

INTEREST EXEMPT, IN THE OPINION OF COUNSEL,
FROM ALL PRESENT FEDERAL INCOME TAXES

Dated: June 1, 1979 $5,000 Denomination
Registrable as to Principal Only   Non-Callable

PURPOSE: Proceeds of the issue will be used for several corporate purposes as follows: $105,000 for constructing and equipping an engine house; $420,000 for constructing and equipping a library; $1,515,000 for improving and extending sanitary sewers system; $1,315,000 for improving and extending storm sewers; and $455,000 for providing street improvements.

SECURITY: Bonds will be the general obligations of the City of Kenosha and will be payable from taxes levied on all taxable property in the City without limitation as to rate or amount.

MATURITIES: December 1

Year	Amount	Year	Amount
1980	$ 35,000	1985	$500,000
1981	275,000	1986	500,000
1982	500,000	1987	500,000
1983	500,000	1988	500,000
1984	500,000		

COUPONS: First coupon payable December 1, 1979 and semi-annually thereafter.

RATING: Outstanding bond issues are rated "A-1" by Moody's. Moody's rating on this issue has been applied for.

Since Kenosha was the first issue scheduled to sell that week, the underwriter turned to a worksheet on it, where he saw the deal's features laid out in convenient form. These are some of the reactions he may have had.

1)	$3.810 million	Small.
2)	Kenosha	O.K. name, but heavy on American Motors. Nicer looking place than you might think.
3)	Wisconsin	Wisconsin local issues scarce right now. A good state to own bonds in.
4)	Due 1980-88	Bank paper.
5)	G.O.	Our customers' favorite.
6)	Moody's Rating: A1	Unchanged. Probably too high, because of car industry problems, but since these bonds have such short maturities, it doesn't much matter.
7)	Dated Date: 6/1/79	Check.
8)	First Coupon: 12/1/79	Check.
9)	Legal Opinion	Good.
10)	Registrable as to principal	Check.
11)	1980—35 Bonds	Spinach.
12)	1981—275 Bonds	No customer interest.
13)	1982—500 Bonds	Half a million, good amount. One of our buyers might pay a 5.30%.
14)	1983—500	Nothing going with us.
15)	1984—500	"
16)	1985—500	"
17)	1986—500	"
18)	1987—500	"
19)	1988—500	"

In such rapid scrutinies the bond designs on which cities labor so long are put to the acid test—a thorough going-over by the dealer professionals who make their living underwriting bonds.

Most competitive syndicates schedule two meetings, a preliminary one on the day before the sale, and a final meeting starting an hour or so before the bidding deadline. However, since Kenosha's sale was scheduled for a Monday, this manager had called only one, final, meeting. Either individually or together at a preliminary, bidding members try to arrive at a working scale before attending the final meeting. What is a scale? The string of yields a dealer group assigns to each of the maturities of a serial loan, representing the interest rates at which investors will be offered the bonds.

The Preliminary Meeting

MAT.	4/24 WISCONSIN	4/30 BALTIMORE	5/7 KENOSHA	
1978				
1979				
1980	5.10	5.40	5.25	
1981	"	"	"	
1982	"	"	5.30 —	
1983	5.15	5.45	5.35	
1984	"	"	5.40	
1985	5.20	5.50	5.45	
1986	"	5.55	5.50	
1987	"	5.60	5.55	
1988	5.25	5.65	5.60	
1989				
1990				
1991				
1992				
1993				
1994				
1995				
1996				
1997				
1998				

We started talking about maturities and yields a few pages back. We mentioned that Wisconsin's 1981 yield was a 5.10%, and that Baltimore, which at the time was worth less than Kenosha, had sold at a 5.40%. Our underwriter was thinking along the same lines, and he put down a 5.25% in 1981. Facing shows us a tentative Kenosha scale constructed with the same kind of logic.

At this stage of underwriting, the person who is to commit a firm's money to a deal begins to think about the margin, and also of how many bonds his sales force can use. Most of the profit on any deal is made by actually selling bonds and thereby earning the takedowns that we talked about earlier. Our man had remembered that one of his salesmen had a bank customer looking for some Midwest bonds due in 1982. He phoned the salesman and told him that Kenosha might come at a 5.30% in '82. The salesman said he couldn't reach his customer until later, but that the 5.30% sounded good to him. By 11:30 our syndicate man had heard nothing back, and he left for the Kenosha meeting, wondering who else might be interested in the loan.

Sales

5/7/79   A1/ NR

Issue: $3,810,000 KENOSHA, Wis., G.O.

Due :   12/1/80-88   Dated: 6/1/79

        1980 –   35   5.25

        1981 –   275   5.30

        1982 –   500   ~~5.35~~   5.30

        1983 –   500   5.35

        1984 –   500   5.40

        1985 –   500   5.45

        1986 –   500   5.50

        1987 –   500   5.50

        1988 –   500   5.55

                                 ~~$9.00~~

                                 $ 9.25

Chapter Fourteen

Underwriting An Issue
(continued)

By 11:40 a.m. on May 7, 1979, the eight member Kenosha syndicate had assembled in a small conference room on the bank's 33rd floor, overlooking LaSalle Street. They were looking intently at copies of the manager's proposed scale. The head of the bank's syndicate department was running the meeting, and he informed the group about the orders the account had received so far, as well as other potential interest in the deal. Then, going around the room in order of participations, he asked for comments and reactions. For his part, as #1 in the syndicate, he said he was willing to underwrite the printed scale. Member #2 said he was unsure and wanted more time to think about it. Our #3 man, in his turn, said his firm might be able to sell all of the 1982 maturity at a 5.30%. He said that he liked the scale, and would make the bid, meaning that his company would underwrite its share of the loan. Since the printed scale in 1982 read a 5.35%, the manager suggested it be raised to a 5.30%, which was accepted by the group.

The Final Meeting

Member #4 said she thought the scale was too high, meaning of course that its yields were too low, and that she would drop. #5 grumbled a bit but said he would stay. The last three members said they would go along, which left six in, one out, and one undecided, as they moved on to the next order of business: setting the profit margin.

The Minors

The manager proposed that they work for a spread of $9.00, that is, a gross profit margin of $9.00 per $1,000, or a little less than 1%. #2, apparently becoming convinced by the orders and other information that the deal had a good chance of making money, said he would go along, but that he would prefer $9.50. Finally the members compromised on $9.25, and that set the bid—the raised scale, less a $9.25 profit. Since #4 had dropped, participations were revised, with the top three members agreeing to absorb her share. Seeing that this would be the final scale, one of the manager's assistants left the room to figure the bid by computer. We will return to see how bids are calculated in Chapter 26.

The Profit

```
FILENAME = KENOSHA


DESCR = KENOSHA WISCONSIN              TOTAL PAR AMT = $  3,810,000

APPROX. DEL DATE =  6/ 1/1979  NIC DATE =  6/ 1/1979  FRST COUP = 12/ 1/1979

   AMOUNT  MATURITY      BOND-YRS COUPON  BASIS  PRICE  C   CALL FEATURE  L

   35,000 12/ 1/80       52.500  5.700  5.250 100.641      3/8    1/4
  275,000 12/ 1/81      740.000  6.900  5.300 103.700
  500,000 12/ 1/82     2490.000  6.900  5.300 105.050
  500,000 12/ 1/83     4740.000  6.000  5.350 102.569
  500,000 12/ 1/84     7490.000  5.400  5.400 100.000

  500,000 12/ 1/85    10740.000  5.400  5.450  99.729
  500,000 12/ 1/86    14490.000  5.400  5.500  99.392
  500,000 12/ 1/87    18740.000  5.400  5.500  99.328
  500,000 12/ 1/88    23490.000  5.400  5.550  98.904

                    ORDERS  2:00  CD7
-----


-----
                    TOTAL       PER $100      PER DAY
PAR AMOUNT   =   3,810,000.00   100.0000
GROSS PROD.  =   3,845,259.35   100.9254
SPREAD       =      35,242.50     0.9250
BID          =   3,810,016.85   100.0004
ACCRUED INT  =                    0.0000       612.42

     NIC*            CIC
  5.613721        5.633464

.05 (PER $100) =     -0.253755   $1 SPRD =  0.016220 NIC

-----

BIDCOMP COMMAND>
```

With thanks to Peggy Alderman and MDCSS.

The next step was to set concessions and takedowns. As we have mentioned, in addition to the underwriting spread, there is another, and usually larger, profit to be made by members who actually take down bonds. And that is the correct term: take down. When you are a member, you take down bonds from the account rather than buy them. Group members can take down bonds at the regular scale price less (minus) two discounts, the concession and the additional takedown. Together these make up the total takedown. If a member sells bonds directly to an investor, he keeps both discounts for himself. However, if he sells them to another dealer, he keeps only the additional takedown. We will return to takedowns in Chapter 20.

Takedowns

After discussion, the account set the concessions at ⅜ of a point for all the maturities, plus an additional takedown of ¼. So the total takedown was ⅝. Although it isn't expressed this way in meetings, setting the takedowns splits the profit between two dealer functions—selling and risking. Since the scale was figured for a $9.25 gross margin, the total takedown (⅝) allocated 68% of the spread to selling. Assuming 75¢ expenses, that would leave $2.25 (24%) for risk taking.

Risks and Rewards

Then the manager suggested that the order period run for an hour, until 2:00. What is an order period? An agreed time, often the one hour after bids are entered, during which the winning syndicate treats all orders as though they were entered simultaneously. When this period is over the manager tabulates the orders, and, using his discretion, confirms the bonds to the members who have entered them. Next he releases a report called the run and balance, showing how many, and in which maturities, bonds are still unsold. From then on members go to work to sell the remaining bonds and may take them down first come, first served, until they are all sold.

The Order Period

This underwriting was quite relaxed and simple, so simple, thought # 3, as he headed back to his office, that they were not bidding high enough. It was an easy-to-read issue selling in a calm market, and the competing accounts no doubt ran similarly. How about the investors? They were even more relaxed. The market was steady, and they could pick from a relatively wide choice of bonds. Once in a while, when the supply of offerings falls off, or interest rates suddenly start to drop, investors stampede to buy. In May 1979, however, they were grazing peacefully, unaware of the tornado which would strike them later that year. In the late '70's, the most likely single class of investors for short-maturity bonds like these was commercial banks. Why? Many bank liabilities, such as longer term certificates of deposit, neatly matched Kenosha's due dates, and since banks were then operating profitably, they eagerly sought tax exemption. The few fire and casualty

Investors

May 7, 1979

Honorable Mayor and Common Council
City of Kenosha
City Hall
625 - 52nd Street
Kenosha, Wisconsin 53140

Gentlemen:

For all but no part of your new issue of $3,810,000 (General Obligation) Corporate Purpose Bonds, Series 1979, which shall be as described in the Official Notice of Sale, we will pay you the par value thereof and accrued interest to date of delivery plus a premium of $ _169.60_ .

December 1, 1980	_6.75_ %		December 1, 1985	_5.40_ %
December 1, 1981	_6.75_ %		December 1, 1986	_5.40_ %
December 1, 1982	_6.10_ %		December 1, 1987	_5.40_ %
December 1, 1983	_5.30_ %		December 1, 1988	_5.50_ %
December 1, 1984	_5.40_ %			

This bid is made for prompt acceptance. Attached hereto is our good faith deposit in the amount of $76,200 payable to the City Treasurer of the City of Kenosha, which is to be held by you uncashed pending compliance with the terms of this bid. Said deposit is to be returned to us promptly if this proposal is rejected.

Sincerely,

First Wisconsin National Bank of Milwaukee

By _____
John B. Eger, Vice President

We, the duly authorized officials of the City of Kenosha, do hereby accept and award the bonds pursuant to the foregoing offer, in legal meeting this seventh day of May, 1979.

Clerk _____   Mayor _____

NOT A PART OF THIS BID: It is hereby represented that the net interest cost, according to our calculations on the above rates of interest, deducting premium, if any, will be $ _1,298,250.40_ , equivalent to an average net interest rate of _5.5269_ % per annum.

134

companies buying short bonds might have been interested in Kenosha, too. Individual buyers were the least likely investors for this kind of loan, since they usually look for longer term bonds with maximum yields.

Entering the Bid

While the members waited for the bidding results, the manager still had a major job to do—getting their bid in to the city. They had arranged for a representative to be in Kenosha with one of the official bid forms, signed and ready, plus a cashier's check for $76,000, the required 2% good faith deposit. At 12:30, a syndicate assistant called the representative and gave him the coupons and the bid price, and the average interest rate bid for, the N.I.C. He filled in the bid form with these figures and took it to the council chambers on the second floor of Kenosha's modern city hall and handed it to Eugene Schulz. Seated next to Schulz was Ken Kerznar, the financial consultant. Schulz asked if there were any other bids, and then at 1:00 sharp announced that the auction was closed. He opened and read out the bids, inspecting each one for completeness and making sure a good faith check accompanied it. The bids were as follows:

FNB Chicago	5.5473%
Citibank	5.5532%
FNB Okla. City	5.73%
First Wisconsin	5.5269%
Northern	5.542%
Continental	5.5908%
Nuveen	5.6441%
Harris	5.6228%

The Winner

The high bid was First Wisconsin at 5.5269%, and second came Northern at 5.542%, giving them an .02 cover (5.542 − 5.5269 = .02). Kerznar checked the two best bids for accuracy, and then he and Schulz spoke privately with the council members about whether to accept the winning bid. Schulz then proposed a vote and the tally was unanimous in favor of accepting the First Wisconsin bid, awarding them the loan. As we saw, First Wisconsin was also Kenosha's municipal financial consultant, and Kerznar was no doubt pleased that his bank's dealer department had submitted the high bid. Their completed bid form is on facing. Their production (average re-offering price) was 100.75. They bid 100, so they worked for a profit margin of $7.50. Concession was ¼, additional takedown ¼, order period 1 hr. If our invented account had bid, it would have come in a respectable sixth out of nine, with a 5.61%.

The Release

By 1:00 the news had traveled around the market that First Whiskey was high on Kenosha. Their account members were flashing the scale and coupons to potential buyers, and orders started coming in. By afternoon,

Summary of Yesterday's Municipal Issues

May 7, 1979 Issuer	Amount (,000 omitted)	Winning Manager	No. of Bids	Bidding Range
King Co., Wash.	38,831	Merrill Lynch, etc.	4	6.408-6.462
Duluth, Minn.	5,275	Northern Trust	8	5.784-5.887
Kenosha, Wisc.	3,810	First Wisconsin Nat'l Bank, etc.	8	5.526-5.730
Emmet Co., Mich.	1,400	State Bk & Trust Co., Petoskey (alone)	3	5.730-6.117

the account had received $945,000 in orders.

By the end of the day there were still $2.855 million, or 75% of the deal left unsold, a slow start. But then sales picked up, prices in the tax-exempt market rose, and the account closed with a profit. How did the investors do? They received their steady 5.25% to 5.50% yields on bonds which maintained their A1 rating. However, the market treated the longer bonds poorly. Their value fell to as low as 63 in 1982, and as of 3/1/85, they were worth about 92. Fortunately, the banks that bought most of the bonds carry them as non-risk assets, and can value them at original cost. But holding on to a 5½% return is certainly no bargain, book value or not. How did the city of Kenosha do? Just fine. They went ahead with their projects, completing all by February 1980, and are still enjoying both them and the low interest rates on the bonds outstanding.

Vermont's New Issue
Chapters 15-27

PRELIMINARY OFFICIAL STATEMENT DATED JULY 3, 1978

New Issue

In the opinion of Bond Counsel, interest on the Bonds is exempt from federal income taxes under existing statutes and court decisions.

$34,450,000

STATE OF VERMONT

GENERAL OBLIGATION BONDS

$26,750,000 Public Improvement Bonds

$7,700,000 Transportation Bonds

Dated: August 1, 1978   Due: February 1, as shown below

Interest on the Bonds will be payable February 1, 1979 and semi-annually thereafter on the first day of August and February of each year. Principal of and interest on the Bonds will be payable at the principal office of Shawmut Bank of Boston, N.A., in Boston, Massachusetts, and for such payments the full faith and credit of the State of Vermont are pledged. The Bonds will be issued in coupon form, payable to the bearer, in the denomination of $5,000 each. The Bonds are not subject to prior redemption or registration.

MATURITY SCHEDULE

$34,450,000 Serial Bonds at   % Interest Rate

Due February 1	Principal Amount	Price or Yield	Due February 1	Principal Amount	Price or Yield
1980	$1,850,000		1990	$1,800,000	
1981	1,850,000		1991	1,800,000	
1982	1,850,000		1992	1,800,000	
1983	1,850,000		1993	1,800,000	
1984	1,850,000		1994	1,800,000	
1985	1,800,000		1995	1,800,000	
1986	1,800,000		1996	1,800,000	
1987	1,800,000		1997	1,800,000	
1988	1,800,000		1998	1,800,000	
1989	1,800,000				

The Bonds are being offered for sale in accordance with the official notice of sale dated July 3, 1978, to which reference is made for the conditions of such sale.

The Bonds will be certified as to genuineness by the Shawmut Bank of Boston, N.A., and are offered subject to the final approving opinion of Messrs. Hawkins, Delafield & Wood, New York, New York, Bond Counsel, and to certain other conditions referred to herein and in the Notice of Sale. It is expected that Bonds in definitive form will be available for delivery in Boston, Massachusetts, or New York, New York, on or about August 8, 1978.

JULY   , 1978

Vermont sold bond issues in each of the years 1975 through 1977, after months and years of planning, and ordering of priorities. In 1978, another issue was proposed, to fund nineteen different projects, the largest for railroad rehabilitation and water clean-up. The vertical type on the left margin of this front page of the preliminary Official Statement is in red, warning that this is only a preliminary Official Statement. We call them red herrings. The final Official Statement, all in black, presents information about the State for bidders and investors to digest.

Chapter Fifteen

Credit Analysis—Vermont

Vermont, which was settled by the French in 1666, and the British in 1690, became the fourteenth State in 1791, and has sturdily and quietly taken its characteristic place in northern New England. Back in 1978, Richard A. Snelling was Governor and Emory A. Hebard the Treasurer. Its bicameral legislature, among other things, debates and approves its budget, imposes taxes and charges, sets expenditures, and authorizes new indebtedness. Vermont sold its first bond issue in 1928 and has never missed paying principal or interest on time. In 1978 about 62% of the state's current expenditures were funded from its own sources, including income and sales taxes and automobile and other fees. The 38% balance came from various payments from the Federal Government. During 1978 the General Assembly authorized a new transportation capital improvement plan whereby, starting in 1980, about $7 million a year would be spent on a variety of state projects in this category. $7.700 million transportation bonds from former plans were included as part of an issue planned for the summer of 1978. In addition, following Vermont's long-range financial plan, the legislature voted to bond the already-voted improvements to the state's infrastructure which are listed on the facing page. After a few revisions, including carry-overs from prior years, the rough shape of the bond issue, which was formed by the State Treasurer's department, assisted by the Shawmut National Bank of Boston's municipal finance department, began to emerge. By May the Assembly approved the sale of bonds totalling $34.450 million, and the Treasurer decided to advertise the issue for sale on July 18, 1978. Although Vermont has the power to borrow by selling bonds at private negotiation, this issue, as usual, was to be put up for public bidding.

The Background

In the Basics section we went in low gear over the whole bond market, and in Kenosha we got up to medium speed. Now let's travel through Vermont covering more ground in less time. Vermont, one of our familiar

The O.S.

OFFICIAL STATEMENT

STATE OF VERMONT

$26,750,000 Public Improvement Bonds
$7,700,000 Transportation Bonds

INTRODUCTORY STATEMENT

This Official Statement, including the cover page and appendices, of the State of Vermont (the "State") is provided for the purpose of presenting certain information relating to the State in connection with the sale of $34,450,000 aggregate principal amount of its General Obligation Bonds consisting of $26,750,000 Public Improvement Bonds and $7,700,000 Transportation Bonds (collectively the "Bonds").

The Bonds will be general obligations of the State and the full faith and credit of the State of Vermont will be pledged to the payment of the principal of and interest on the Bonds. Pursuant to State law, the Treasurer of the State is required to pay such principal and interest as the same become due without further order or authority. The amount necessary each year to pay the maturing principal of and interest on the Bonds is required to be included in and made a part of the annual appropriation bill for the expense of State government, and such principal and interest on the Bonds as may come due before appropriation for the payment thereof has been made is required to be paid from the General Fund or from the Highway Fund.

For the payment of principal and interest on general obligation indebtedness, including the Bonds, the State has the power to levy taxes, including taxes on all taxable property and income in the State, without limitation as to rate or amount. For a description of the State's sources of revenues and accounting thereof, see "Nature of State Funds and Revenues" and for a more complete discussion of the authorization of general obligation bonds and the provisions for payment thereof, see "State Indebtedness — Nature of State Indebtedness and Procedure for Authorization."

All quotations from and summaries and explanations of provisions of laws of the State herein do not purport to be complete and are qualified in their entirety by reference to the official compilations thereof and all references to the Bonds and the procedures for issuance thereof are qualified in their entirety by reference to the definitive forms of the Bonds and their statutory authority.

market names, expected no problems getting good bids for its bonds. Shawmut estimated that they would come in somewhat under 6%, a satisfactory rate at that time. As we have mentioned, in the 'seventies investors had started insisting on better quality research for tax-exempt issues. So, the state got busy, and by May had produced a 52 page Official Statement covering more points in greater detail than they had in more relaxed times, emphasizing, among other things, the status of their pension funding, an item it was the fashion to closely scrutinize in that period. A number of dealers turned out independent reports on the state's financial condition, among them one by Harris Bank of Chicago, a manager of one of the syndicates which usually bid on Vermont. Let's make up a credit report of our own, using the methods we developed with Kenosha.

*Legal
Items*

First, what proof was there that the bonds were valid and binding obligations of the state? The Official Statement cited Chapter 13 of Title 32, Vermont Statutes (the General Obligation Bond Law), under which full faith and credit bonds could be issued. On page 3 of the O.S. it was stated that Vermont had the power to levy taxes on all property and income, unlimited as to rate or amount, in order to pay principal and interest on its G.O. bonds. And how about tax-exemption? The front page of the Official Statement affirmed that the sale was subject to the opinion of Hawkins, Delafield & Wood, N.Y.C., a well-known bond counsel firm, that this issue was exempt from Federal income taxes. So all was well on the legal front.

*State
Boards*

We talked a lot about the real estate in Kenosha, since its bonds were largely serviced from property taxes. But we won't spend much effort on Vermont's real estate, because, although its Constitution permits such a levy, in practice it is not made. In fact few of our states directly tax property holders to any appreciable extent, leaving that power to local municipalities. For comparison purposes, in 1978, Vermont's assessed valuation was $2.642 billion, and its estimated true valuation $8.454 billion. Vermont's population was then 492,000, so its *per capita* valuations were $5,370 and $17,183, respectively, compared to the U.S. figures of roughly $5,000 and $15,000. It may comfort bondholders that Vermont has this authority, but since it is not used, you can see one way in which state bonds stand apart from other municipals. States are different from towns and cities, a lot different. They enjoy sovereign immunity (the right not to be sued without its consent), they can pass whatever taxes they choose, they can create agencies and authorities to issue surrogate debt, and can even run deficits with only themselves to account to. Some people even think that state bonds should be rated separately from those of localities.

Per Capita Income

	State of Vermont			U.S.
	Total Personal Income in Thousands of Dollars	Population in Thousands	Per Capita Income	Per Capita Income
1976	$2,577,000	476	$5,411	$6,399
1975	2,336,000	471	4,960	5,902
1974	2,152,000	468	4,602	5,486
1973	2,002,000	466	4,296	5,049

Source: U. S. Department of Commerce.

Over the last five years, unemployment in Vermont has been at approximately the mid-point of the New England region as a whole.

Unemployment Rates

	Twelve Month Annual Average				
	1973	1974	1975	1976	1977
United States	4.9%	5.6%	8.5%	7.7%	7.0%
Vermont	5.7	6.9	9.7	8.8	8.1
Other New England States:					
Connecticut	5.7	6.0	9.2	9.5	7.1
Maine	5.9	6.7	9.4	8.9	8.5
Massachusetts	6.7	7.2	11.2	9.5	8.1
New Hampshire	2.6	3.6	6.5	5.0	3.8
Rhode Island	6.2	7.3	13.9	8.1	8.6

Source: Federal Reserve Bank of Boston "New England Economic Indicators" (May 1978) and U. S. Bureau of Labor Statistics.

The total labor force in Vermont for March, 1978, the most recent data available, was 219,900, with 202,400 employed and 17,500 unemployed, for a total labor force unemployment figure of 7.9%. The Vermont total labor force unemployment rate is not seasonally adjusted.

In any case, it is soundest to compare their credits with bonds of other states.

When most people hear Vermont, they think of New England: conservative, plenty of snow and skiing, maple syrup, small cities and tiny villages, colleges, and dairy farms. And for those of us who get to visit there often, that picture is outwardly correct. But prosperity is another matter, and for that we have to look at the economic figures. The 1970 census put Vermont as the most rural of all the states, in the sense that 68% of its people lived in places of fewer than 2,500 population. Median age was 26.8 years, 1.3 years younger than the national average, and the median educational level was 12.2 years, just above that of the U.S. as a whole. In 1976, manufacturing accounted for 27% of the state's personal income, distribution 16%, business services 30%, government 17%, and agriculture only 5%, though cash income figures certainly understate farming's true importance in Vermont. 8.1% of the work force was unemployed, compared to the U.S. average of 7.0% in that post-recession year. Vermont's 1975 per capita income was 84% of the U.S. average, and its median family income was $8,929, or 93% of the national number. In 1976 total income in the state amounted to $2.577 billion, and it was growing at about the overall U.S. rate, with tourism and recreational activities contributing a major share. What summary can we make about Vermont's economy at that time? Fairly well diversified, below the average of national income, growing at a satisfactory pace; healthy, if not rich, and perhaps a bit more vigorous than its somewhat tranquil image suggests.

From its beginnings through the post-war years, Vermont was dominated by its agricultural and land-owning interests acting through the Republican party. In 1965, following the Supreme Court's issuance of the one person, one vote ruling, Vermont's House of Representatives, which had formerly been apportioned geographically, regardless of population, was redistricted into 150 equal-sized constituencies. So in a sense the Court brought the modern age to Vermont, and the voices of the sharply increasing numbers of suburban citizens there, quite a few arriving from out-of-state, began to be heard. In the middle seventies one of their chief concerns was the upgrading and extension of local services, especially education, which brought them into some opposition with the more budget-conscious rural folk and their friends, who were more concerned with the large number of farms in default in the state. When industry began moving into Vermont in a serious way, the professional sorts, joined by some students at the State University at Burlington, began questioning it on environmental grounds, while the less esthetically minded farmers were

Economic Factors

Social and Political Factors

145

GENERAL FUND

COMPARATIVE STATEMENT OF BUDGETARY OPERATIONS

	1973	1974	1975	1976	1977
Revenues:					
Taxes:					
Cigarette	$ 7,838,966	$ 8,171,520	$ 8,478,928	$ 9,337,552	$ 9,339,099
Corporate Income . . .	7,921,724	8,023,998	9,921,361	13,289,745	16,900,246
Personal Income	49,747,897	52,661,892	55,140,451	58,922,538	70,333,938
Liquor	8,449,120	8,549,161	8,918,418	8,933,085	8,655,137
Meals and Rooms . . .	6,140,122	6,441,913	7,588,148	9,232,023	9,845,755
Sales and Use	25,465,140	26,503,572	26,523,418	28,031,739	32,496,918
Other Taxes	22,854,685	21,077,083	21,793,444	23,529,809	24,203,914
Total Taxes	$128,417,654	$131,429,139	$138,364,168	$151,276,491	$171,775,007
Non-Tax Revenues (1) .	9,239,117	12,557,519	10,558,046	10,311,889	10,059,231
Total Revenues . .	$137,656,771	$143,986,658	$148,922,214	$161,588,380	$181,834,238
Appropriations (Net) (2):					
General Government . . .	$ 8,041,277	$ 8,345,448	$ 9,496,339	$ 9,073,179	$ 11,841,342
Protection to Persons and Property	8,012,114	8,996,540	9,526,445	9,896,769	10,160,030
Human Services	43,175,449	45,626,646	51,585,843	52,729,289	50,590,117
Education	57,540,553	63,260,369	66,657,579	67,865,666	67,907,302
Environmental Conservation	4,372,792	4,977,100	3,740,990	3,516,705	3,298,832
Development and Community Affairs	1,234,029	2,030,571	2,542,498	2,288,127	2,154,392
Debt Service	13,377,472	15,296,425	15,877,812	16,156,675	16,769,352
Other (3)	139,434	91,079	36,362	82,314	90,158
Total	$135,893,120	$148,624,178	$159,463,868	$161,608,724	$162,811,525
Excess (Deficiency) of Revenues over Net Appropriations	$ 1,763,651	$ (4,637,520)	$(10,541,654)	$ (20,344)	$ 19,022,713

mostly in favor. A look at the maturity schedule may prove interesting, especially in view of our hypothesis that rapid bond retirement indicates willingness to repay. Average length of maturity? Under 6 years, about half the U.S. state's average.

Our summary of the socio-political climate? A blending of more demanding younger suburbanites into a more conservative rural landscape, accomplished in some conflict, but with harmonious results.

Vermont, like all states, gets its money from a variety of taxes and charges, plus receipts from the Federal Government. In 1977 it was imposing an income tax (equal to 25% of the Federal personal income liability, plus a temporary surcharge of 9%) and also a 3% sales tax, thereby collecting 30 and 14% of its internally generated income. It also taxed liquor and cigarette sales (for 9% of its revenue), electric, insurance and other franchises (13%), auto fuel, registration and ownership (22%). The remaining 12% came from miscellaneous fees and charges, including income from its lottery. In addition, $162 million came from Washington. For the fiscal year ending 6/30/77, total revenues were $258 million, and disbursements $244 million. After adjustments, the state's general fund (their main operating account, and kept separate from the highway fund) showed a surplus of $17 million, up almost $20 million from the previous year's deficit of $2 million. Looking back at 1975, we can see a deficit of $11 million, partly caused by the recession of 1974-75. To correct this the Legislature had passed the 9% income tax surcharge, resulting in an $11 million increase in income from that source, and in addition, expenditures, which had risen by 6% a year from 1973 to 1976, were held to an increase of just 1.5% in 1977. These moves were successful, and though the surcharge was eliminated for 1978, revenues increased substantially, and it seems that Vermont had returned to a sound financial footing. So let's add up the whole asset side.

The Financial Side

1. Legal—Clean.
2. Economics—Steady, balanced growth.
3. Social—Moving smoothly from farm conservative to modern.
4. Political—Stable, progressive.
5. Financial—Good rebound.

Summary: Strong. Somewhere in the A 1 to Aaa range, depending on what we find about debt levels.

When we were looking at the city of Kenosha we saw that a good part of its debt liabilities came from its proportionate share of the underlying school district and overlapping county debts. The equivalent for states is

Bonded Debt

FINANCIAL STATEMENT AS OF   June 30   19 78 **POP 19** 70 **FED CENSUS** 444,330   **EST** 492,000 (1978)

EQUALIZED ~~ACTUAL~~ VALUATION (ESTIMATED) (1977)	$	5,283,939,000.00

ASSESSED VALUATION, 19 77 (June 30th)   50   **% OF** EQUALIZED ~~ACTUAL~~ $ 2,641,989,751.00

REAL PROPERTY	$ 2,412,517,075.00
PERSONAL PROPERTY	229,472,676.00
SPEC. FRANCHISES, ETC.	

TOTAL FUNDED DEBT INCLUDING THIS ISSUE $ 258,167,000.00

LESS: WATER BONDS	$	
SINKING FUND (WATER EXCLUDED)	$	-0-

NET FUNDED DEBT (9.77 % OF ASSESSED: $ 524.73 PER CAPITA) $ 258,167,000.00

FLOATING DEBT (TAX ANTIC. NOTES, ETC.,) (NOT INCL. ABOVE) $

OVERLAPPING DEBT $

COMBINED NET DEBT ($ PER CAPITA) (% OF ACTUAL) $

REMARKS:

NOTE: The Net Funded Debt Figure of the State shown above does not include Limited or Contingent Liabilities as follows: $24,932,175 Vermont Home Mortgage Guarantee Board Guaranteed Mortgages; $690,000 University Agricultural College Bonds; $9,480,000 Whey Pollution Abatement Authority Bonds Lease Rental Obligation; $3,000,000 Vermont Industrial Development Authority Insured Mortgages; $65,485,000 Vermont Municipal Bond Bank; and $51,825,000 Vermont Housing Finance Agency.

NOTE: As of June 30, 1977, the Total Equalized Fair Market Valuation of the State amounted to $8,454,302,000.00.

Courtesy of *The Bond Buyer*

the extent of their contingent liabilities. Vermont, in 1978, had $234 million in direct G.O. bonds outstanding. In addition, it had created two substantial bond-issuing agencies, the Vermont Municipal Bond Bank, and the Vermont Housing Finance Agency, both of which were designed to be, and in fact were, self-supporting. However, if the income received by these two state creatures were ever to fall below what is needed to service their bonds, the Legislature has the power, and a moral obligation, to appropriate enough money to keep their debt service reserves filled. This system, originated in part by John Mitchell, the same of Nixon days' fame, for New York State, enables Vermont to stand back of (and therefore benefit from lowered interest rates), but not directly behind these bonds, which are not counted as part of its debt. In Vermont's case this helps, because in 1975 it passed quite an unusual debt limitation for itself, partially stemming from the deficit it ran that year, a debt limitation which might possibly be instructive in light of the proposals being advanced in 1985 advocating a no-deficit amendment to the U.S. Constitution. But in any case, municipal bond analysts such as ourselves have to make an allowance for indirect state obligations. Let's look at its whole debt to see.

Vermont's Bonds

As of 6/30/78 the state had $224 million in direct G.O. bonds outstanding, and the true value of its real property was $8.454 billion, which gives us a B.D./E.T.V. percentage of 2.6%. The comparable national average was 2%. How about debt per capita? $224 million divided by 492,000 comes out to $455 per head, compared to a national average of about $250. What happens if we add in the contingent moral obligations? An increase of about 50%, whereas the U.S. average at the time was about 100%. So, although the Green Mountain State's G.O. per capita debt was almost twice that of its sisters, overall it was only about 50% greater.

Total Debt Levels

Although Vermont's per-person debt was relatively high, it is one of the few states where most bonds are issued at the state level, and where localities rarely sell their own bonds. In 1977 the 50 states had $87 billion bonds outstanding, while their local governments had $157 billion, or close to twice as many. But in Vermont the picture was quite different. Local issues there totalled only $152 million, one-third that of their State's bonds, including its contingent liabilities, and so the debt load on its residents came to $1,175 each, almost exactly the same as the national average ($1,190). On balance how does the balance of Vermont's assets and liabilities strike you, my reader? If you were to say that the debt load seemed easily manageable, and was backed by adequate assets, you would not hear an argument from me. Moody's was in this corner, too, and in early July confirmed its high grade, Aa rating.

Dealer	The Vermont Managers		The New Hampshire Managers	
	1976	1978	1976	1978
Citibank	Citibank	Citibank	Citibank	Citibank
Chase	Chase	Chase	Chase	Chase
Harris Bankers F.N.B.C. C.I.X. T.N.T.	T.N.T.	Harris	Bankers	Bankers
Chemical	Chemical	Chemical	Bankers	Bankers
F.O.B.	F.O.B.	F.O.B.	Citibank	Citibank
Bache	Chase	Chase	Bache	Bache
Lehman	Chase	Chase	Citibank	Citibank

Chapter Sixteen

Setting Up an Account

Many municipal issuers sell bonds quite regularly, and the same underwriting syndicates usually enter bids on them every time one comes to market. When, for example, Vermont announced a sale in 1979, the five managers that had led syndicates on its previous issues (Chase, Chemical, Citibank, First Boston, and Harris) prepared to do so again. Each of those Vermont groups was composed of one or more managers and from 20 to 60 members who had bid on it together year after year, more or less automatically. This system of so-called historical accounts greatly simplifies dealers' lives—otherwise there would be a mad scramble for members and managers every time a deal was announced, or rumored. And when a brand new issuer announces its first competitive sale, that's just what does happen: would-be managers hustle around for members, especially strong ones; members go out looking for a good home, and eventually the new teams get organized. Then when the issuer sells a second time, everything is pretty well set; the same managers are in charge, and most of their original members stay in their lineups.

Historical Accounts

However, don't assume that the members of an historical Vermont syndicate necessarily bid together when other names come to market. When, for example, New Hampshire sold in 1978, only two of the five dealers who led accounts on Vermont that year (Chase and Citibank) also headed groups on the state next door. The other three bid as members of other accounts. So dealers who bid in one account on Vermont may, or just as easily, may not, bid with it on New Hampshire. It's like a baseball league in which different sets of teams are formed for each series of games, and where the players switch positions all the time—exciting for the fans, but tough on the managers.

Distinction

When a new issue is announced, members look up their records, and if they see they have bid on that name before, they can safely expect to be included in the same account. When a dealer without a history of bidding

Continuity

$34,450,000
STATE OF VERMONT
Various Purpose Bonds

Sale - July 18, 1978

Membership and Participation

Harris Trust and Savings Bank)	Joint	$1,600,000
The Northern Trust Company)		1,600,000
Bankers Trust Company)		1,600,000
Continental Illinois National Bank)		
and Trust Company of Chicago)		1,600,000
The First National Bank of Chicago)		1,600,000
Goldman, Sachs & Co.)		1,600,000
Drexel Burnham Lambert Incorporated)		1,600,000
Donaldson, Lufkin & Jenrette)		
Securities Corporation)		1,600,000
United California Bank)		1,600,000
First National Bank in Dallas)	Managers	1,600,000
Mercantile Trust Company N.A.		1,600,000
First National Bank of Oregon		1,600,000
Dean Witter Reynolds Inc.		1,600,000
The Connecticut Bank & Trust Company		1,600,000
A. G. Becker		
Municipal Securities Incorporated		1,600,000
Loeb Rhoades, Hornblower & Co.		1,600,000
The Bank of New York		1,600,000
Hartford National Bank and Trust Company		1,600,000
J. C. Bradford & Co.		1,600,000
Trust Company Bank		1,600,000
The Fidelity Bank		1,600,000

Total	$41,700,000
Over syndication	7,050,000
PAR VALUE	$34,450,000

PRICE MEETING

A price meeting will be held at the New York Office of the
Investment Department, Harris Trust and Savings Bank, 39th
Floor, One Chase Manhattan Plaza on Monday, July 17, 1978
at 3:00 P.M. (EDT). Those members who cannot attend the
meeting are requested to appoint a proxy to represent them.
Please execute the enclosed proxy form and return together
with your signed contract. IF WE DO NOT HEAR FROM YOU PRIOR
TO THE TIME OF THE FINAL MEETING, DIRECT OR THROUGH YOUR
PROXY, YOU WILL NOT BE INCLUDED AS A MEMBER OF THE FINAL
ACCOUNT.

Undivided Account

on a credit wants to participate, he may call a manager and ask to join his syndicate. If that manager has room, he may let him in; if not, the dealer may try another. What about a new dealer? The historical system is fairly open: new firms who act responsibly and who sell their share of bonds are welcome into most accounts.

Syndicate Formation

After a sale is announced, the managers, too, check their records, and inform their members that they will function. Some of their old members may not wish to bid this time; some may request either higher or lower participations; some new dealers may ask to join, and adjustments are made accordingly. If the new deal is much larger than the ones before, or if the market is shaky, the managers may merge their account with one or more others. After all the changes have been made, syndicate letters, with a list of the participations, go out to the members to be signed and returned to the manager. Although syndicate letters legally bind the group together, it is doubtful that the fine print of one in a thousand is ever read. However, once in a blue moon, something does come up that calls its terms into play, and its language may settle the question. The letter does not obligate bidders to commit. Members may drop from a group any time before the bid is entered, and are thereby released from liability. If the group wins the issue, the manager sends out a short letter confirming the purchase and the amount of each member's final participation.

Managers

The syndicate manager acts as the group's chief executive. He takes the initiative in setting up the account, researches the credit, conducts underwriting meetings, figures and enters the account bid, takes orders, sends out confirmations, places advertisements, and handles the bookkeeping. Sometimes there may be a number of joint managers, but usually this is for form's sake, and the top manager is the real leader. Typically, a manager takes 5 to 25% of the total underwriting.

Majors

Just below the managers comes a set of members we informally call majors. Because of their selling power and judgment capacity, majors may be consulted about the bid by the manager before the meetings, and later about how to handle the unsold bonds. The manager and the majors together usually have majority control of an account, rather like the operating officers of a corporation. Each major generally has 3 to 15% of the underwriting.

Minors

The rest of the account is made up of minors, that is just plain members. Some companies who are minors in one account are majors, or even managers, in others. Wm. R. Hough & Co. of Florida, a firm which regularly manages accounts there, may be a major in a Georgia deal, but only a minor in a Washington loan. Minor members resemble the small

Morgan Stanley Shuns I.B.M. Issue

To the surprise of Wall Street, the $1 billion debt offering that the International Business Machines Corporation announced yesterday will not be managed by Morgan Stanley & Company, I.B.M.'s traditional investment bankers. Salomon Brothers and Merrill Lynch, Pierce, Fenner & Smith will handle the offering instead.

Morgan Stanley was offered the opportunity of being the lead co-manager, based on its "long-standing and productive relationship" with the computer manufacturer, but the securities firm declined "as a matter of policy," an I.B.M. spokesman disclosed yesterday.

I.B.M. wanted more than one manager because of the relatively large size of the offering, the spokesman said, adding that I.B.M. still planned to continue to do business with Morgan Stanley.

The firm, which has acted as the lead investment banker to many blue-chip industrial corporations, declined to elaborate on its decision.

THE NEW YORK TIMES

stockholders of a corporation; each owns shares in the company, but lets the directors and executives run the show. They are supposed to give the account selling power in their regional or local markets, and often do; but at other times they just seem to ride along for the underwriting profit. Typically their participations will run from .1 to 2% of a larger deal, up to 20% of a small one.

The relative order of the syndicate members' participations would seem to be an easy thing to fix. However, this determines whose name will appear before or after that of other dealers in the advertisements. And since certain members may feel that some others are smaller, or newer, or more or less something than they themselves are, the manager may have a major problem putting everybody in satisfactory rank. In fact, the Wall Street pecking order can run to extremes. Morgan Stanley would never appear in any syndicate, no matter what the size, unless they were on the first line alone, or at least, left and foremost. Never. They even declined to be number two in the then largest deal in corporate bond history, and only later changed their policy. Other firms take a more relaxed attitude. Merrill, bidding from a local office, will often appear in the middle of a tax-exempt syndicate lineup, with no apparent damage to its reputation.

The Order of Appearance

Long ago, one dealer who ran the appropriately named John Small & Co., had a different perspective. John said he preferred appearing at the bottom of an ad because many readers read just its first and last names, and skipped all the ones in between. Although these rivalries may seem silly, who can criticize your pride when your company's name has a handsome position in a fine syndicate ad? And if you spot it in the morning newspaper, your feelings of warm and proper smugness may even overcome Conrail's shortcomings for a moment or two.

Rivals and Cooperators

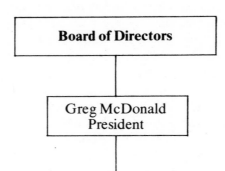

Syndicate	Public Finance	Sales	Trading
Kate Gilbert V.P.	Jim O'Toole Sr. V.P.	Huck Ostler V.P. Joe Smithers	Gary Black V.P.

Operations
Stephen Clearance V.P.

Johnson and McDonald's organization chart looks something like this. (Like most Wall Street firms, it also has some corporate affiliates which dabble elsewhere.) In our Vermont example, we are seeing the syndicate and sales departments at work. Operations handles the administrative work of the company—the books, and delivering and paying for bonds.

Chapter Seventeen

Pre-Sale Work on Vermont

In June, 1978, Vermont announced a bond sale for that July 18, and in real life the issue was bought by one of its five usual bidders—Harris Trust, of Chicago. But for our purposes, we have invented another syndicate, managed by First National, with some typical, even though imaginary, members, including the bond firm of Johnson & McDonald, Inc., New York City.

First National, perhaps a giant medium-sized New York City bank, had for many years maintained a rather slow-moving municipal bond dealer department. Then in the late seventies the bank management decided to enlarge and strengthen it, promoting its chief underwriter elsewhere and bringing in some new talent. Maybe we can go back and root for this account since it would be their only chance ever to buy a deal.

Enter First National

Although the State of Vermont's financial people had for several months been busy designing their issue, the news only reached Wall Street on June 27, 1978, when *The Bond Buyer* printed a short paragraph announcing the sale. Bob Swenson, V.P., the head of First National's new issue department, spotted the Vermont sale announcement, and he, like his counterparts managing the actual groups, started up the four phases of underwriting most new issues require: syndication (forming the account); research (how sound is the bond?); pricing (how much to pay for it); and entering the bid (filing the proposal with the issuer). Bob simply put a big checkmark on the notice and handed it to his young assistant, setting in motion the historical bidding account processes we talked about in the last chapter.

A Little Squid in the Paper

Now let's meet Johnson & McDonald, Inc., a fictional medium-sized dealer. The firm concentrated on the secondary market, but was also active in both competitive and negotiated new issues. So back we go to 1978 to take a silent and non-paying seat in their syndicate department, headed by Kate Gilbert, V.P. In recent years J & Mc had risen to the major bracket of

Johnson & McDonald

$34,450,000
State of Vermont

Selling 7/18/78

First National Bank		$6,450,000
Two		6,000,000
Three	Jt. Managers	6,000,000
Four		6,000,000
Five		2,500,000
Seven		2,500,000
Johnson & McDonald, Inc.		2,500,000
Eight		2,500,000
Nine		2,500,000
Eleven		1,000,000
Thirteen		1,000,000
Fourteen		1,000,000
Fifteen		1,000,000
Sixteen		500,000
Seventeen		500,000
Eighteen		500,000
		$42,450,000
		34,450,000
	Over—Underwritten	$ 8,000,000

Preliminary Meeting—Monday, July 17, 1978
Room B—44th Floor

The rear view of First Nat's syndicate letter, with 14 of the same 16 members who were invited to bid on the prior issue still in the lineup. The participations add up to $8 million more than the issue—this excess is called the over-underwriting, or oversyndication. Most members will come to the final meeting with these amounts authorized and in place in their own minds, and the manager can feel confident the account could absorb $8 million in drops without a tremor.

most underwritings, but they were still stuck down low in First Nat's Vermont account, formed so long ago no one could recall its origin. Kate had also seen the Vermont announcement. She called Bob Swenson to see if he was bidding on Vermont as usual. He said that he was, and Kate asked him if J & Mc could have a larger participation in the account. Bob seemed receptive to the request and said that he would try. By late June, about 150 other interested municipal dealers had joined one of the bidding groups (the regular five, plus First Nat's), and syndicate letters were on their way.

Most managers automatically refer every issue they plan to bid on to their research departments, who usually prepare reports on the credit in question, along with their conclusions. The shorter write-ups may be quite useful to their salesmen, and to the other members of the syndicate, helping them price and sell the bonds. First National had four people in its municipal bond research department, headed by an A.V.P. And it got to work on Vermont right after the Fourth of July. Johnson & McDonald had only one person in its research section—he worked on some primary analysis, but relied on the managers for information on Vermont. How much can one man accomplish? Smaller firms get along well enough without full-time research people; they analyze bonds informally at best, and rely heavily on subscriptions to Moody's *Bond Survey*, Standard & Poor's *Credit Week* and the like. Their salesmen soon learn to forage for themselves.

Credit Research

A week before the sale, each of the managers started on the third phase of pre-sale work, pricing, which is closer to the heat of Wall Street. If syndication is hiring the farmhands, and research is surveying the field, then pre-sale price work is the cultivation before planting. First National's Swenson was glad to have the credit report in hand by July 10; no proper bank group would bid without one. His real job, however, was to buy the bonds and make a profit, not to dwell on the state's transportation facilities, or even its debt ratios. He saw to it that a conference room was reserved for the meetings and that the members were notified. He asked Charley Stone, who had been with the bank for three years, and who was anticipating an A.V.P. title soon, to oversee the technical work; Bob would concentrate on locating investor interest and on pricing the deal. He had made one decision earlier—raising Johnson & McDonald to the $2.500 million major bracket. They were good sellers, better than some of the old-line majors, and he wanted to move with the times. He left the rest of the account just about the way it had always been, adjusting only for the size of the issue. After all, it had bought and made money on Vermont many a time—"If it ain't broke, don't fix it," he thought.

Progress

PROPOSAL FOR BONDS

July 18, 1978

Hon. Emory A. Hebard, *State Treasurer*
State of Vermont
c/o Shawmut Bank of Boston, N.A.
Municipal Services Department
Eleventh Floor
One Federal Street
Boston, Massachusetts 02211

Dear Sir:

In accordance with the provisions of your Notice of Sale dated July 3, 1978, which Notice is hereby made a part of this proposal, we offer to purchase $34,450,000 Public Improvement and Transportation Bonds of the State of Vermont bearing interest at the rate of   % and to pay therefor the price of
and accrued interest to date of delivery for each $100 par value of bonds.

The undersigned hereby acknowledges receipt of the Preliminary Official Statement referred to in the aforementioned Notice of Sale.

. . . .

. . . .

. . . .
(Manager)

. . . .

. . . .
(Mailing Address)

The Shawmut Bank would be pleased to assist you in entering your bid on these bonds if you will mail your signed bid form in advance and telephone figures to Mr. Daniel J. Shields, Vice President, about one-half hour before the time of sale. Telephone: 617-292-3192.

This is the last of Vermont's four page Notice of Sale, and it serves as the bid form, or as they call it here, the Proposal for Bonds. It is a deceptively simple way to spend $34 million—not much harder than making out a traveler's check.

A bid form is usually signed and sent to a local representative, in advance. He then fills in the interest rate and coupon blanks just before he hands it in. Most have one more blank, for the N.I.C., or average interest rate. But since Vermont only permits one coupon, it is not necessary here.

Every municipal new issue, in addition to its own specific credit qualities, has a unique maturity amount and bidding specification shape, so each one has to be set up and calculated accordingly, custom-style. And in practice, one of a manager's most demanding tasks is to effectively process the large number of issues for sale. We are looking at Vermont, which had a simple structure, but First Nat was also bidding on 15 other deals that week alone, and setting and figuring all the bids regularly and accurately is a challenge to any department. Mistakes are relatively rare, although they are not unknown. Once, back in 1973, Salomon and Donaldson, Lufkin bid on and bought a nice new issue of New York Job Development Authority State Guaranteed Bonds. At least they assumed that the deal was one of the guaranteed series. The competing accounts bid much lower, since that issue was in fact a straight revenue bond. They are probably sick of hearing about it, and plenty of worse mistakes have been made, but few stick out so far. That errant little syndicate took its loss quickly and went on to better things.

In the week before the sale Charley turned to figuring the bid. Since the early seventies, new issue set-ups have been available to feed into in-house or time-sharing computers, making much of the computation on them automatic. But Charley did it his way; he went to the horse's mouth—the State's Official Notice of Sale—and made up his own bidding sheet. And from this he entered the data into the bank's computer system. Other managers do it differently, some using the outside service organizations who sell this information all packaged up and ready to use.

On Thursday, July 13, Charley got around to his final pre-sale job: arranging for the bid to be entered. Two items are usually involved—the bid form, and the good faith check. Most new issue bids have to be submitted on an official form and physically presented to the community itself—and so each manager has to get one of the forms, and then find someone to fill it out and deliver it. (Vermont does it differently. Shawmut National Bank acts as its agent, and receives all the bids at its Boston office—a very sensible and efficient procedure.) Charley sent a blank form to member FOURTEEN, who had a Boston office, to present to Shawmut at sale time. Most issuers require a good faith deposit, in the form of a bank check, to accompany each bid. So each manager either sends out his own check or wires funds to the bid submitter's bank. The commonest good faith amount is 2%, sometimes more, sometimes less. Vermont requires none at all, and they have never suffered from it. After Charley had that in place, he ran over everything, saying to himself, set-up checked, bid form, and good faith, and so on the Friday before the sale he knew that he was ready. The meetings were scheduled for Monday and Tuesday, and the account was rolling ahead.

		1983	1982	Percent Increase (Decrease)
Per Share Data*	Net Income	$ 4.47	$ 4.57	(2.2)
	Dividends Declared	1.79	1.79	—
	Book Value at December 31	35.49	33.46	6.1
	Average Common Shares Outstanding	9,284,172	9,136,161	1.6
Operating Results	Net Interest Income	$153,763	$138,801	10.8
($ in Thousands)	Other Income	58,400	55,045	6.1
	Other Expense	145,465	129,070	12.7
	Provision for Possible Loan Losses	15,955	14,397	10.8
	Provision for Federal Income Taxes	9,198	8,675	6.0
	Net Income	41,545	41,704	(.4)
At Year End	Total Assets	$5,508,208	$5,691,332	(3.2)
($ in Thousands)	Loans and Leases, Net of Unearned Income	2,930,545	2,598,153	12.8
	Investment Securities	884,508	683,188	29.5
	Deposits	4,120,824	3,713,055	11.0
	Shareholders' Equity	347,260	306,571	13.3
	Shareholders of Record	10,667	10,852	
	Employees	3,875	3,572	
	Banking Offices	83	68	
	Automated Teller Machines	41	36	
Selected Ratios	Return on Assets	.82%	.83%	
	Return on Equity	12.93	14.16	
	Equity to Assets	6.34	5.84	
	Dividend Payout	39.90	39.20	

Mercantile Bancorporation Inc.

Mercantile Bancorporation Inc. is a $5.51 billion asset regional multi-bank holding company providing complete banking and related financial services primarily in the 8th and 10th United States Federal Reserve Districts, through a network of affiliated banks in the state of Missouri. Mercantile's lead bank is the 129-year-old Mercantile Trust Company N.A. in St. Louis, which has total assets of $3,429,860,000. Mercantile's 42 other affiliate banks have combined total assets of $2,171,012,000. Services include commercial, retail, correspondent and international banking, corporate and personal trust management, and bond investment and underwriting activities.

From the 1983 annual report to the shareholders of Mercantile Bancorporation, Inc., whose lead bank, the Mercantile Trust of St. Louis, is definitely *not* our fictional 'Mobank.'

Chapter Eighteen

A Bank Investor

If in early 1978 you had been driving up the Interstate highway just a few blocks from the business center of the second or third largest city in Missouri, you might have seen a new and impressive building outlined against its modest skyline. Part office tower and part bank building, it radiated confidence, and well it might have; by all standards the Bank of Missouri, N.A., which we are hereby inventing for our example of an investor, was a prosperous outfit. On the edges of the Midwest, the East, and the South, the State of Missouri had taken its own direction of growth, and this, one of its largest banks, had contributed to it and had benefited, too. Mobank started in 1910 as a strictly local enterprise, and slowly developed into a state-wide holding company, owning 25 banks in 45 cities and 2 abroad. Like most commercial banks, it devotes most of its time and effort to servicing the financial needs of its customers, both individual and business. In 1978, it had 2,325 employees, and over 150 officers with the title of Assistant Vice-President or higher.

All of these people were working on Mobank's day-to-day corporate banking and trust department operations, contributing to earnings. Mobank's policy was to steadily increase its common stock dividend, distributing about 40% of its earnings in dividends to its stockholders, and retaining the balance for capital purposes. Retained earnings had reached $136 million at the end of 1977, up $12 million from the prior year, bringing Mobank's total shareholder equity to $208 million. This capital base supported $3.1 billion in deposits and other liabilities, a conservative 6.7%. The bank's assets were distributed in loans (52%), short term securities (18%), bank premises, cash and other items (15%), and also in almost half a billion dollars worth of bonds held for investment (15%).

Every busy corporation has its investment aspects and problems; in some they play a major part in the company's profitability, in some they don't. But with a commercial bank, whose product is money itself, investing

Exhibit 11
Analysis of Asset and Liability Maturities and Rate Sensitivity
($ in Millions)

December 31, 1983

	1-30 Days	31-90 Days	91-180 Days	181-365 Days	Total 1 Year or Less	Over 1 Year	Total
Assets							
Due from banks-interest bearing	$ 180	$ 105	$ 107	$ 1	$ 393	$ —	$ 393
Federal funds sold and repurchase agreements	319	—	—	—	319	—	319
Taxable securities	22	43	65	162	292	225	517
Tax-exempt securities	22	13	7	17	59	309	368
Loans and leases							
Commercial, financial, agricultural	1,091	99	79	56	1,325	214	1,539
Real estate-construction	112	13	3	3	131	28	159
Real estate-mortgage	107	26	44	67	244	305	549
Consumer	18	31	31	55	135	294	429
Foreign	123	62	55	3	243	65	308
Total Loans and Leases	1,451	231	212	184	2,078	906	2,984
Total Interest-sensitive Assets	$1,994	$392	$391	$364	$3,141	$1,440	$4,581
Liabilities							
CDs over $100,000	$ 425	$168	$108	$ 62	$ 763	$ 57	$ 820
Foreign deposits	88	55	35	6	184	—	184
All other time deposits	674	275	267	97	1,313	269	1,582
Short-term borrowings	615	8	5	—	628	—	628
Long-term debt	—	1	1	2	4	125	129
Total Interest-sensitive Liabilities	1,802	507	416	167	2,892	451	3,343
Interest Sensitivity Gap	$ 192	$(115)	$ (25)	$197	$ 249	$ 989	$1,238
Cumulative Interest Sensitivity Gap	$ 192	$ 77	$ 52	$249			
Cumulative Ratio of Interest-sensitive Assets to Interest-sensitive Liabilities:							
1983	1.11	1.03	1.02	1.09			
1982	1.07	1.07	1.03	1.09			

From the 1983 annual report to the shareholders of Mercantile Bancorporation, Inc., whose lead bank, the Mercantile Trust of St. Louis, is definitely *not* our fictional 'Mobank.'

is central. The effectiveness of its daily matching of shorter term investments against its liabilities is one of a bank's largest profit-making determinants. And buying and selling longer term securities can also result in substantial profits, or losses; in fact, investment decisions may affect a bank's earnings in any given year more than all the efforts of its whole commercial division. Mobank showed a pre-tax net income of $30 million in 1977; at the same time it owned $460 million in taxable and tax-exempt bonds. If they had been sold at seven points below cost, the bank would have had a loss year. And, of course, if they had been sold at a profit, then the bank would have benefited by that amount. Mobank had a six-person department set up for handling its long-term investments—headed by Mr. Arnold Freihofer, Sr. V.P., who reported directly to the Board of Directors.

In our earlier chapters, we spoke mostly about the income bonds provide. However, since market values do change, and since their holders' need for tax-exempt income also shifts, investors often sell some of their bond holdings, realizing profits or losses. In the case of commercial banks these capital gains and losses are separated from other operating results. This enables a bank's shareholders to see how it is doing on the operating side, eliminating the effects of a changing bond market (or a losing investment strategy).

Security Transactions

Although, of course, interest on municipal bonds is tax-exempt, if a bank ever sells them at a profit, the gain is taxable at the regular corporate rate—because corporations get no capital gains tax advantage. So, if Freihofer bought a bond at say, 90, and Mobank either sold it at a higher price or held it to maturity, it would have to pay a tax on the gain. Consequently, when we dealers offer discount bonds, we are selling a combination of tax-exempt income (the coupon), and taxable income (the profit eventually made between the discount and 100). To quote the tax-exempt yield properly, the capital gains tax effect has to be allowed for. If, in July 1978, a salesman offered Mobank a State of Louisiana 4% bond due in 1989 at a 5.60% gross yield, he would have to explain that this would actually produce only a 5.15% yield, assuming that the 46% corporate tax would apply. Don't worry about Freihofer and taxes, though; he never bought discounts.

Capital Gains and Taxes

Mobank was doing very well back in the late seventies—bank stock analysts might well have said that it was nearing a mature stage. In 1977, the holding company's net income had reached $25 million, after taxes, on total revenues of $315 million. In the first quarter of 1978 its operations had turned even more profitable because the spread between its interest costs and its return on earning assets had widened. It looked like 1978 would be a banner year, partly the result of some acquisitions it had recently made. The

Bank Capital and Earnings

Investment Securities

Total investment securities were $884,508,000 at December 31, 1983, an increase of $201,320,000 or 29.5% from the previous year. Taxable securities grew by $143,905,000 or 38.6% while state and municipal holdings increased by $57,415,000 or 18.5%. Approximately $98,000,000 of the increase was added from the investment portfolios of acquired banks and the remaining $103,000,000 came from purchases. The recent mix of the portfolio is graphically portrayed in Exhibit 22.

The investment portfolio represented 17.8% of earning assets during 1983 compared with 16.8% in 1982. On average, taxable securities grew by $77,000,000 while tax-exempt actually declined by $23,716,000. Mercantile manages its investment portfolio based on the liquidity and interest sensitivity needs of its banks.

As noted in Exhibit 20, the average maturity of the U.S. Government portfolio declined for the fourth consecutive year to one year and five months from one year and ten months at the prior year's end. The average maturity for tax-exempt securities was likewise shortened and at December 31, 1983, was six years and nine months versus eight years at December 31, 1982. The reduction in the average holdings of tax-exempt securities reflects the fact that during 1983 the yields on short-term state and municipal securities were not as attractive as other tax-sheltered investments such as leases, industrial revenue bonds, and taxable investments.

Exhibit 21
Securities of State and Political
Subdivisions by Quality Rating
($ in Thousands)

	December 31, 1983	
Moody's Ratings	Par Value	Percent
Aaa	$ 35,833	9.7%
Mig 1	1,075	.3
Aa	117,562	31.9
Mig 2	1,400	.4
A1	62,950	17.1
A	69,663	18.9
Baa1	7,325	2.0
Baa	9,606	2.6
Ba	3,165	.8
Caa	3,260	.9
Not rated	56,881	15.4
Total	$368,720	100.0%

From the 1983 annual report to the shareholders of Mercantile Bancorporation, Inc., whose lead bank, the Mercantile Trust of St. Louis, is definitely *not* our fictional 'Mobank.'

Board of Directors estimated that earnings would probably reach $30 million, or over $3 per share.

Naturally, one concern was its effective tax rate. Justice Brandeis said that it is the duty of all citizens to minimize their own taxes, and Mobank was certainly no dissenter. The bank had already gone into leasing and related fields, but no further relief was in sight there. Another possibility was pretty obvious: tax-exempt interest. Every year, when expenses and taxes cut every other income dollar down to a few pennies, this stands untouched. No wonder that commercial banks were then our best customers.

Taxes on Corporate Earnings

At the last Board meeting, the Chairman and Chief Executive Officer, and the restless younger Vice-Chairman, both originally from Illinois, had said they thought Mobank was under-invested in municipals, pointing out that while the average bank's holding of tax-exempts was 9% of total assets, theirs was under 6%. And if they increased their holdings of tax-exempts to 9%, the bank's net income would go up by about $2 million, or about 20¢ per share, an increase of 7%.

Tax-Exempt Holdings

They looked at Arnold Freihofer, and Freihofer, as usual, shot it back to them straight. He didn't like the bond market right then; in fact, it seemed he never liked the bond market—he was from Missouri. He said that the municipal market was too darn high, and that in his opinion, Mobank was doing just fine on its investments, taxes included. He pointed out that their bond portfolio's cost was near the current market value. If they had to sell, they wouldn't have any embarrassing losses—not like some other banks he could mention. He said that short-term municipals yielded only 50 basis points more than governments, after tax; and added that if 1978 were a loss year for the bank, then Treasuries would actually return them more. He was right, financially; but politically he had slipped. Neither the Chairman nor the Vice-Chairman had any intention of losing money. And although the Chairman who had retired a few years back didn't know what a basis point was, this one did.

Discussing Investment Policy

"What about long-term municipals?" he asked. "How do they compare?" Freihofer said he always bought short; he'd have to look into the long term market. The Vice-Chairman did a little figuring on his yellow pad, and said, "It would take $100 million to get us to the 9% average." The thought of buying $100 million long tax-exempts would have curled Freihofer's hair, if he had had any. The meeting then turned to other subjects, but it was understood that information and decisions were expected at the next week's meeting. Distrust of long bonds or not, Hof was not one to resist the boss—his retirement was scheduled in only three years.

At December 31, 1983, the estimated market value of the portfolio was $833,165,000, a depreciation of $51,343,000 or 5.8% from the carrying value of $884,508,000. A year earlier the depreciation was 6.5%. Most of the unrealized depreciation in the portfolio relates to tax-exempt securities. Management believes that the Company has sufficient liquidity in the portfolio and from other sources to preclude the sale of securities at a loss unless economic opportunities warrant sale.

As noted in Exhibit 21, 78.3% of the state and municipal bonds held were rated single A or higher by Moody's Investors Service. Many of the non-rated bonds are part of small local issues purchased by our affiliate banks and those bonds are evaluated internally for creditworthiness.

Mercantile's commitment to its region is partially exemplified by its holdings of securities issued by its home state of Missouri and its municipalities, although bonds of virtually every state are held in the portfolio. At December 31, 1983, Missouri securities had a par value of $102,307,000, representing 27.8% of total tax-exempt securities. This concentration is spread throughout the state; in fact, the securities issued by any single Missouri political subdivision did not exceed 2.4% of shareholders' equity. The bonds of any single issuer outside the state of Missouri did not exceed 2.8% of shareholders' equity.

Exhibit 22
Average Investment Securities
(Millions)

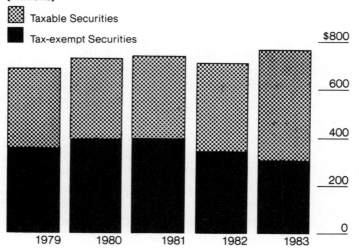

From the 1983 annual report to the shareholders of Mercantile Bancorporation, Inc., whose lead bank, the Mercantile Trust of St. Louis, is definitely *not* our fictional 'Mobank.'

Although the term itself did not come up, the concept of spreads surfaced twice at the board meeting. Our Missouri bankers first looked at the spreads, or yield differences, between municipals and governments, with an eye on the tax advantage of buying the former. Later, they decided to examine the spreads between short and long term municipals, trying to balance the long maturity bonds' greater risk against their higher income. The Chairman pointed out the importance of these spreads most clearly—a difference of 7% in the per share earnings, a figure uppermost in his mind, if not in Hof's.

Yield Spreads

Next morning, Hof arrived at the office as usual, a few minutes before James Winderman. Freihofer was the overall head of the investment department, but Winderman handled its day-to-day operations, including trading the municipal and government bond positions. Hof said, "It looks like the board wants us to take on some long tax-exempts." Windy's heart took a little jump—he had been in favor of that for a long while. And he would be the one to do it.

"We have $193 million now," Windy replied. "Do they want to go up to $200 million?"

"Well, not exactly—the President mentioned $300 million. What do you think?"

"Wow! That would be some program. $100 million more!"

And so it went. Hof, with Windy's willing help, got to work on two charts: one on the spread between municipal and government yields, and the other on long municipal yields versus short. The following Monday the Board looked them over, discussed them in detail, and agreed to think some more. During the week several members consulted with the bank's economist, who was predicting a slowdown in the economy and lower interest rates, and talked it over with their Chicago and New York correspondents. The following Monday the Board approved a $20 million program for then, with more to come later, and Windy was brought into the discussion. After a contest between Hof, on one hand, who wanted to stick to Aaa and Aa state names, and Windy and the Chairman, who wanted to buy some medium-grade revenues for their higher income, a compromise was struck: $10 million in Aaa and Aa G.O.'s, with maturity dates of 15 to 25 years; and $10 million in revenue bonds due out to 2000, A 1 or better, but nothing in New York, Michigan, or California. Windy looked forward to it with pleasure and even thought of a few salesmen he would surprise. Seven years with the bank, and here was a real chance—$20 million to spend, just for starters. Maybe he could help turn the bank's investment performance around, and assure himself of Hof's job when he retired.

A Buying Program

DATE	DESCRIPTION	AMT.	COUP.	MATURITY	YIELD	$ PRICE
6-22-7_	Wayne Co. has Been Cancelsd — Has Ky. Tpr. Bonds ordered					
6-27-72	No. Hospital Rev					
7-24-	N.Y.S Whran — (said we'll be bidding) wants to wait & see what they look like No Lakeland Fla —					
7-25	Call Back Later No Bonds					
7-26	No P.R.					
8-2	Conn — Looked no price not right due to mtg.					
8-3	No. Grand Hospital					
8-28	Holz — Snow on vacation					
9-29	Fulton Dome P.R. WRA in 84 Rather op longer					
10-11	No N.Y. City			(2003)		
11-17	Has an order for 3,000,000 Group P NET H.F.A. May shd ? Pt Him					
11-27	No P.R. @ 5½ — would have to be 5.10					
12-11	May look at NYS Dorm — No N.J. HFA 5¼ Will keep an eye on Richmond — nothing yet or for sale					
1-5-73	Richmond Mthis Dec .50		5½		8.13	Par
1-24-73	Bearish					
4-18-23	Out of funds for a few weeks					
6-4	No interest Culinary Inst NYS Dorm					
9-17	Dos Dorm 5⅝ Not selling					

Typical scribbles in a salesman's account book.

Chapter Nineteen

New Issue Sales Work
July 17, 1978

We just visited a bank investor at his office, and saw some of his problems; earlier we started with some underwriters, particularly First Nat and Johnson & McDonald. How do investors and underwriters like these get together? Not by reading ads in the newspapers, and not by delivering prospectuses. Most communication between dealers and investors comes through the dealers' salesmen, who pass along information to their customers every working hour. It is their principal function, and their rewards are orders and the commissions they bring. Sales information takes many forms—how the bond markets are acting, what new developments are occurring in municipals, predictions of interest rate changes, among others. Sales people are also supposed to bring back information to their buying departments—which customers are in the market, what kinds of bonds they are looking at, and the levels of yields they might pay.

Sales and Information

Serious efforts by dealers to sell competitive new issues usually begin only a day or two before the sale, when their probable yields can be estimated accurately. Our Vermont example issue was scheduled for sale on Tuesday, July 18, and it wasn't until the morning before that Joe Smithers, a salesman in Johnson & McDonald's Philadelphia office, looked at a preliminary price sheet showing Kate's prediction of a Vermont scale. Joe's customers were mostly high-grade buyers—banks and insurance companies—and he himself was most comfortable selling Aa and Aaa bonds. Joe decided he would call Kate in New York later that morning to ask her about their chances of buying the issue, the coupon it was likely to carry, and so forth—his customers were closely stalked by the competition's salesmen and he wanted some ammunition. One of his customers was Windy Winderman, Mobank's portfolio buyer. Windy seemed to like him, but so far they had done very little business. One of these days, thought Joe, and one of these days was almost here.

The Approach Begins

Windy arrived at work that same Monday morning, wearing his best

7/17 – 8/15/78

1– G.O.

- 10# TOTAL
- 5# STATE BONDS
  - NO NY, CAL, MASS, PA
- 5# LOCAL BONDS, Aa or AAA
- 1993 – 98
- MIN 250

2 – REV.

- 10# TOTAL
- 5# Aa
- 5# A1
- NO NORTHEAST, CAL, MICH
- 1990 – 98
- MIN 250

brown suit, his new narrower figured tie, shoes all polished—very bushy-tailed. He had a job to do. After the expected struggle with Hof, who wanted to tip off an old bank pal in Chicago about Mobank's buying program, Windy claimed his responsibility—he would do the buying him-self; it was so decided, and Hof retreated to think about longer-range plans. Windy wanted to show how a modern buyer works—keep intentions quiet, use a number of dealers, especially some of the smart New York ones, and choose from the best and cheapest available bonds. Over the weekend he had decided to buy $3 to $5 million right away. He wrote out two program descriptions, like shopping lists, one for the G.O.'s and one for the revs, and planned to start buying the G.O.'s first. Windy decided not to make any calls himself—he'd just wait and talk to whoever calls in. That's the way to play it cool.

8:55 a.m., C.D.T., and his phone rang. "Hi, this is Jim Handy. How are you today, Windy?"

"O.K., so far. What's up?"

"The market. Ha, ha."

"Oh, yes? Like what?"

"Well, the Oregons '90 to '94 that traded up .05 Friday are selling up .10 this morning. Any interest?"

"No, not a thing."

"Anything else this week?"

"Nope, not now."

"O.K. Thanks, so long."

Windy was playing it so close to the vest that that salesman didn't even see the back of his cards. So it goes. Again the phone, and on came Bill Thompson. Bill sold for a big New York bank and called in all the time.

"Hi, Windy. Bill Thompson here. How are things?"

"Pretty fine, Bill."

"What are you up to?"

"What do you have today, any tax-exempt securities?"

"Huh, very funny, Windy. Just about $25 million. Things are pretty strong here. Oregons are trading up .10, but we still have some nice looking Californias, only .10 higher. How about some Cals in the ten year range?"

"Nope. No California."

"We had some Illinois. We bought a million 6's of '92 this morning and sold them right away at a 5.50."

Windy said, "An .05 cheaper than Oregon—that doesn't sound bad."

"Would you be interested in some at that level? I think I might get some more out there."

173

ORETON

1988   5.20

89   30

90   35 30 25

91   45 40 35

92   55 50 45   ILL 6e 5.50

93   60 55 55

94   70 65 65

95   80

96   85

97   90

98   95

99

2000 00
    01

    02

    03

Keeping up with the prices of serial bonds is one problem you have to accept if you want to be in municipals. Windy had an Oregon scale, and as the market changed, kept it current. The first column has the original scale. After the account was closed, they were raised in price by some dealers by .05, as the first cross-out shows. Then on Monday morning they traded up another .05—the 1992's sold at the up .05 price—a 5.50—and were offered at a 5.45. Windy jotted the new scale down, and noted the Illinois trade too—he was as up-to-the minute as he will ever be.

174

"Might take a look, Bill. See what you can do."

"O.K. Sure will. How about Vermont? $35 million selling tomorrow and they might look good if they came at Oregon original."

"Never bought Vermont," said Windy, thinking over his list. But before he could say anything, Bill started to say good-bye. Windy had $10 million in his pocket, and neither salesman had sniffed it out.

"O.K., guy, I'll see what I can do. Bye."

With this bit of information, Bill called his trader, and told him he had a nibble for Illinois in 10 years. 250 to 500, he guessed, current coupon, .05 cheaper than Oregons. His trader noted it, and asked him the obvious— would any other state do—Cals, or Vermonts, for instance? Bill said no, he wanted Illinois, and his trader, with a smirk, knowing how scarce that name was, remembered to forget it. What a salesman, he thought, but promised him to look anyway. *Market Data*

Does it seem odd that two supposed professionals, salesmen who depended on commissions for a living, walked right past a good sized buying program and failed to recognize it? Why did they miss? Because they forgot one of the fundamental rules of selling: before you place a call, assume the customer is going to buy. Make 20 calls, get 19 kinds of No, and you're in good shape. But if you assume you will fail, you probably will. Windy was not trying to be coy. He really wanted to buy some bonds, and although he was playing it tight, that's the way poker is played, and bonds, too. *The Rule*

Again, Windy's phone rang. On average, he got around ten calls a day from bond salesmen, even when he was out of the market. In the following few weeks, this would double or triple, as dealers found out that he was buying.

"Hello, Windy, this is Joe." It was Smithers from J & Mc's Philadelphia office.

"Hi, Joe, what's doing?"

"Nothing much, they're trying to take this market up again. But I don't think they will get too far. How much higher do you think it will go?" Notice that Joe tried to get Windy to do the talking. He meant business.

"Maybe another .10 or so."

Joe continued, "A couple of interesting new issues coming this week, Windy—Ohio Eds and Vermonts might be O.K. Suppose Vermont came at a 5.25 in '90, how would that look to you?"

He had hit the nail on the head, though he didn't know it yet. Notice that he loaded his question with information and phrased it to require a direct answer.

```
JULY 17, 1978    STATE OF VERMONT
SELLING $34,450,000 G.O. BONDS ON TUESDAY, JULY 18,1978   RATINGSXX
RATINGS MOODYS  AA
COMMENT:
VERMONT HAS TURNED THE CORNER IN DEALING WITH TWO OF ITS MOST SERIOUS
NEGATIVES: GERNERAL FINAN CIAL POSTION AND DEBT LOAD.
1.  IN FISCAL YEAR 1977 THE STATE RECORDED ITS LARGEST GENERAL FUND
    SURPLUS IN AT LEAST TEN YERS AFTER HAVING BEEN IN A DEFICIT POSI-
    TION IN ATXX FOR THE TWO PRIOR YEARS.  EVEN THOUGH THE STATE LEGIS-
LATURE RESPONDED TO THE LARGE SURPLUS WITH A TAXCUT PACKAGE WHICH
WAS EFECTIVE IN FIXCAL YEAR 1978, STATE OPERATING FUNDS ARE EXPECTE
    TO CARRY OVER A REDUCED BUT STILL A SATISFACTORY SURPLUS.
2   THE SATE'S DEBT LOAD HAS TAKEN A TURN FOR THE BETTER IN THE LAST
FIVE YEARS.  STATE DEBT EXXX ESCALATED IN THE FIRST PART OF THE SEXX
    SEVENTIES DUE LARGELY TO THE CONSTRUCTION OF THE STATE'S INTERSTATE
    HIGHWAY PROGRAM.
TODAY, THE STATE'S INTERSTATE HIGHWAY PROGRAM IS NEARLY 100% COMPLE-
TED. IN ADDITION THE STATE LEGISLATURE ENACTED A DEBT ISSURANCE LIMIT
IN 1975 WHICH IMPOSES A TOUGH CONSTRAINT ON NEW G.O. DEBT AUTHORIZATO
AS A RESULT, STATE G.O. DEBT RATIOS HAVE SHOWN MARKED IMPROVEMENT
AND SHOLD CONTINUE TO DECLINE AS LONG AS THE LIMIT IS NOT ALTERED
 BY THE STATE ASSEMBLY.
OTHER POINTS OF INTEREST:
PENSION PLANS ARE IN GOOD SHAPE.  THE TEACHER'S RETIREMENT SSTEM,
THE LARGEST, SHOWS VERY GOOD ACTURARIAL FUNDING RATIO OF 87%L.
UNEMPLOYMENT STILL REMAINS A PROBLEM IN THE STATE; HOWEVER, TOTAL
EMPLOYMENT INCREASED BY OVER 8% BETWEEN 1975 AND 1977 AZX WITYH
THE GRETEST GAINS OCCURING IN THE MANUFACTURING AND SERVICES SECTORS
SUMMARY:
VERMONT IS IN MUCH BETTER SHAPE THAN THEY WERE A COUPLE OF YEARS AGO.
THE IMPROVEMENTS IN FINANCIAL OPERATIONS AND DEBT OUTSTANDING ARE
NOTABLE AND SERVE OX TO STREANGTHEN THE STATE' CREDIT QUALITY.
RAC:PHL
```

Harris's research department had turned out this report on Vermont before the sale in 1978. It could have answered one of the questions that came up across the way, and as you can see, it can make an interesting sales tool.

"Pretty good. I might have interest there."

"You said you might be buying a bunch of high-grades some day. Are you starting a program now?"

"No, just shopping around to replace a few runoffs. I don't think we have any Vermonts, so give me a buzz. I might go for 500 if they came at a 5.25."

"O.K. I'll keep on it—you know me."

"Yup, I sure do. One thing I have a problem with, Joe; what is the unemployment picture in Vermont these days? Any improvement recently?"

Joe stopped a second. "I'll check it out. My impression is that it's not too bad, but I'll get some figures for you this afternoon."

And that was that for then. Joe told Kate that he had an interest in 500 Vermonts of 1990 at a 5.25, but that he needed some unemployment figures. Kate said she would watch that maturity and would try to get him the dope on Vermont.

While Joe and Windy had been talking, other J & Mc salesmen were also making their calls, and so were the salesmen of other members in First National's group, and in the competing accounts, too. A total of six syndicates were bidding on Vermont, with an average of 30 members. If each member had five high-grade salesmen, each of whom made five calls on Vermont, that adds up to 4,500 conversations, so it's not hard to figure why downtown N.Y.C. has so many phone exchanges. Welcome to the free enterprise system. Telephone expense is the third highest most financial outfits bear, after salaries and interest, with $1,000 a month per salesman not unusual. Results of the Vermont phone campaign went on to the first meetings, where preliminary prices started to jell, as the pace quickened.

Syndicate Selling

SCALE SHEET

ISSUE _____

DUE _____   DATED _____

MAT.	7/11 OREGON aaa/AA	7/12 WPR#2 aaa/AAA	7/13 WISC S.C. A/	7/13 N.Y.S. A/AA	7/13 SALT aa/A
1976					
1977					
1978					
1979			5.00	4.70	
1980			70	90	
1981			40	5.00	
1982		4.85	60	15	
1983		95	75	30	
1984	5.00	5.00	90	40	
1985	05	10	6.00	50	
1986	10	70	10	60	
1987	15	30	70	70	5.70
1988	70	40	25	80	80
1989	30	50	30	90	90
1990	35	60	35	11	95
1991	45	70	40	6.00	6.00
1992	55	80	50	11	10
1993	60	90	60	10	70
1994	70	6.00	70	15	30
1995	80	10	75	20	40
1996	85	70		25	50
1997	90	30		30	60
1998	11	40		40	65
1999		50		45	70
2000		60		50	75
2001					"
2002					80
2003		06 — 680			"
2004		10 — 67/8		5.1/2 6.75	
2005					18 — 7.00
2006					
2007					
2008					

Chapter Twenty

The Preliminary Meeting
July 17, 1978

Bob Swenson had set the preliminary meeting of his Vermont account for Monday afternoon for 3:30, asking syndicate members to send representatives to First National's office on Broad Street to present scale ideas and discuss the deal in general. In stable periods, and for general market names, nothing much seems to happen at preliminaries, except for the manager maneuvering the account around to make the bid it wants. But in tough markets, or on more obscure names, members often make genuine contributions at the first meeting, helping the account to move in the right direction.

Setting a working scale on this issue of Vermont figured to be quite an easy job. The high-grade market had been steady, there were a number of comparable state names that had sold recently, and the secondary was full of offerings and trades. Oregon provided the best standard. This state, then rated Aaa/AA (Aaa by Moody, AA by S&P), had issued $150 million bonds on the prior Tuesday, July 11. On July 17, the Oregons were trading in the secondary at what we call up .10, that is lower in yield by ten basis points. So when Vermont came to be priced, it boiled down to setting its scale in the right relationship to Oregon's current worth. What was the right relationship? The differential investors would pay for Vermont versus Oregon. Some dealers would have put Vermont .05 to .10 cheaper than Oregon, some would have scaled them both the same, while others figured that Vermont, despite its lower rating, was worth .05 more. Why the difference of opinion? From different points of view, from talking to different customers, and from a variety of past experiences. All of these opinions and experiences produced a range of only 20 basis points, a deviation of about 2%.

All in all, the narrow spread of opinions made it obvious that it would take a highly competitive scale, and a narrow profit margin, to buy the bonds. In unsettled or rapidly changing markets, or with less familiar credits, there are often much wider differences of approach. But not on

PRELIMINARY BIDDING VIEWS

$34,550,000
STATE OF VERMONT
SELLING JULY 18, 1978

.05 equals

Average Life

MEMBERS		1980	1983	1988	1993	1998	MARG.
FIRST NATIONAL BANK	6,450	4.50	4.85	5.10	5.50	5.90	7
TWO	6,000	4.60	.90	5.20	.60	6.00	9
THREE	6,000	4.50				6.00	11
FOUR	6,000	4.60	5.00	5.25	5.60	6.00	8-9
FIVE	2,500	4.70	5.00	5.20	.60	6.10	3/4
SEVEN	2,500						
Johnson & McDonald	2,500	4.50	4.90	5.20	5.50.	6.00	3/4
EIGHT	2,500						
NINE	2,500	4.75				6.25	11
ELEVEN	1,000	~~4~~					
THIRTEEN	1,000						
FOURTEEN	1,000	4.70	5.00	25	60	6.20	12
FIFTEEN	1,000	4.60	5.00	20	50	6.00	14½
SIXTEEN	500						
SEVENTEEN	500	4.75				6.25	1½
EIGHTEEN	500	4.70	5.00	5.30	5.90	6.30	1½

Bob thought the best strategy for this meeting was to ask the members to spot their scale—just read off their ideas in the five year maturity hops we see above. As usual, the lowest members presented the cheapest views, and the thickest spreads.

Vermont; it was going to be hard to buy the loan right, for the very reasons that made it easy to price. Bidding on high quality bonds in a tight market is like the old game of chicken—let the car roll down the road until you don't dare go a second more, then grab the wheel and hope everything will be all right. Some call it courage, some call it foolishness, but on Vermont that was the game to play. And if First Nat's Vermont meetings develop typically, you will see some firms that genuinely wanted to buy the loan drop out because they figured the price was too high for them to make a profit. That's competition. Bid until it hurts.

At half past three, Bob went into the meeting room and found eight members there, a slim half of the account—though a couple of others had phoned in their ideas. The room was respectably, if not opulently, furnished; its chief feature was a modern oak table, at which Charley and the seven other members were seated, and on which pencils and yellow pads had been laid out. On the pencils was printed, "First National hits first". By 3:40, 10 members were present. Two were women, and if this seems like a small proportion, consider that until 1967 meetings were invariably male only. Sally Winston, of Wilson White, Inc., broke the precedent, attracting considerable notice. By custom the underwriters from larger firms sit near the head of the table, and so on down, roughly in order of their participations. Kate sat in the middle, on one of the long sides. Suits are the prevailing syndicate uniform, although a sport jacket creeps into meetings now and then; it is impossible, however, for a man to bid on a municipal new issue without a tie.

The Preliminary

Bob handed out blank view forms and the faithful ten spotted their ideas, that is, read off their scales in the first maturity, 1980; then in the fifth, tenth, fifteenth and twentieth years. Next Bob read out his whole scale and mentioned $7 as a possible spread, depending on how much business the account saw by the following day. Most of the members privately thought that his scale was too high, but first meetings usually start like that—perfunctory and too rich. In preliminaries discussion is usually limited to rough ideas of scale and profit margin, and the finer points, such as concessions and takedowns, are left for the final meeting. As we brought out in Chapter 14, in municipals we use a discount system to pay dealers who sell bonds. Let's see how this works.

Scale Ideas

We operate with two commissions, or discounts, from each maturity of a new issue scale: the concession and the additional takedown. Together they are called the full takedown, or just the takedown. Takedowns reward members for selling bonds directly to investors, and, to a lesser degree, for selling bonds to other, non-member dealers. Let's suppose that the conces-

The Takedowns

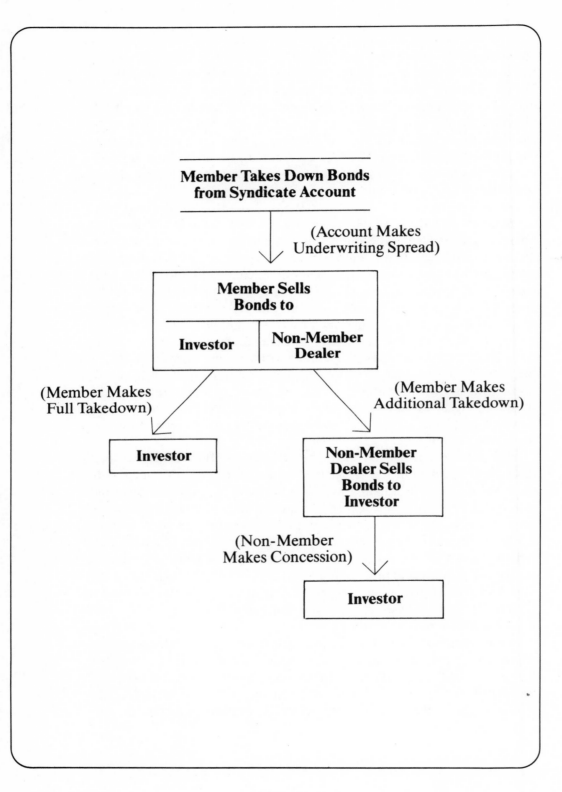

Member Takes Down Bonds
from Syndicate Account

(Account Makes
Underwriting Spread)

Member Sells
Bonds to

| Investor | Non-Member Dealer |

(Member Makes
Full Takedown)

(Member Makes
Additional Takedown)

Investor

Non-Member
Dealer Sells
Bonds to
Investor

(Non-Member
Makes Concession)

Investor

sion on Vermonts in the 1983 maturity would be set at ¼, and the additional takedown at ⅛. Members would take bonds down from the account less the full takedown, so Vermonts of 1983 would be taken down at less a ¼ concession, plus an extra ⅛, or ⅜ total. So if J & Mc got an order for 100 bonds directly from an investor, they would take them down at the regular scale price (perhaps a 4.85%) less ⅜. Then they would sell them at a 4.85% net (no concession) and make $375.

A Dealer Order

However, if a dealer outside of the account (a non-member) got the order instead, he would have to buy the bonds from a member. If he were to come to Kate, she would take the bonds down, again at a 4.85% less the same total takedown, ⅜. She would then sell them to the non-member dealer at a 4.85% less the ¼ concession, and keep just the second discount, the additional ⅛, as her profit. In both cases, the bonds would be taken down at a 4.85% less ⅜, and the investor would buy them at a 4.85%. But on one sale the account member would reap both discounts, the whole takedown, and on the other would give up the concession to the selling dealer. Naturally, members who figure to get more dealer orders prefer larger additional takedowns, and the other way around.

Meetings, Meetings

After all the ideas had been presented the members stayed seated for a few minutes and the talk drifted to other things. Then the meeting broke up; Kate headed back to her office, but some, now that it was after four o'clock, went on to Harry's, to do some serious thinking. The five competing Vermont accounts also held preliminary meetings that day, all in New York. Five other big issues were selling that week, and since they drew an average of eight bids, managers would hold something like 50 sets of municipal syndicate meetings, 40 or so in New York, perhaps five in Chicago, and the rest in local markets.

AMOUNT	2/1	BOND YEARS	RATE	BASIS	PRICE	RATE	BASIS	PRICE
	1978			5·½				
	1979							
$ 1,850,000	1980	2775		4.50				
1,650 ~~1,850,000~~	1981	7400		65				
1,850,000	1982	13875		75				
1,750 ~~1,850,000~~	1983	22200		85				
1,850,000	1984	32375		90				
0 ~~1,800,000~~	1985	44075		95				
1,800,000	1986	57575		5.00				
1,800,000	1987	72875		05				
1,800,000	1988	89975		15				
1,800,000	1989	108875		20				
1,800,000	1990	129575		25				
1,800,000	1991	152075		30				
1,800,000	1992	176375		40				
1,300 ~~1,800,000~~	1993	202475		100				
1,800,000	1994	230375		11				
1,800,000	1995	260075		60				
1,800,000	1996	291575		70				
1,800,000	1997	324875		80				
1,750 ~~1,800,000~~	1998	359975		90				
	1999							
	2000			101.016				
	2001							
	2002							
	2003							

Kate's worksheet showing scale A. Above the 4.50 yield on the first maturity is the projected coupon—5½. At the bottom of the scale is the production, 101.016, the average dollar price of the reoffering yields. She later reduced the amounts in years where bonds were spoken for—including 1983, where she had an order for 100 bonds.

Courtesy of *The Bond Buyer*

Chapter Twenty-One

The Final Meeting
July 18, 1978

On Tuesday morning, after they had finished their coffee, Bob and Charley grabbed a minute to talk together about Vermont. 1978 had been a pretty decent year for them so far—nothing spectacular, but the times weren't great either. Bob wanted to better last year's department results—his bonus was at stake. He was looking at Vermont with $50,000, tops, in mind. Maybe a $20,000 underwriting profit, plus $25,000 or so if First Nat sold $10 million bonds themselves. They talked about the scale that they had suggested at the preliminary meeting, and agreed that it was high enough for a start. "How about orders?" Bob asked. Charley looked over the scale sheet, and said he could probably sell the 1985's at a 5.00 basis. They looked at the 1985 maturity and saw that the scale read a 4.95%. Both minds went to work on the .05 difference it would take to cut price to a 5.00%. They calculated that if they took the bonds down at a 4.95% less ⅜, they could sell them at a 5.00%, make a few cents, and start the account moving. Bob winced at the necessity for a price cut so early in the game, but did not resist as Charley went off to see if he could firm up the order. Before 10:00 a.m. the 5.00 basis order was definite, and one of their salesmen got a legitimate order for 500 of the 1993's—as 5½'s at 100. At least they had a little something to show the account.

A Pre-Sale Huddle

Conference Room B, on the forty-fourth floor of the First National Building right off Wall Street, had been reserved for the Vermont meeting. At 10:00 a.m., five of the Vermont syndicate members' representatives had drifted in. By 10:05 Charley saw that only eight of the 16 on the original account letter were present, and hoped more would arrive soon. The syndicate was actually down to 15 members, since NINE had told Bob he didn't want to bid this time. In former years, a $35 million syndicate might have had up to 50 members, and a few larger ones still do. But, starting around 1970, a number of very small high-powered accounts began to challenge the traditional large groups. We called them Guerilla (or Gorilla)

The Group Assembles

185

$34,450,000
State of Vermont

Selling 7/18/78

		OUT ON SCHE A	ADDL. OUT ON SCHE B $620
First National Bank	$6,450,000		
TWO	6,000,000		
THREE	6,000,000		
FOUR	6,000,000		
FIVE	2,500,000	− 2,500	
SEVEN	2,500,000	− 2,500	
JOHNSON & McDONALD	2,500,000		
EIGHT	2,500,000		− 2,500
~~NINE~~ (Pre-sale)	~~2,500,000~~	− 2,500	
ELEVEN	1,000,000		
THIRTEEN	1,000,000		
FOURTEEN	1,000,000	− 1,000	
FIFTEEN	1,000,000		− 1,000
SIXTEEN	500,000		
SEVENTEEN	500,000		
EIGHTEEN	500,000		

	$42,450,000	42,450 −8,500	42,450 −12,000
	34,450,000	33,950	30,450
Over-Underwritten	+8,000,000	− 500	− 4,000

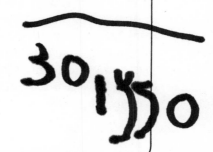

groups, among other things. Although that particular species has since returned to its caves, in 1985 most accounts bidding for an issue of this size now have from 20 to 40 members, with an average participation of about $1 million each. First Nat's band was small, but definitely not a wild one. At 10:10 three more members appeared, and Bob started the first order of business, the roll call. In larger meetings, all the names in the account are read out and checked for attendance, but since Bob knew most of the people there, he checked the roll by eye. Three of the remaining members were absent: EIGHT, a New York firm that had more meetings today than people to cover them, ELEVEN, and THIRTEEN, of Memphis. THIR-TEEN had phoned Kate, who agreed to vote for him by proxy. The missing member ELEVEN slid in, and the group was ready.

Charley passed out worksheets with the scale he proposed bidding. Scale A, he called it. Getting the ball rolling, Bob Swenson said, "As for me, I like the market. We have going-away orders for all of the 1985's, half a million of the 1993's, and we have some other buyers looking on the fence. I think it will take at least this scale to buy the loan." Kate looked at Scale A, wanting to hear about other buyers, but she heard nothing more, and took Bob's speech with at least one grain of salt.

Scale A

Kate put in for 100 of 1983 for Johnson & McDonald, and some other members entered a few more orders, too. She jotted them down and tried to assess what they indicated about the prospects of the deal. She knew that managers usually write the highest possible reoffering scale, increasing the probability that they will buy the bonds. Somewhat more puzzling, the manager often pushes for the lowest possible profit margin. Why? The lower the profit, the higher the bid, and the better the chance that they will win the issue. Not only do managers want to buy issues in order to earn underwriting profits, but also, more pointedly, to control the deal, which will give them a number of substantial built-in advantages. This was not discussed, of course, but it was in the minds of both Bob and Kate. A more dangerous motive pushing managers to buy is pride, that deadly sin, which dwells on the annual published lists of leading underwriters and the like. Members beware. On the other hand, managers certainly do provide re-search, leadership, and many other services, and these have to be paid for.

Motives

After those early orders had been entered, Bob polled the account, asking each representative whether or not his or her company would bid that scale. The three other joint managers said they would go along. Members FIVE and SEVEN said they would not. "Sorry, No," is one of the standard phrases. At her turn, Kate said that she would stay, and that so would THIRTEEN, for whom she was proxy. Bob continued his poll to the

Polling the Account

$34,450,000
State of Vermont

Selling 7/18/78

		FINAL PRTK.
First National Bank	~~$8,450,000~~	8,000 ~
TWO	~~6,000,000~~	7,950
THREE	6,000,000	6,000
FOUR	6,000,000	6,000
~~FIVE~~	~~2,500,000~~	
~~SEVEN~~	~~2,500,000~~	
JOHNSON & McDONALD	~~2,500,000~~	3,000
~~EIGHT~~	~~2,500,000~~	
~~NINE (Pre-Sale)~~	~~2,500,000~~	
ELEVEN	1,000,000	1,000
THIRTEEN	1,000,000	1,000
~~FOURTEEN~~	~~1,000,000~~	
~~FIFTEEN~~	~~1,000,000~~	
SIXTEEN	500,000	500
SEVENTEEN	500,000	500
EIGHTEEN	500,000	500

$42,450,000
34,450,000   34,450

Over-Underwritten 8,000,000

end, and all the rest stayed except FOURTEEN, who hesitated and then dropped. The drops added up to $8.500 million, which the rest of the account could easily absorb, since they had started out over-syndicated by $8 million. Then, at 10:20, one of First National's syndicate assistants entered the room and handed Bob a note saying that they had received an order for a million of 1988, and that two other buyers were looking at the 1989 and '90 maturities. An order for 250 of the first maturity, 1980, had come in, too. At this point Bob suggested that they raise the scale an .05 in the 1983, '89, and '90 maturities. That would lower those offering yields by an .05, and so raise the price, giving the account a little better chance to buy the issue. So the price of those three years would be raised from a 5.15%, 5.20%, and a 5.25%, up to a 5.10%, 5.15%, and a 5.20%. All the remaining 12 members, in response to the definite signs of interest, went along with the change.

Then Bob raised one of the tough questions on any underwriting deal: profit. How much to work for? He proposed $6, a spread of .6%, or just over ½ of 1%. Once again a poll was taken; a few said Yes, but most objected. Eventually a compromise was reached—$6.20. Kate still liked it, and said that she would go along, but EIGHT (who had phoned in) and FIFTEEN declined to take the risk for that small a reward. They dropped from the underwriting, but not permanently. The next time Vermont came to market they could expect to bid with First National again.

Profit

So the original account had now lost six members, with a total of $12 million in participations. Why was Bob pushing so hard? Because he knew that the other accounts would also be straining to buy the loan, and that every dollar and dime (and sometimes even every penny) can make the difference between buying and missing. There was another thought at work in his mind, too—if a bid doesn't force some members out, it isn't high enough. Now that the scale and the profit were set, the next order of business was to reassign the $4 million slack in underwriting participations. He asked each member how many more he was willing to take, and when it was Kate's turn she said, with some enthusiasm, "I'll take three million." Bob simply said, "O.K., we are underwritten," which meant that he was willing to take a total of $8 million. So the deal was syndicated—$34.450 million, on a scale from a 4.50% to a 5.90% for 5½'s, with a $6.20 spread.

Participations

Then Bob asked the remaining underwriters if they would like to try bidding the same scale and profit, but using a 5.45% coupon. No one moved a lip, and so the subject was dropped. Although a bid for 5.45's made mathematical sense, and might have enabled them to buy the bonds, the members felt that the odd-looking rate would have been so much harder to

The Bid and the Coupon

189

	CONCESSIONS		ADD. TAKEDOWN		TOTAL TAKEDOWN
1980	1/4	+	1/8	=	3/8 ($3.75)
81					
82					
83					
84	3/8				1/2 ($5.00)
85					
86					
87					
88					
89					
1990					
91					
92					
93					
94					
95					
96					
97					
98					

sell that it was not worth taking the additional risk. Let someone else do that, said Bob to himself. It was 10:35 and Charley took the bid inside to have it calculated and entered with Shawmut. If you wish to see how the bid was figured, go to Chapter 26. What we call the municipal bond market is really no more than a long series of practical decisions such as these. If you get the chance, ask a syndicate man to let you tag along with him to a few meetings, and you will get some feel for it. Meetings are an invaluable learning experience, and incidentally, a good place to make yourself seen and known.

The scale, spread, and underwriting were all set, and it was time to set the takedowns. As we discussed in the Kenosha example, the larger the takedowns, the smaller the underwriting profit, and the other way around. This account was bidding for a $6.20 gross profit per bond, and there would be about 40¢ per bond in various expenses, leaving $5.80 net. For example, if an average of $3.80 is paid out in takedowns, there will be $2 a bond left in the underwriting. *Takedowns*

Bob suggested these takedown terms: a concession of less a quarter through '83; three-eighths on the balance; plus an additional takedown of an extra eighth all the way. In translation, members would take down bonds due 1980, '81, '82, and '83 at the set scale, with two discounts (¼ plus ⅛%) totaling three-eighths of one percent, or $3.75 per bond. And take down bonds due 1984 through 1998 at ⅜ plus ⅛, or a total of one-half of one percent, $5 per bond. Kate mentally calculated that those takedowns would average about $4.75; and since there was only $5.80 to work with, there would be only about a dollar a bond left in the account. She said, "That's too much," meaning that the takedowns were too high. Several other voices were raised in her support, and manager Bob backtracked a bit. "O.K. How about less a quarter, plus an eighth all the way?" This was three-eighths of a percent, or $3.75, on all the bonds, leaving about two dollars in the underwriting, twice as much as in his first proposal. The remaining members accepted these takedowns, with a few grumbles from those who figured to sell more bonds than average and who liked the bigger takedowns, and a few mutterings from the other members.

Let's go back to see what had passed through Kate's mind. She and the other members had a decision to make—whether or not to stay. All of them were trained and experienced people and were there to make a profit; but some dropped, some stayed along with no change in participation, and some, like Kate and Bob, took more bonds. What made up their minds so differently? A set of complex evaluations of internal and external factors, and how they figured to interact. The internal ones included actual and *To Stay or Not to Stay*

AMOUNT	2/1	BOND YEARS	RATE	BASIS	PRICE	RATE	BASIS	PRICE
	1978			5·½				
	1979							
1,608 ~~1,850,000~~	1980	2775		4.50			1/4	1/8
1,650 ~~1,550,000~~	1981	7400		65				
1,850,000	1982	13875		75				
1,750 ~~1,850,000~~	1983	(100 cpm 22200)		85				
1,850,000	1984	32375		90		~~~~		
O ~~1,800,000~~	1985	44075		95				
1,800,000	1986	57575		5.00				
1,800,000	1987	72875		05				
800 ~~1,800,000~~	1988	89975		~~15~~	10			
1,800,000	1989	108875		~~20~~	15			
1,800,000	1990	129575		~~25~~	20		(NOON)	
1,800,000	1991	152075		30				
1,800,000	1992	176375		40				
1,300 ~~1,800,000~~	1993	202475		100				
1,800,000	1994	230375		11				
1,800,000	1995	260075		60				
1,800,000	1996	291575		70				
1,800,000	1997	324875		80				
1,750 ~~1,800,000~~	1998	359975		90				
	1999							
	2000			~~101.016~~				
	2001			101.07 39				
	2002			.62				
	2003			100.4 539				

192

possible future orders, the position of each member in the syndicate, and how much other bond inventory each owned at the time. The external factors included scale, profit, takedowns, and each member's guess about the direction of the bond market. Since their internal situations were quite disparate, and since outside forces were perceived by each member differently, each one solved the problem according to his own lights. So staying along might have been right for one member and wrong for another. Making these decisions is not easy, and although no one freshly entering any business really likes to hear it, experience helps determine the winning answers.

In Kate's case, she had just one small order (the 100 of 1983) and one good possibility, Windy, for 500 of 1990. With $2.500 million in underwriting, and $2 a bond in net profit, J & Mc would earn $5,000 if the deal sold out at list. She tried to estimate the probability that it would sell, what the loss would be if it didn't, and what other orders she might get. She came to a positive decision, and even took a few more bonds. If there were no business in sight, or if she hadn't liked the direction of the bond market, her solution might have been to join the six who declined to underwrite. *Decisions*

In addition to the profit motive, a number of political factors enter into account strategies. Dropping, for instance. Since dealers bid together to make money, and since presumably their colleagues are not completely crazy, most dealers drop with some degree of reluctance. Among other things, it may seem to show weakness. Majors tend to drop less often than smaller members; joint managers, who have more status to lose, still less often; managers, almost never. As a compromise, members sometimes go along, but for fewer bonds. On the other hand, members who support accounts and go up in participation can enhance their own standing in the industry. It was a good thing for Kate that she liked the bid, since it would have looked odd for her to first ask to be made a major, and then to drop. Decisions are not often so clear-cut. *Wall Street Politics*

Now let's see how they wrapped it all up. The takedowns were set, and attention moved to order handling. First, Bob said that he thought all the pre-sale orders should be honored. Agreed and done, and so those $3.900 million bonds were confirmed. Bob added that the order period would be for one hour, a usual limit, and there were no disagreements. There was nothing more to discuss, and the meeting was over. Kate headed for the phone bank on the side wall and called her office with the scale, concessions, takedowns, order period, and the pre-sale business. *Pre-Sale Confirmations*

Gross Margin of Profit	$6.20
Estimated Expenses	−.40
Net Spread	5.80
Takedowns	−3.75
Underwriting Spread	$2.05

Risk-Taking $\dfrac{\$2.05}{5.80} = 35.34\%$

Selling $\dfrac{\$3.75}{5.80} = 64.66\%$

Here's how the profit we were discussing in the prior chapter was divided between underwriting and sales.

Chapter Twenty-Two

Entering the Bid

Beginners in municipals are often given the job of entering their syndicate's bid with a municipality, or, as we call it, covering a sale. Back in 1954, when I thought it was a great honor to cover a $2 million sale all by myself, my first boss, Mr. Richard Rand, told me how to do it right:

How To Enter a Bid

1. Make sure you have the three items required in the notice of sale: the bid form, the good faith check, and an envelope typed out according to instructions. Also bring a watch, set to the exact time.
2. One hour before the deadline, find the room where the bids will be received. Then locate a phone you can use and check in with your office (where the bid is probably still being determined) to agree on the time you want to call back for the numbers. Return to the bid room, and keep to yourself; why give the other bidders any knowledge about their competition?
3. Call your office back, and write all the numbers dictated to you directly onto the bid form. Read them back, every single number, slowly. Yours is not to reason why; yours is but to do or die. Put the bid and the check in the envelope and seal it.
4. Before the official sale time, hand in the envelope to one of the city officials. If a competitor tries to submit a bid even one second after the time limit, scream bloody murder—he would do the same to you.
5. Listen to the bids as they are read off, write them all down, and make up your own mind which one is high.
6. If it's yours, identify yourself, sign what they ask you to, and notify your office.
7. If another bidder is high, get your good faith check back, and return it and yourself to your office.

Particularly at smaller-sized sales, the town officials and local lawyers fumble around a bit—bond auctions only come once every few years for them. In New Jersey, for instance, many sales are scheduled at night, to

A Bond Sale

PROPOSAL FOR BONDS

July 18, 1978

Hon. Emory A. Hebard, *State Treasurer*
State of Vermont
c/o Shawmut Bank of Boston, N.A.
Municipal Services Department
Eleventh Floor
One Federal Street
Boston, Massachusetts 02211

Dear Sir:

In accordance with the provisions of your Notice of Sale dated July 3, 1978, which Notice is hereby made a part of this proposal, we offer to purchase $34,450,000 Public Improvement and Transportation Bonds of the State of Vermont bearing interest at the rate of _5 1/2_ % and to pay therefor the price of _100. 4539_ and accrued interest to date of delivery for each $100 par value of bonds.

The undersigned hereby acknowledges receipt of the Preliminary Official Statement referred to in the aforementioned Notice of Sale.

Robert W Swenson
....

Robert W. Swenson
Vice - President
by First National Bank
(Manager)

First National Bank
and associates

Box 1087
....

New York, N.Y. 10005
....
(Mailing Address)

The Shawmut Bank would be pleased to assist you in entering your bid on these bonds if you will mail your signed bid form in advance and telephone figures to Mr. Daniel J. Shields, Vice President, about one-half hour before the time of sale. Telephone: 617-292-3192.

coincide with regular city council meetings, where the usual gatherings of casually attired citizens interested in zoning variances, school closings, stop signs, and other vital, if purely local, matters are for once joined by a dozen or so New York and New Jersey dealers, who wait until the mayor suspends the ordinary business and carefully opens and reads off the bids. This may go on for half an hour or more, including time out for a financial huddle with the town's advisors. Finally, a vote is taken and, well over 95% of the time, the council accepts the bid and makes the award. The losing bidders get up to go, shake hands with the winner, who is all smiles, wish him luck (and may privately think he will need it, at so high a cost), collect their good faith checks, and head out, perhaps wondering how they could have made the winning bid themselves.

In about 2 or 3% of all sales, the vote goes against accepting the bid because the interest rate seems too high, or because of internal political reasons. In these cases, it's back to the drawing board with the issue. In another small fraction, maybe 1%, a syndicate enters a bid which, though high, does not conform to the required specifications. Sometimes in these cases the issuer waives the irregularity, but more often the high bid is thrown out, and the deal is awarded to the cover. *Exceptions*

Returning to our Vermont example, the First Nat member's man had stationed himself in a phone booth around the corner from Federal Street, Boston. He called Charley at 10:40 and got the figures—100.4539 for 5½'s—repeating them to make sure they were correct. Since he had five minutes to spare, he stayed on the phone, chatting, in case there were any last minute changes. There were none, so off he went, into the small room where the bids were to be received, with five minutes to spare. A bank officer, a friend, smiled at him, and announced officially that bids could then be entered. One by one the six bidders handed in their sealed envelopes, each marked Proposal for Bonds, and each containing a filled-out bid form. He asked if there were any more, and at exactly 11:00, cut the bidding off. If someone had rushed into the room after the time limit, his bid would have been rejected. Sometimes bids do come in late, and every couple of months a deal is awarded to the second (or the third) highest bidder. *The Bid Is In*

Right after 11:00, Shawmut's man counted the six envelopes and opened them, first checking each bid for completeness. One usual thing he didn't have to bother with: a good faith deposit, which, as we mentioned, Vermont did not require. Then he read the bids off, each of the bidders writing them down. They were all for 5½'s and here is how they came in: First Nat, 100.4539; Chase 100.07 (pretty far away); F.O.B. 100.15 (closer); *Tabulating the Bids*

When Issued and Regular Delivery Dates

TRADE DATE	EVENT	STATUS	SETTLEMENT DATE
7/18 - 11:00	First Nat. high bidder	W.I., subject to award	-
7/18 - 11:30	Award Made	W.I.	W.I.
7/19 to 7/26		W.I.	W.I.
7/27	Delivery set	W.I.	8/15
7/27 to 8/8		W.I.	8/15
8/9		W.I.	8/16
8/10		W.I.	8/17
8/13		W.I.	8/20
8/14		W.I.	8/21
8/15	Bonds delivered	Regular	8/22
8/16		Regular	8/23
Etc.		Regular	Etc.

Citibank 100.18; Chemical 100.20; and Harris, the cover bid at 100.2359. First Nat was high by $2.18 a bond. By 11:10 the official announced that First Nat was indeed high, and excused himself to phone where the State Treasurer and some other officials held a short meeting, and as expected, voted to award the loan. Shawmut's man returned to the room at 11:30 and told the group that the bonds were awarded to First National, and thanked all of the bidders for their efforts. Very proper, that Bostonian.

As we will see shortly, First Nat's account did not wait for the award, or even for official confirmation from Boston that they were high. They just checked the other five bidders and started offering the issue right at 11:00, subject to award. If for some reason the bid had been rejected, any trades would have automatically been cancelled. But the award was made promptly, with sales made on a when issued basis.

When issued, or W.I. for short, means just that. New deals, right up to the time the bonds are actually printed and delivered, are offered with that special condition—when, as, and if issued, and received by us. We send out special confirmations for them, marked W.I., without the usual money figures, since the settlement date is not definitely known. If everything goes according to plan, the bonds are duly delivered. But once in a long while, a legal technicality surfaces after the award, and the deal falls through. If that happens the syndicate and any other dealers who sold the bonds are released from liability to deliver them. So we see that a bond's life has four stages:

1. Before the sale: unborn, so to speak.
2. After the high bidder is known, when the bonds are offered when issued, and also subject to award.
3. After the award, when the bonds are offered W.I. This stage usually lasts for one to four weeks.
4. Regular delivery, when the new bonds are traded with money and a fixed settlement date.

Now we will take a look at sales. Sales takes up more energy than any other part of our business, and dealers with the strongest sales forces often collect the most profit, and the most respect. Bonds sometimes drop into dealer's laps so cheaply that they seem to sell themselves, but all too rarely—usually they have to be pushed hard, or they don't sell at all.

7/18/78   11:05 AM
A GROUP HEADED BY FIRST NATIONAL BANK IS APPARENTLY HIGH ON

$34,450,000 STYATE OF VERMONT GENERAL OBLIGATION VARIOUS PURPOSE BONDS

$34,450,000 STYATE

$34,450,000 STATE OF VERMONT GENERAL OBLIGATION VARIOUS PURPOSE BONDS

DUE 2/1/80-98, ON THEIR BID OF 100.4539 FOR 5 1/2%, A NIC OF 5.456562

SCALE: 4.50,4.65,4.75,4.85, 4.90,4.95,5.00,5.05,5.10,
5.15,5.20,5.30,5.40,100, 100,5.60,5.70,5.80,5.90

CONCESSIONS: 1980-98 1/4
ORDER PERIOD: NOON EDT
PRE-SALE: 1980-250, 1981-200, 1983-100, 1985-1,800,
          1988-1,000, 1993-500, 1998-50

Chapter Twenty-Three

Sales
July 18, 1978—11:00 a.m.

Just before the sale, the underwriters sent the final Vermont scales out to their branch offices, and all good salesmen prepared to contact their customers if their account was high. A few minutes before sale time, the competing syndicate departments in New York called each other to compare bids, and by 11:00 Bob and Charley had heard that they were high by a little more than $2 a bond—a respectable, if not great, cover. It amounted to about $75,000. They could have had $2 a bond more spread and still bought the issue, but that is how the competitive system works. Bob sang out, "We're high, by two bucks. Go get 'em." The salesmen hit the phones, offering the bonds when issued and subject to award.

Right after 11:00, First National's underwriting people got busy releasing the scale to the financial public. And the managers, majors, and minors all started the big push to sell Vermont, using the mechanisms we have discussed—scale, concessions, takedowns, order period, the works. Charley Stone called the *Bond Buyer*'s Munifacts syndicate wire desk and gave them the coupons, bid, scale, concessions, order period, and the pre-sale business, and this news appeared on their subscribers' machines in four or five minutes. The scale was also printed on the Dow Jones ticker and a First Nat specialist went to work calling in the ad material to *The New York Times*, hoping to meet their Wednesday morning deadline.

In the first half-hour, First National's 20 salesmen made about 200 calls, trying to be the first to contact the buyers. It's great to work for a manager of a deal; you can speak with some authority in your voice, and even intimate that an investor has a better chance to get his order filled from the outfit that runs the books. At Johnson & McDonald, Kate flashed the branch offices to tell them that their account was high, and Joe Smithers, in Philadelphia, got moving. Joe had 105 accounts assigned to him, 40 of which might be interested in this issue. Of these, 15 had bought municipals that year, and he planned to call every one of them. Four customers had money right then;

The High Bid

Releasing the Scale

Branch Office Sales

	Aa Vermont	A1 West Virginia	Aa Indianapolis Gas Rev.
1983	4.80		
1984	4.90		
1985	4.95		
1986	5.00		
1987	5.05		
1988	5.10		
1989	5.15		
1990	5.20	5.20	
1991	5.30		
1992	5.40		5.65
1993	100		
1994	100		
1995	5.60		
1996	5.70		
1997	5.80		
1998	5.90		

Comparisons between trading levels of various municipals are the constant pre-occupation of traders, underwriters, and investors. We saw some new issue scales, particularly Oregon, enter the bond minds, and here we have a couple of actual trades with which Vermont could have been compared. Most people would have thought that Vermont was worth more than West Virginia, and so when Joe heard that West Virginias of '90 had traded at a 5.20, he tried to use that as a sales point for Windy to buy Vermont. On the other side of the fence, Smythe bought a Midwest revenue name at a 5.65 in '92 and was using that to contrast the higher priced Vermonts unfavorably.

two had bought bonds the day before and were looking at Vermont, but he knew whom to call first—Winderman. He had talked to Windy earlier that morning and passed on the unemployment figures for Vermont, 7.9% that year. He said that was only .9% higher than the 7% national number, the way a salesman talks, though, of course, 7.9 is actually 13% higher than 7. But in any case, 7.9% didn't look too bad to Windy. Joe got past Windy's secretary at 11:03 and said that he was in Vermont and Ohio Eds, too. Windy said he would pass on the Ohios, and Joe read him the Vermont scale. "A 5.20 in '90, Windy. Sorry about that. I know we were talking a 25 yesterday." Windy had written down the scale and was looking at it, saying nothing. Encouraged by the silence, Joe said, "A block of A-rated West Virginias of '90 just traded in the secondary at a 5.20—Vermonts at the same price look cheap to me."

"Not bad," Windy said. "I'll take a good look at 250 or 500."

Joe sensed that Windy didn't want to be pressed any further, so he said, "I'll keep on top of it. Talk to you later, Windy," and got off quickly. His call had lasted about two minutes. Right away Joe called Kate and told her that Windy was on the fence for maybe a half a million 90's and asked her to let him know how that maturity was going. She said she would try.

Then Joe called Otto Smythe, a buyer for a medium-sized casualty company in Detroit. Smythe had bought 500 Aa-rated Indianapolis Gas Revenues of '92 the day before at a 5.65%, and Joe thought Otto just might pay more for a good state name. Smythe's secretary put Joe on hold for a minute, and he fidgeted a bit, knowing that someone else was talking to him already, probably about Vermont.

"Hi, Otto, we bought Vermont and Ohio Eds. How do they look?" He figured Otto had the scale already—which he had.

"Vermont's too high for me," said Smythe, testily. "I want a six, or something like that, in '92." Joe was a little disgusted to hear how cheap he was, but thanked him anyway. Next he phoned his third best possibility, got her reaction, and continued down his list, all the while thinking about Windy.

After Winderman hung up he had a lot of thinking to do, and asked his secretary to hold his calls so he could get some peace and quiet. Windy was facing his central problem: uninvested money to spend, and a large variety of bonds to choose among. Mobank would probably keep whatever he bought for years, if not decades, and Winderman's career would be affected by the results. It's a lonely decision to make, something like buying a house, where present needs have to be balanced against long-term considerations. A good real estate salesman informs potential buyers about that market,

The Buyer's Choice

	7/11 Oregon	7/14	7/17	7/18	7/18 Vermont	7/18 West V.
1988	5.20				5.10	
1989	5.30				5.15	
1990	~~5.35~~	30	~~5.35~~	5.20	5.20	5.20
1991	~~5.45~~	~~40~~	~~5.35~~	30	5.30	
1992	~~5.55~~	~~50~~	~~5.45~~	40	5.40	
1993	~~5.60~~	~~55~~	~~5.55~~	50	5.50	
1994	~~5.70~~	65			5.50	
1995	5.80				5.60	
1996	5.85				5.70	
1997	5.90				5.80	
1998	5.90				5.90	
1999						
2000						

Here we have another round of comparisons that traders and investors and syndicate people were working on. The market as a whole was rising—we see that Oregons of 1990, which came out the week before at a 5.35, marked up again on the morning of the Vermont sale—to a 5.20, up a total of 15 basis points. And in the First Nat final meeting, Vermont was also upped to a 5.20. Windy heard, in Missouri, that a New York dealer traded a block of West Virginias of '90 to a Florida dealer bank, who had an order from an Alabama retail bank. How municipal news does travel.

and a good bond salesman should be able to do it more precisely. However, in the end the buyer must make up his own mind. Windy had the last few weeks' scales of high grades in front of him, and his notes about recent trades, too. He thought over his shopping list again, and came back to Vermont. It fit his requirements perfectly, and furthermore, the bank had none of that name on its books. He recalled his talk with Bill, who had said that the best gauge of the market was Oregon. Windy had expressed interest in Illinois at an .05 cheaper than Oregon, but there were no Illinois available. So for Windy it boiled down to whether a 5.20%, the same price as Oregon, was cheap enough for Vermont. Here you can see one complication to buying municipals, compared to buying Governments. All U.S. Treasuries have the same credit, and so it is only a matter of picking which maturity and coupon suits best. But there are hundreds of well-known municipals, and choosing the right one at the right price isn't easy.

10:30 central time came, and only a half hour remained in Vermont's order period. Windy went to the water cooler to clear his head, and then back to his desk to think it out. First: he had been directed to buy $100 million municipals, starting then. Second: Vermonts of 1990 matched his requirements. They were at a 5.20 basis, which he thought was a pretty decent level. Third: if he did buy Vermont, it would be from Joe. Fourth: before giving Joe an order, he would find out how the deal was going. Now, he was organized, and felt better; he looked at the clock—10:40. He was confident that Joe would call him back, and at that moment his secretary said, "Joe Smithers, Mr. Winderman." He nodded Yes, he would take the call. "Winderman."

"Hi, Windy! Joe. Listen, Vermont looks pretty good—not out the window, but moving well from 1980 to '85, and definitely half-sold overall. Shall we put in for some 1990's?"

Windy liked what he heard, and perhaps as important, how it was said. He was sliding off the fence, but said nothing. Joe knew the meaning of his pause and kept his mouth shut tight. Like a fisherman who feels a nibble, he wouldn't move a muscle until the hook was in. Finally, it was Windy who spoke. "Do you think I could get 250?"

The Decision

"Sure will try, Windy. Let's go get them."

Joe had swung up his pole, and the hook was set.

"O.K. 250 of 1990 at a 5.20, right?"

"Right. Thanks, Windy. Bye."

Joe hung up fast, before Windy had a second thought. A less experienced salesman might have talked on when Windy paused, and pushed his man back onto the fence, but Joe had waited out many a hesitating buyer.

The following day *Bond Buyer* shows all the bidding accounts and lists the members who stayed in the underwriting groups. Naturally, they did not report our fantasy that First National bought the bonds. In fact, Harris Trust bought them and Chemical was the cover. They say truth is stranger than fiction, and you can be sure that the action in the actual bidding syndicates was more complex than in the one we invented.

Almost before Windy knew it, he had made his decision.

The whole thrust of sales is to make an undecided buyer say one little word: Yes. A salesman has to wait for the buyer to make the commitment, which often comes unexpectedly, or even half-heartedly. Then the salesman must hit him hard, turning a simple "O.K." or a "Yup" into an order by confirming it in explicit detail. As soon as he got off the phone Joe called Kate and told her that Winderman would take a quarter of a million 1990's. Then he had another idea—if he could sell Windy, why not call Otto again, even if he was cranky that day? As he waited for him he did a little arithmetic on his Compucorp. 250 times ⅜—$937.50—with one third for himself, that's $312—not a bad start on the day.

Closing a Sale

How much can an institutional municipal bond salesman make? In 1984 we were hiring good inexperienced prospects for about $20,000-$25,000 a year. Then, after a year or so of training, we put them on commission, with 35% an average pay-out. As soon as a salesman starts to gross $300,000 or so for his firm, with $100,000 a year for himself, we figure he is a worthwhile producer; and perhaps 500 men, and a very few women, earn $250,000 a year in this field. From there the sky is the limit, with $1 million a year not unheard of.

Sales Earnings

SCALE SHEET

ISSUE ___ VERMONT

DUE ___ DATED 7/18/98

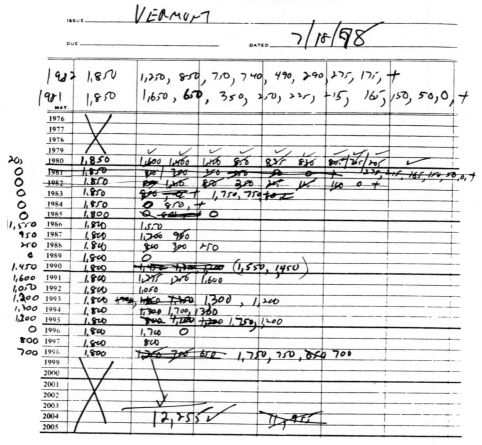

	MAT.									
	1982	1,850	1,250, 850, 750, 740, 490, 290, 275, 175, +
	1981	1,850	1,650, 650, 350, 250, 225, 215, 165, 150, 50, 0, +
	1976		
	1977	X	
	1978		
	1979	✓ ✓ ✓ ✓ ✓ ✓ ✓✓ ✓
20;	1980	1,850	1,600 1,400 1,100 850 825 820 800 765 205 ✓
0	1981	1,850	800 300 350 300 50 0 + 225, +F, 165, 150, 50, 0, +
0	1982	1,850	800 1,100 800 250 225 115 140 0 +
0	1983	1,850	800, 0, + 1,750, 750, 0
0	1984	1,850	0 450, +
0	1985	1,800	0 450, + 0
1,550	1986	1,800	1,550
950	1987	1,800	1,700 950
250	1988	1,840	800 300 250
0	1989	1,800	0
1,450	1990	1,800	1,450 1,700 1,200 (1,550, 1,450)
1,600	1991	1,800	1,275 250 1,600
1,050	1992	1,800	1,050
1,200	1993	1,800	1,400, 1,800 1,700 1,300 , 1,200
1,300	1994	1,800	1,700 1,700, 1300
1,200	1995	1,800	800, 1,700 1,200 1,750, 1,200
0	1996	1,800	1,700 0
800	1997	1,800	800
700	1998	1,800	1,750 700 650 1,750, 750, 850 700
	1999		
	2000		
	2001		
	2002	X	
	2003		
	2004		2,755 ✓ 1,955
	2005		

Chapter Twenty-Four

Orders and Allocations
July 18, 1978—11:00 a.m. to 1:30 p.m.

Back at First National, things had been hectic. Not only were they running Vermont, but they were a joint manager of the Ohio Ed. deal, which also sold at 11:00, and were managing a small Bismarck, North Dakota, account, too. All ten new issue department people were pitching in, Charley and two others concentrating on Vermont. By 11:30 about 20 orders, totaling about $10 million, had been entered. Adding in the $4 million pre-sale, the account was almost half sold.

The New Issue Buzz

Then member SEVEN called in with orders for 100 of '93, and 50 of '98. Next a call from Kate—she put in for 250 of '90 (against Windy's order, but of course only J & Mc knew that) and also for 100 of '94. First National's people jotted down each order on a printed form and Charley transcribed them onto a master sheet showing the bonds remaining in each maturity.

You can see here how running the books gives the manager one of the advantages we spoke of earlier—he can see the maturities in which orders are heaviest, and which dealers have entered them. A fair manager keeps his account informed about where the orders are coming in; however, it is all too easy to withhold this information from members (who, after all, are competitors) and to direct his salespeople, and also to make his own takedowns, in maturities where he sees demand building. The standard phrase to cover this: orders are still being tabulated. Bob had resolved to avoid such practice himself—he was a young man. The phones went on ringing, and at 11:45 Vermont seemed headed for a reasonably good deal. Orders kept coming in until noon, with quite a few entered at the last minute.

Managers' Business

This syndicate, like most, had more orders than bonds in some maturities and only a few orders in others. In oversubscribed maturities we use a number of common-sense allocation procedures, hammered out by long experience, to determine which orders get filled. There is also M.S.R.B. Rule G-11, which appears to promote regularized order treatment. We

Allocation Procedures

FNB

Issue *VT*

Date

Mat. 1980

Orig. 1,850

Group 500   500 ✓

Desig.

Bal. 1,350

Member	Entered		Confirmed
PN	(250)	PRE-SALE	250 ✓
2	200		200 ✓
FOUR	250		250 ✓
PN	300		300 ✓
EIGHTEEN	15		15 ✓
11	5		5 ✓
ELEVEN	25		25 ✓
TWO	100	STRIP	100 ✓

Tot. 1,145 ✓

Total 1,145 ✓   Bal. 205
                         500
                        1,850 ✓✓

recognize three classes of orders: group, designated, and member. Group orders are placed by investors for the benefit of the syndicate as a whole; they are entered at the net price (no concession) and get first confirmation preference. Designated orders are given to two or more members (who may be credited with the concession) and receive second preference. Together, group and designated orders are called priority orders. Last come the members' own orders; they go out at the full takedown and get last preference. We can see the descending price level in the three classes: from net, to concession, down to takedown. The number of members included also descends: from all, to some, down to one. And often the largest orders are for the group, the medium-sized are designated, and the smallest come from members.

The rules do make sense on paper, and, by and large, investors are well served by them. However, member dealers do not fare as well, for all too often their rights are abused to the managers' advantage. As for G-11, for members, it is like the rules of boxing: shake hands first, sit down every three minutes, and abide by a vote at the end, but in between it's legal mayhem. Managers' ways of allotting bonds vary greatly. A few try to balance practicality with equity, but most are consistent only in flagrant self-service. However, there is another side to this—among the very fairest managers were Ira Haupt, Phelps, Fenn and Harriman Ripley. They usually gave their members a good shake. And gave is right—they went out of business or merged into other firms in 1963, 1966, and 1973, respectively.

Now let's take a look at allotting in practice. At 12:15, Bob and Charley went into a small conference room to get away from the members they anticipated would be calling them to ask for favored confirmation treatment. They had been through this dozens of times before—balancing order pressures as smoothly, and as profitably to First National, as possible. They looked at the master sheet, which showed an unsold balance of $12.255 million. Charley started with the 1980 maturity, and saw that 250 had been confirmed pre-sale. There was one group net order for 500, and seven smaller member orders, altogether only $1.645 million. So the allocation here was easy; since 1980 started with $1.850 million, everybody was confirmed the bonds they put in for, and there were 205 left unsold. Charley took the original order slips, marked each one CFM, clipped them together, and went on to the next maturity. Bob was keeping in mind the word Strip marked next to one of the orders.

Bob found slips totaling $1.975 million for 1981, which had started with $1.850 million bonds. Or, as he would say, orders for a million nine seventy-five, against a million eight-fifty to start. More orders than bonds, so they

FNB

Issue **VT**   Mat. 1981

Date _____   Orig. 1,850

Group _____

Desig. 1,000   1,000 ✓

                    Bal. 850

Member	Entered		Confirmed
FOUR	200	—(PRESALE)	200 ✓
THIRTEEN	300		300 ✓
TWO	100	STRIP	100 ✓
EIGHTEEN	10 + 25		X
SIXTEEN	25		X
FOUR	50		X
SEVENTEEN	15		X
THREE	100		100 ✓
PN	150		150 ✓

                    Tot. 850 ✓

Total 975   Bal. 0

                    1,000
                    1,850 ✓

had some decisions to make. 200 had been confirmed pre-sale, and there was one priority item, a designated order for a million. The million would be sold at net, and $2,500 ($2.50 x $1,000) eventually credited to the dealers that the customer designated. (Bob hoped First Nat was included; however, he didn't know for sure—to help keep things honest, designees are usually disclosed only after confirmations are made.)

1981, Cont.

Bob checked off the pre-sale and designated business as confirmed, but with 775 in member orders and only 650 bonds left, they remained over-subscribed by 125 bonds. Bob and Charley glanced at the order slips; two of them were conditional. Bob had seen that one order was marked Strip. This tied together 100 bonds a year, 1980, '81 and '82, one kind of conditional order we permit to help investors buy precisely what they need. Since the strip order had helped the account move unsold bonds in the 1980 maturity, it had already been put aside and Bob checked it as confirmed.

The Decisions

Looking at 375 in orders, and only 250 bonds left, Charley knew that something had to go. He eliminated the 10 and 15 bond orders, putting their slips aside. Now came another moment of truth. There were five orders left, for 25, 25, 50, 100, and 150—a total of 350. Who would get the remaining 250, and the profit their takedown would bring? There were two round lot orders, for 100 and 150, and these could be given the nod. Or, they might confirm the 150 and the three smaller orders, making four dealers happy instead of two, depending. They may have felt some special heat from their own sales force or from dealers to whom they owed something. Bob and Charley talked it over, and marked a total of $1.850 million confirmed. The 200 pre-sale, the million designated, the 300, the 100 Strip, and the others they selected. Perfectly fair? Quite fair. Anyway, the 1981 balance was zero.

1982

1982 presented another allocation problem. There were orders for $2.225 million bonds against the original $1.8 million—but again, it was a nice problem to have to solve. All too often deals are slow throughout, like the longer maturities of this one. On the 1982's, Bob gave group and designated their preferred treatment, and confirmed that million. The Strip got 100, leaving 750 more to be filled, and 375 to miss out. One order was marked A.O.N. (All or None), another conditional order device, used to accommodate buyers who have minimum size requirements. In this case, they could look at the conditional order quite differently, since they could sell the whole maturity without it. They made their decisions, checked off their choices, and continued for all the maturities. After they finished, they would probably look over all the confirmed orders to see if they had treated any members more or less favorably than they had intended. If so, they might have gone back to make some adjustments. Since customers often

FNB

Issue *VT*

Date

Mat. 1982

Orig. 1,850

Group	600	600 ✓
Desig.	400	400 ✓
	Bal.	850

Member	Entered		Confirmed
TWO	100	STRIP	100 ✓
SEVENTEEN	10		X
THREE	250	AON	X
FNB	200		200 ✓
SEVENTEEN	15		X
PN	100		100 ✓
FOUR	300		200 ✓
FNB	250		250 ✓
		Tot.	850 ✓
Total	1,225	Bal.	0
			1,000
			1,850 ✓

give dealers some maturity latitude, they also could have called some members to suggest they move orders from one year to another, to get them bonds and help the account, too.

Managers may also look at business which comes in after the order period is over. If one maturity has a balance of 700 bonds and a late order comes in for a million A.O.N, it would take a staunch man indeed to turn it down. Bob and Charley got it all done, added up the unsold bonds in each maturity, checking the master sheet, and verifying a balance of $12.255 million. 36% were unsold—they still had plenty of work to do.

Just after one o'clock they returned to the syndicate room and gave their junior people the run and balance and the allocations. On some deals, particularly large negotiated ones, members pick up their allotments in writing, but on Vermont, as on most deals, the manager confirms by phone. The assistants called the financial media, and the run and balance went out over the wires, providing the market with a significant price indicator. First Nat had proved the Vermont scale, at least 64% of the way.

Releasing the Run and Balance

Down in Philadelphia, Joe received word at 1:20 that he had been allotted his 250 bonds and that there were $1.450 million left in 1990. His heart sank a little. Only 100 other bonds had sold in that year. However, he called Windy with a brave heart, and was little relieved to find that he was out to lunch (O.T.L.). He confirmed the 250 to Windy's secretary, and resolved to get him another 250 the following day, at a cheaper price—he had mentioned 500, and Joe was not one to forget.

Confirming to the Customer

VERMONT 7/18/78

1980	2~~05~~ *0*		1990	1,450
1981	0		1991	1,600
1982	0		1992	1,050
1983	0		1993	1,2~~00~~ *1,150*
1984	0		1994	1,3~~00~~ *1,250 1,225*
1985	0		1995	1,200
1986	1,5~~50~~ *1,450 1,445*		1996	0
1987	950		1997	800
1988	250		1998	7~~00~~ *600*
1989	0			

Balances

1:15 P.M.	1:20	5:00
12,255 ✓	11,950 ✓	11,720 ✓

Most managers keep blackboards like this going, because so many calls come in asking for the runs and balances of the deals they are heading. Anyone getting one of these calls just swings around in his chair and reads it off. Although only half a million Vermonts moved after the order period, a steady patter of little orders sometimes encourages the account, and seems to keep a deal's momentum going.

Chapter Twenty-Five

Closing Vermont
July 18-19, 1978

Closing an account, a process which extends from the time the first run and balance is released until the syndicate is terminated, is the last major job of underwriting. The excitement of buying is over and the presale work is long forgotten, but the price it takes to dispose of the unsold balance often makes the difference between a syndicate's profit or loss. If the syndicate cannot sell the rest of the bonds at the original scale, it eventually will have to lower its price or sell the balance by methods we will return to later. So the members of our Vermont account had their work cut out for them; with one-third left, its fate was very much in doubt. We saw how an order period works, but after it is over a different set of confirmation rules applies. Members can call their manager to get the current run, and if bonds are still unsold, they have the right to take down any they wish—first come, first served. As members take down bonds the run is changed and the balance reduced; no waiting, and no priorities. *After the Order Period*

As we saw, Vermont's balance after the order period was $12.255 million. At 12:15, two more orders came in, 350 of 1980, and 100 of 1998, and stayed in limbo until the allotment was finished. As soon as the first run was released, a junior hand called member FOUR to confirm the 100 of '98. And also member ELEVEN, who agreed to accept just the 205 of 1980; so he crossed out 1980, reduced 1998 to 600, and changed the balance to $11.950 million. Nothing much more came in by 2:15, and so Bob went out to lunch, leaving Charley in charge of First Nat's syndicate desk. Charley had eaten there earlier—a ham and American on rye, with a little plastic packet of mustard for sauce and a quarter of a limp pickle for garnish, and a diet soda. *Late Orders*

At 2:30 the phone rang for perhaps the three hundredth time since 11:00. It was Willis, head trader for member THREE, on their direct wire. He said, "Charley, I have a joint account bid for you on Vermont. Down .05 less ½ for 1991 through 1995." So instead of a 5.30, 5.40, 5.50 twice and a *A Bid Against the Account*

217

AMOUNT	2/1	BOND YEARS	RATE	BASIS	PRICE	RATE	BASIS	PRICE
	1978							
	1979							
$ 1,850,000	1980	2775	5½	4.50	¼	+⅛		
1,850,000	1981	7400		65				
1,850,000	1982	13875		75				
1,850,000	1983	22200		85				
1,850,000	1984	32375		90				
1,800,000	1985	44075		95				
1,800,000	1986	57575		5.00				
1,800,000	1987	72875		05				
1,800,000	1988	89975		10				
1,800,000	1989	108875		15				
1,800,000	1990	129575		20				
1,800,000	1991	152075		30	5.35			
1,800,000	1992	176375		40	5.45		457	457
1,800,000	1993	202475		100	5.55	-½	-⅞	-½
1,800,000	1994	230375		''	''			
1,800,000	1995	260075		60	5.65			
1,800,000	1996	291575		70				
1,800,000	1997	324875		80				
1,800,000	1998	359975		90				
	1999							
	2000							
	2001							
	2002							
	2003							

5.60%, less ⅜, he was bidding the account a down price, a 5.35, 5.45, 5.55 twice and a 5.65%, less ½. The market felt pretty good to Charley, but with $12 million left he had a real problem. He estimated that down .05 was about a half point ($5) in those years, and with the less ½, the bid was about one point below list. Since the account's spread was only $6.20, it would show about a ⅜ loss on the $6.350 million bonds that the joint account was bidding for.

"I'll poll the account, Willis, but I don't know how the vote will go."

"O.K., Charley, as soon as you can, O.K.?"

"Yup," and they both hung up.

Charley thought it over and decided to oppose the sale. He wondered if the joint account had some orders for the bonds, but he couldn't figure out from whom. He put in a call to Bob, but couldn't reach him. Then he called member TWO, who thought the bid was too cheap, and suggested that they counter it with a special offer: the same list yields, but at less ⅝, or ¼ more than the regular ⅜, which would be about break-even. We would say it was a list less ⅝ counter to a down .05 less ½ bid. Charley called member FOUR and also Johnson & McDonald, both of whom liked TWO's suggestion. Charley called THREE back, and said, "No go at down .05 less a half, Willis, but we would do list less ⅝." Willis checked with his joint account partners, and after a few minutes called back, "No interest at that price, but thanks." And that was that for then. After a few minutes Bob called in, and agreed with Charley's decision. Some more small orders straggled in, but the day's closing balance was $11.720 million—still quite a load.

A Counter Proposal

Next morning, Wednesday, July 19, some high-grades traded in the secondary and the market definitely felt better. Vermont was under $11 million, and Willis called Bob at 10:00.

He said, "O.K., Bob, we'll take them." (The Vermonts 1991 to '95 at list less ⅝ were understood.) However, that cut price had been only a temporary special offering, and both Bob and Willis knew it. Willis was obviously trying to get yesterday's counter renewed, now that the market was stronger. Bob talked it over with Charley and they agreed that they should not sell them at less ⅝. They called the six top account members, and found a sharp difference of opinion. Three members wanted to hold strictly to list, but three wanted to sell the bonds at less ⅝. "Can't you make up your mind, and stick to it?" one of the latter asked.

A New Bid, Higher

It was a virtual tie, and so it was up to manager Bob to make the decision. As he said it to THREE, "List is best." Willis didn't like it, but what could he do? The vote, based on participations, was narrowly in favor of holding to list, and so list it was. Charley called all the members and told

The Bid Is Turned Down

VERMONT   7/19/78

1980	0		1990	1,450 *FNB*	
1981	0		1991	1,600	
1982	0		1992	1,050	
1983	0		1993	1,150 *1,125*	
1984	0		1994	1,225 *1,025*	
1985	0		1995	1,200	*J/ACCT.* 7,270
1986	1,445 *1,345* *1,045*		1996	0	
1987	980 *940*		1997	800 *770*	
1988	200 *200*		1998	600 *500*	
1989	0				

Balances

9:00 A.M.	10:00	10:15	10:30
11,720 ✓	10,905 ✓	3,635 ✓	2,185 ✓

220

them that a list less ⅝ bid had been turned down, the news traveled around the Street, carried fastest by the brokers, and the account members had something good to tell their customers. Joe got the idea, and called Windy right away. Windy was out on his coffee break, and Joe banged down his phone. "Coffee!" he groaned. The market heated up a bit more—some Californias of '95 traded in the secondary at a 5.55%, and at 10:15 back came Willis again.

"O.K., we'll pay less ⅝ for all the bonds 1991 and out." He was bidding the same price, ¼ under the takedown, but now for the last seven maturities, over $7 million bonds. Bob was non-committal, and made a quick check of the top members. Five of the six agreed to stick to list, and Bob turned Willis down again. In a minute he returned with a new bid of list less ½, ⅛ higher, and just $1.25 under the regular takedown, for 1991 and out. He was tough, Willis. Bob said, "Why don't you just take them at list?" but Willis didn't budge. Bob checked his members again, and they supported him in holding to list. Willis had stayed on the wire, and Bob figured he would buy. "List—that's it," he said, and Willis said, "You win, send them in." He was taking down all the bonds 1991 through 1998, a total of $7.270 million, at the regular scale less the regular ⅜ takedown. Bob ran over all the amounts, and to make sure, repeated the price: "The original scale, less ⅜. Good luck with them, and thanks." Word went out that all the long Vermonts had traded at list, fresh news confirming the market's strength.

More Bids, and a Trade

The remaining Vermonts started to move, and Charley, though he had no actual orders, began to like the looks of the 1990's. He and Bob consulted, and at 10:30 they took them down, $1.450 million, just before J & Mc called in to do the same, no doubt hoping that Winderman would buy some more. As it turned out, Windy's thoughts were on other bonds, and the 250 of 1990 were all the Vermonts he bought. First Nat offered the 1990's at the net price and sold them all there before the day was over, making themselves $5,400. Buying like this, without orders, is called taking bonds down for stock, or for inventory, and like Willis' joint account action, is part of the speculative processes we will return to in a later volume.

Takedowns for Stock

At noon the balance was down to $2.185 million, all on the short end, but the market continued upward, and at 4:00 the last bonds were taken down and the account was closed. Every bond went out at list, a rarity, producing the hoped-for underwriter profit of $2 a bond. Charlie removed the syndicate price restrictions, and Vermont was officially free to trade according to supply and demand. The primary phase was over, and the issue had entered the secondary. It was a neat deal—bought by $2, and closed on the second day. The joint account did well, too, finally making

The Account Is Closed

4:20 EDT

FIRST NATIONAL BANK ANNOUNCES THAT THEIR ACCOUNT ON
$34,450,000 STATE OF VERMONT VARIOUS PURPOSE BONDS
PURCHASED 7/18 AT COMPETITIVE BIDDING IS ALL SOLD
THE BONDS ARE FREED FROM SYNDICATE RESTRICTIONS
ESTIMATED DELIVERY DATE 8/8/78

4:21 EDT

about half a point a bond, or $36,000. For a while it was touch and go, but all's well that sells well. Something like 300 people worked in the pre-sale phase in the six accounts, and about 75 salespeople got orders. Five insurance companies, about 30 banks (including Mobank), and 50 individuals eventually invested in Vermont. We can hope they were happy with their bonds. Now for a chapter let's go back to see how the bid was calculated.

STATE OF VERMONT

$34,450,000

Sealed proposals will be received by the State of Vermont at the Shawmut Bank of Boston, N.A., Municipal Services Department, 11th Floor, One Federal Street, Boston, Massachusetts on Tuesday, July 18, 1978 until 11:00 A.M., (E.D.S.T.) at which time they will be publicly opened and announced, for the purchase of the following issue of Bonds of the State of Vermont, dated and maturing (without option of prior redemption) as follows:

$26,750,000 Public Improvement Bonds, dated August 1, 1978, payable February 1, $1,430,000 in each year 1980 to 1984, inclusive, and $1,400,000 in each year 1985 to 1998, inclusive.

$ 7,700,000 Transportation Bonds, dated August 1, 1978, payable February 1, $420,000 in each year 1980 to 1984, inclusive, and $400,000 in each year 1985 to 1998, inclusive.

The Bonds will bear interest at the rate per annum specified by the successful bidder therefor in accordance herewith, payable on February 1, 1979, and semi-annually thereafter on each August 1 and February 1 until maturity.

The Public Improvement Bonds are issued pursuant to No. 269 of the Public Acts of 1973, Adjourned Session, No. 194 of the Public Acts of 1975, Adjourned Session, No. 98 of the Public Acts of 1977, and No. 246 of the Public Acts of 1977, Adjourned Session. The Transportation Bonds are issued pursuant to No. 109 of the Public Acts of 1971, Nos. 87 and 98 of the Public Acts of 1977, and No. 246 of the Public Acts of 1977, Adjourned Session.

The Bonds will be of the denomination of $5,000 and will be issued in bearer form with a single coupon attached for each installment of interest thereon. Both the principal of and interest on the Bonds will be payable in lawful money of the United States of America at the principal office of the Shawmut Bank of Boston, N.A., Boston, Massachusetts.

Each proposal for the Bonds must specify in a multiple of ⅛ or 1/20 of 1% the single rate of interest which the Bonds are to bear. No bid of less than par and accrued interest to the date of payment of the purchase price will be considered. Award will be made to the bidder who offers to purchase the Bonds pursuant to a legally acceptable proposal at the lowest named rate of interest, or, as between legally acceptable proposals specifying the same rate of interest, to the bidder complying with the terms of sale and offering to pay therefor the highest price. If two or more such bidders offer to pay the same highest price the Bonds will be awarded to one of such bidders selected by lot from among all such bidders.

Each proposal should be enclosed in a sealed envelope marked on the outside "Proposal for Bonds", and, if mailed, addressed to Hon. Emory A. Hebard, State Treasurer, State of Vermont, c/o Shawmut Bank of Boston, N.A., Municipal Services Department, 11th Floor, One Federal Street, Boston, Massachusetts 02211.

Award of the Bonds, which is subject to confirmation by the Governor, or rejection of all proposals is expected to be made promptly after opening of such proposals.

The Bonds will be delivered at the Shawmut Bank of Boston, N.A., Boston, Massachusetts, or at an agent or place designated by said bank in New York City on or about August 8, 1978, against payment in Federal Reserve Funds.

The Treasurer reserves the right to reject all bids and any bid not complying with the terms of this notice.

The successful bidder will be furnished, without cost, with the approving opinion of the law firm of Hawkins, Delafield & Wood, New York, New York, to the effect that the Bonds are valid general obligations of the State

Chapter Twenty-Six

Figuring the Bid

We spent several chapters on competitive new issue bidding, seeing one group strain to top the competing syndicates while somehow keeping the scale attractive enough to sell the bonds and turn a profit, a clash of brains and financial muscle. Syndicate work is like a stock-car race—148 m.p.h. around the curve, and you lose; 150, and you spin into a wall. Too dangerous? Look elsewhere—there is plenty of other work in municipals; but whether as a member in the stands or as a manager right there behind the wheel, competitive bidding is a fascinating contest. Now let's take a look at the people who crouch in the municipal pits—the support staff who figure scales, enter bids, and complete syndicate details.

The Bid Figurers

When a City Hall is to be refurbished, or salt for roads bought, most municipalities are required by state legislation to award contracts for them through public competitive bidding. The same goes for bonds. Each bid process—whether for painting or for supplying long-term funds—is governed by a set of specifications, all legal and proper, which spell out exactly what has to be delivered, how much, and when. Bond sale bidding specs, which govern the maximum number and size of coupons, dates of interest, maturities, call features, and many other conditions, are contained in Official Notices of Sale. We saw Charley referring to Vermont's when he was preparing to bid.

Bidding Specifications

We all learned how to figure interest in secondary school by using some variant of this formula: principal x rate x time (I = PRT). Simplifying it somewhat, in the bond bidding process the community specifies two of these factors: the principal (in Vermont's case $34.450 million); and the time, on that issue an average of 10 years, five months. It's up to the bidders to enter the third factor, the rate. And that's what new issue bidding comes down to—naming just one number—the average interest rate.

Interest Calculations

In the chapter on yield we saw how total return is figured according to a formula which includes maturity, coupon and dollar price. A similar sys-

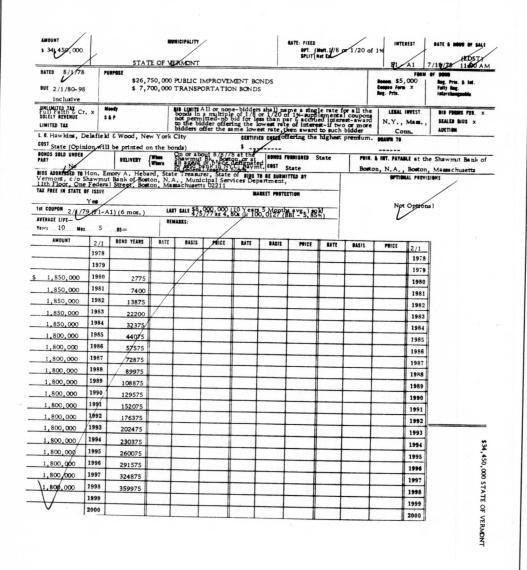

AMOUNT						
$ 34,450,000	MUNICIPALITY	RATE: FIXED	INTEREST	DATE & HOUR OF SALE		

AMOUNT $ 34,450,000

MUNICIPALITY STATE OF VERMONT

RATE: FIXED OPT. { Mult. 1/8 or 1/20 of 1% SPLIT { Not Ex.

INTEREST F1 A1

DATE & HOUR OF SALE 7/18/78 11:00 AM (EDST)

DATED 8/1/78

PURPOSE $26,750,000 PUBLIC IMPROVEMENT BONDS $ 7,700,000 TRANSPORTATION BONDS

DUE 2/1/80-98 inclusive

FORM OF BOND Denom. $5,000 / Coupon Form x / Reg. Prin. — Reg. Prin. & Int. / Fully Reg. / Interchangeable

UNLIMITED TAX Full Faith & Cr. x / SOLELY REVENUE / LIMITED TAX

Moody / S & P

BID LIMITS All or none—bidders shall name a single rate for all the bonds in a multiple of 1/8 or 1/20 of 1%—supplemental coupons not permitted—no bid for less than par & accrued interest—award to the bidder offering the lowest rate of interest—if two or more bidders offer the same lowest rate, then award to such bidder offering the highest premium.

LEGAL INVEST. N.Y., Mass., Conn.

BID FORMS FUR. x / SEALED BIDS x / AUCTION

L. O. Hawkins, Delafield & Wood, New York City

CERTIFIED CHECK

DRAWN TO

COST State (Opinion will be printed on the bonds) $ ....

BONDS SOLD UNDER PART? No

DELIVERY When / Where

On or about 8/8/78 at the Shawmut Bk. Boston or at an agent or place designated by said bank in NYC.

BONDS FURNISHED State / **COST** State

PRIN. & INT. PAYABLE at the Shawmut Bank of Boston, N.A., Boston, Massachusetts

BIDS ADDRESSED TO Hon. Emory A. Hebard, State Treasurer, State of Vermont, c/o Shawmut Bank of Boston, N.A., Municipal Services Department, 11th Floor, One Federal Street, Boston, Massachusetts 02211

BIDS TO BE SUBMITTED BY

OPTIONAL PROVISIONS

TAX FREE IN STATE OF ISSUE Yes

MARKET PROTECTION

Not Optional

1st COUPON 2/1/79 (F1-A1) (6 mos.)

LAST SALE $5,000,000 (10 Years 5 Months avg.) sold 4/5/77 as 4.80s @ 100.0127 (BBI = 5.85%)

AVERAGE LIFE— Years 10 Mos. 5 .05=

REMARKS:

AMOUNT	2/1	BOND YEARS	RATE	BASIS	PRICE	RATE	BASIS	PRICE	RATE	BASIS	PRICE	2/1
	1978											1978
	1979											1979
$ 1,850,000	1980	2775										1980
1,850,000	1981	7400										1981
1,850,000	1982	13875										1982
1,850,000	1983	22200										1983
1,850,000	1984	32375										1984
1,800,000	1985	44075										1985
1,800,000	1986	57575										1986
1,800,000	1987	72875										1987
1,800,000	1988	89975										1988
1,800,000	1989	108875										1989
1,800,000	1990	129575										1990
1,800,000	1991	152075										1991
1,800,000	1992	176375										1992
1,800,000	1993	202475										1993
1,800,000	1994	230375										1994
1,800,000	1995	260075										1995
1,800,000	1996	291575										1996
1,800,000	1997	324875										1997
1,800,000	1998	359975										1998
	1999											1999
	2000											2000

$34,450,000 STATE OF VERMONT

Courtesy of *The Bond Buyer*

tem prevails in figuring the interest cost of a new loan. Bidders are required to name one or more coupon rates and also one dollar price for the whole issue. The group that proposes the lowest overall interest cost is high. There are several methods of calculating which bid represents the lowest interest cost; the simplest is one where bidders must name a single coupon for the entire issue, and the lowest rate wins the bonds. And if more than one group bid that same lowest rate, the winner is the one among them which bid the highest dollar price.

How the Winning Bid Is Determined

This, a one-coupon bid specification, was Vermont's system on their 1978 issue. However, using only one rate for 20 years of maturities is usually inconvenient for bidders. They can often market bonds more effectively, and bid lower interest costs, if they can use several coupons. So most issuers permit different coupons for different maturities. The easy way to figure the lowest average interest cost in these cases is by the net interest cost (N.I.C.) method. To figure N.I.C. you can multiply the number of each maturity's bond years by its coupon rate, total this, then subtract any premium (or add any discount) in the bid price, and finally divide by the total number of bond years. Or, you can enter the N.I.C. code on your computer console, push the return key, and get the answer that way. We shall return to N.I.C., and its more modern version, T.I.C., in the next volume.

N.I.C., T.I.C.

We sat in on First National's Vermont meeting where two scales appeared—Scale A and the final one. Charley had taken charge of the bidding procedures on Vermont, and like any good executive he delegated the technical work, in this case to Henry, an assistant in the department, who had a way with scales. Let's pretend that First Nat's computer was down at ten o'clock that Tuesday morning and see Scale A figured the old-fashioned way, by hand. Although he could use a computer as readily as anyone, Henry followed the same old four-step routine he had learned from Harry B., his first boss; the computer's problem didn't bother him a bit.

Figuration

Step 1—Check the worksheet against the Notice of Sale. Once in a coon's age, even (or especially) in these electronic days, an error appears in them, and there is hell to pay. The day before the Vermont sale, Henry compared every single box on the *Bond Buyer* worksheet against the N.O.S. until he was satisfied that its bid specifications were accurate. As usual, the sheet was O.K., but you never know. As a check he added up the maturity years to see if they matched the issue amount. $34.450 million. Right. From then on he could trust the thing.

Check the Sheet

Step 2—Estimate a trial coupon. At 10:00 a.m. on Tuesday, Henry looked carefully at the amounts in each year and at the preliminary scale. He had worked on thousands of scales in the past 15 years, and without

A Trial Coupon

AMOUNT	2/1	BOND YEARS	RATE	BASIS	PRICE	RATE	BASIS	PRICE
	1978							
	1979			5½				
S 1,850,000	1980	2775		4.50	101.434			
1,850,000	1981	7400		65	101.984			
1,850,000	1982	13875		75	102.392			
1,850,000	1983	22200		85	102.599			
1,850,000	1984	32375		90	102.862			
1,800,000	1985	44075		95	103.025			
1,800,000	1986	57575		5.00	103.095			
1,800,000	1987	72875		05	103.078			
1,800,000	1988	89975		15	102.603			
1,800,000	1989	108875		20	102.403			
1,800,000	1990	129575		25	102.137			
1,800,000	1991	152075		30	101.811			
1,800,000	1992	176375		40	100.949			
1,800,000	1993	202475		100	100 —			
1,800,000	1994	230375		100	100 —			
1,800,000	1995	260075		5.60	98.931			
1,800,000	1996	291575		70	97.803			
1,800,000	1997	324875		80	96.623			
1,800,000	1998	359975		90	95.401			
	1999				101.015	95		
	2000							
	2001							
	2002							

much thinking, a coupon of 5½% popped into his mind. Maybe it was too low or too high, but it was close enough for a test. Like most issuers, Vermont required a minimum bid of 100, so to get the $6.20 profit that Charley wanted, Henry had to find a coupon which on that scale produced an average price of at least 100.62. If 100.62 were in fact the average re-offering price, and the bid 100, First Nat's spread would be $6.20.

The Production

Step 3—Produce the scale using the trial coupon. To do this, first calculate the dollar price for each year's yield. Next multiply the dollar price of every maturity by the number of bonds in that year. After this is done for every maturity, add them all up; then divide by the total number of bonds. This is the production. Henry used his little calculator, and facing shows how it came out, or as he soon called Charley to say, "Scale A is 101.01 for 5½'s." For the mathematically talented, it's easy to see that a production is just a weighted average. Naturally, the price of the $1.850 million bonds in 1984 affected the production a little more than the $1.800 million in 1985.

Trial and Error

Step 4—If the production is too low (with a premium lower than the desired profit) or too high (with a premium far above it) then pick another coupon until the production minus the profit is higher than the specified minimum bid price.

Since Vermont allowed only one coupon, and there were 18 different yields on the scale, some maturities (with yields lower than the 5½% coupon) would be priced above 100, or even above 100.62—premium bonds. And some (with yields higher than the coupon) would be priced below 100—the discounts. It's like a wholesale butcher who bids $500 for 200 pounds of beef ($2.50 a pound) when sirloin sells at $5.00 and ground round at $2.00. He hopes to make a profit selling at an average of $3.00, a spread of 50¢, or 20%. In bonds we make smaller percentage mark-ups, so we have to be more exact, but the math is essentially the same. Notice that we first figure our average re-offering price (the production) and then work back to the bid. Henry calculated the dollar price for each year, and as you can see, his prices started at 101.434, rose up to 103.095, and later went as low as 95.401. Porterhouse, filet, and chuck. He looked at the dollar prices with a practiced eye, and estimated that the production would be 101. Then he did the actual multiplication, and he came up with 101.01595. An excellent guess, his 101. In this case, 101.0159 minus $6.20 was over 100, the minimum, but not too far over it, so Henry had picked a valid trial coupon. A possible next step would have been to the next lower allowable rate— 5.45's, but Henry didn't think Charley would like that odd a coupon. He brought the numbers to Charley, who wondered about 5.45's, too, but said nothing more.

To repeat, you figure backwards to bid on a new issue. First you

```
DATED          8/ 1/78
DELIVERED      8/ 8/78

      DUE        AMT      B/Y    RATE    SCALE    PRICE   EFFECTIVE CALL
                 (000)   (000)

  1   2/ 1/80   1850     2775   5.500   4.500   101.415
  2   2/ 1/81   1850     4625   5.500   4.650   101.968
  3   2/ 1/82   1850     6475   5.500   4.750   102.379
  4   2/ 1/83   1850     8325   5.500   4.850   102.588
  5   2/ 1/84   1850    10175   5.500   4.900   102.852

  6   2/ 1/85   1800    11700   5.500   4.950   103.016
  7   2/ 1/86   1800    13500   5.500   5.000   103.087
  8   2/ 1/87   1800    15300   5.500   5.050   103.071
  9   2/ 1/88   1800    17100   5.500   5.150   102.598
 10   2/ 1/89   1800    18900   5.500   5.200   102.399

 11   2/ 1/90   1800    20700   5.500   5.250   102.133
 12   2/ 1/91   1800    22500   5.500   5.300   101.808
 13   2/ 1/92   1800    24300   5.500   5.400   100.947
 14   2/ 1/93   1800    26100   5.500   5.500   100.000L
 15   2/ 1/94   1800    27900   5.500   5.500   100.000L

 16   2/ 1/95   1800    29700   5.500   5.600    98.932B
 17   2/ 1/96   1800    31500   5.500   5.700    97.803B
 18   2/ 1/97   1800    33300   5.500   5.800    96.624B
 19   2/ 1/98   1800    35100   5.500   5.900    95.402B
TOTAL          34450   359975.0000
B = COUPON IS BELOW THE LOWER LIMIT OF THE OPTIMIZATION CONSTRAINT.
L = COUPON AT LOWER LIMIT OF OPTIMIZATION CONSTRAINT.

TOTAL PAR      34,450,000
GROSS PROD     34,797,997.00   101.01015
PROFIT            213,590.00     0.62000
BID            34,584,407.00   100.39015
PREMIUM           134,407.00
GROSS INT      19,798,625.00
PROD EXCESS  +    134,407.00
NET INT        19,664,218.00 % 5.462662
AVG. LIFE 10 YEARS,  5 MONTHS, 11 DAYS
 ** DATA FILE USED IS VERMANT
```

Courtesy of *The Bond Buyer*

calculate your selling price—the production. Then you subtract your spread, and the difference is the bid.

Production (estimated)	101.000
Spread	.620
Bid	100.380

At 10:20 Henry tried the computer again, and the right lights went on. He punched in his security pass-words, and when on line asked it to retrieve the Vermont set-up he had entered the day before. Out it came. He entered scale A, the $6.20 spread, and, specifying a 5½% coupon, asked for that solution. A few seconds later the printout appeared and he was not surprised at the answer—101.01015, as the computer said, GROSS PROD. Then Henry entered a different command, and the computer picked the mathematically optimum rate—5.45%. That production was 100.645. At 10:30 Charley came in and asked Henry to figure a new scale. 1988, '89, and '90 were each to be raised an .05, to a 5.10, 5.15, and 5.20%.

Henry had kept the computer on line and entered the three changes. He estimated 101.09, pushed the return button, and in two seconds out came the answer—101.0739. Pretty close, he was. Why did he bother to make estimates? To make sure no gross error had been made, such as a typo on the dated date, retrieving the wrong issue entirely, or any of the hundreds of things that can go wrong when man teams with machine.

As we mentioned, Vermont did not use net interest cost, but just for fun, Henry guessed Vermont's N.I.C.—a 5.44%. A glance at the printout showed a 5.4565%, which was .016% off—close, but not one of his better tries. At 10:45 Henry called back Charley and just said "par four five three nine," which was the final bid. Charley read back the whole scale, the coupon, and the bid, and Henry grunted Yes. Their man in Boston was waiting on the phone and Charley gave him the bid himself, going over every detail carefully and slowly, with the results we have already seen.

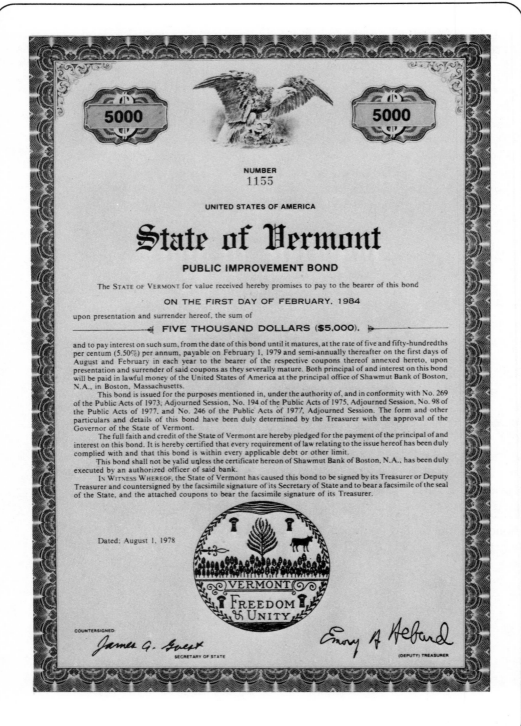

NUMBER
1155

UNITED STATES OF AMERICA

State of Vermont

PUBLIC IMPROVEMENT BOND

The STATE OF VERMONT for value received hereby promises to pay to the bearer of this bond

ON THE FIRST DAY OF FEBRUARY, 1984

upon presentation and surrender hereof, the sum of

FIVE THOUSAND DOLLARS ($5,000).

and to pay interest on such sum, from the date of this bond until it matures, at the rate of five and fifty-hundredths per centum (5.50%) per annum, payable on February 1, 1979 and semi-annually thereafter on the first days of August and February in each year to the bearer of the respective coupons thereof annexed hereto, upon presentation and surrender of said coupons as they severally mature. Both principal of and interest on this bond will be paid in lawful money of the United States of America at the principal office of Shawmut Bank of Boston, N.A., in Boston, Massachusetts.

This bond is issued for the purposes mentioned in, under the authority of, and in conformity with No. 269 of the Public Acts of 1973; Adjourned Session, No. 194 of the Public Acts of 1975, Adjourned Session, No. 98 of the Public Acts of 1977, and No. 246 of the Public Acts of 1977, Adjourned Session. The form and other particulars and details of this bond have been duly determined by the Treasurer with the approval of the Governor of the State of Vermont.

The full faith and credit of the State of Vermont are hereby pledged for the payment of the principal of and interest on this bond. It is hereby certified that every requirement of law relating to the issue hereof has been duly complied with and that this bond is within every applicable debt or other limit.

This bond shall not be valid unless the certificate hereon of Shawmut Bank of Boston, N.A., has been duly executed by an authorized officer of said bank.

IN WITNESS WHEREOF, the State of Vermont has caused this bond to be signed by its Treasurer or Deputy Treasurer and countersigned by the facsimile signature of its Secretary of State and to bear a facsimile of the seal of the State, and the attached coupons to bear the facsimile signature of its Treasurer.

Dated: August 1, 1978

COUNTERSIGNED:

James G. Guest
SECRETARY OF STATE

Emory A. Hebard
(DEPUTY) TREASURER

Chapter Twenty-Seven

Account Settlement

By July 19, 1978, Vermont had come and gone. The bonds were all sold, our imaginary account was closed, and the underwriters turned their attention to other things. However, the manager's operations department still had work to do, in fact, the three things underwriting accomplishes: getting money to issuers, delivering bonds to investors, and distributing syndicate profits.

The Money Flows

Vermont's finance people had estimated in their Notice of Sale that the bonds would be ready for delivery about August 8, 1978. First National's chief operations person in New York got in touch with his counterpart at Shawmut in late July and started talking about the delivery. They tentatively agreed that the bonds would be sent down to New York on August 8. By July 28, it became apparent that the printing process was running late and on that day August 15 was decided on as the definite settlement date. So on August 1 First Nat sent out regular-way confirmations, with the usual money figures, using August 15, 1978 for settlement, and accruing interest up to that date.

Settlement

Instructions were sent to the printer, for all of the maturity amounts as 5½'s. The legal formalities proceeded smoothly, directed by Hawkins, Delafield & Wood, of New York City. Then, on August 10, 6,890 paper bonds and the closing documents were delivered to the signature company where they were duly signed. In the meanwhile, First National had sent redelivery instructions to its clearing bank, Chase, as did the real-world winning syndicate, Harris Trust. As is customary on new issues, members were required to pick up their bonds at the settling bank, rather than following the secondary market practice where sellers deliver to buyers. So by the morning of Tuesday, August 15, 1978, Chase had counted out 108 packages of bonds, representing all of the separate takedowns of the issue, each with its own individual amount due, and the total amount due from each member. First Nat, acting for the syndicate, handed a check for

Delivering The Goods

233

First National Bank

State of Vermont
7/18/78

GROSS PROFIT $213,590.00   ($6.20 x 34,450)

TAKEDOWNS   — 123,312.50

(⅜ x 31,950 = $119,812.50)
(¼ x   1,400 =   3,500.00)
$123,312.50

PROFIT FROM
SALE OF BONDS   90,277.50

EXPENSES   −17,742.83

Clearance	$ 8,612.50
Fed. Funds	7,441.75
Other	1,688.58
	$17,742.83

NET PROFIT $72,534.67

$34,680,053.27 to Chase, who credited it to the State of Vermont's account, and the issuer received its money. This was immediately put into short term investments the treasurer's office had arranged to buy in the weeks before payment was due, and started earning interest that same day. Eventually, as the investments came due and as the money was needed to pay for the capital projects for which the bonds were floated, the funds were moved into one of Vermont's checking accounts, to be disbursed to its suppliers.

On August 15, the runners (delivery men) from each syndicate member delivered Chase checks or credit slips. The joint account picked up the physical bonds and brought them to the members' clearance facilities, where they were inspected for accuracy. No mistakes were found, and all the bonds were paid for on schedule. The joint account picked up the largest pile, $7 million, 1,400 individual pieces of paper. Then, in turn, each member of the First Nat account redelivered to their customers. So Johnson & McDonald picked up one of the bundles, the 50 pieces of paper representing the 250 bonds it had taken down from the 1990 maturity at a 5.20% less ⅜, and had sold to Winderman at a 5.20% net, paid Chase $256,004.72, ($255,470 principal and $534.72 interest), and Chase credited that amount to the syndicate. Then J & Mc redelivered the bonds to Mobank's agent in New York, picking up a check for $256,942.22 ($256,407.50 principal and the same $534.72 for interest). And if you look sharp enough you will see that the difference in J & Mc's two checks was the $937.50 Joe Smithers had calculated would be the credit on his sale.

Bonds for Dollars

How did our First Nat syndicate get its underwriting profit? As we saw, it paid Chase 100.4539 for the $34.450 million bonds, $34,606,368.55 plus interest. Its members picked up their bonds through the processes we followed, paying Chase and the account $34,696,645 plus the same amount of interest. The difference was $90,277, the account's profit before expenses. First Nat's expenses were exactly the same as Harris Trust's in the real world—$17,742.83. Subtract this from $90,277 and we have the net profit of the First National syndicate—$72,534.

The Underwriter Collects

The $72,534 net profit belonged to the underwriters in exact proportion to their participations, regardless of the number of bonds each took down. First Nat got $16,842.55 (on $8 million participation), J & Mc got $6,316.52 on its $3 million, down to member EIGHTEEN, who was in for 500 bonds, who made $1,051.75. All in all, not a bad deal.

The Net

Let's see how the actual underwriting profit compared to what the account had estimated at the meeting. The gross spread was $6.20, and expenses were estimated at 40¢, leaving $5.80 profit before takedowns.

The Underwriting Profit

First National Bank
$34,450,000
State of Vermont
7/18/78

Distribution

Members	Participations	Sales	Profit
F.N.B.	$8,000,000	$12,765,000	$16,844.05
Two	7,950,000	2,850,000	16,738.77
Three	6,000,000	10,020,000	12,633.03
Four	6,000,000	1,330,000	12,633.03
Johnson & McDonald	3,000,000	2,255,000	6,316.52
Eleven	1,000,000	980,000	2,105.51
Thirteen	1,000,000	1,075,000	2,105.51
Sixteen	500,000	185,000	1,052.75
Seventeen	500,000	150,000	1,052.75
Eighteen	500,000	340,000	1,052.75
	34,450,000	31,950,000	72,534.67
	Group & Desig.	$ 2,500,000	
		$34,450,000	

The actual expenses ($17,742.83, divided by $34.450 million) came to 52¢ a bond. The original $5.80 estimate, less ⅜ takedowns, was to have left $2.05 in the underwriting. Since the account got some priority business, the actual takedowns were slightly lower, $3.58 per bond. 52¢ and $3.58 make $4.10, which left $2.11 for the underwriters, versus the $2.05 estimate. Very close to the guesstimates, and well it might be on such a straightforward deal.

On September 29, 1978, First Nat sent out the profit checks to its members, strictly observing Rule G-12, which states that syndicate profits must be distributed by 60 days after delivery date, so finishing off Vermont's 1978 issue. That was that, until next time it came to market, which in fact occurred on 7/10/80, when a $51 million issue drew bids from the usual syndicates, but none from First Nat. And that concludes Vermont for us, too.

Glossary

Account. 1.) An underwriting syndicate, as in First National's account; 2.) An investor covered by a salesman, as in "That's my account, Tom Large."

Additional takedown. One of the two discounts or commissions which a member receives from an underwriting account. *See* Takedown.

Ad valorem. According to its value, referring to a method of levying a tax on real estate.

Agency. A unit of municipal government usually formed to accomplish a single regional goal and empowered to issue revenue bonds, such as the Illinois State Housing Authority.

A.O.N. All or none. A condition set on an order for bonds, specifying that only the whole amount named will be accepted.

Assessed valuation. A community's measure of the worth of its real and personal property, usually a defined fraction of market value.

Asset allocation. A technique used by commercial banks, splitting up their various liabilities and buying securities which match them.

Authority. *See* Agency.

Balance. Total number of bonds remaining in a new deal.

B.A.N. Bond anticipation note. A short-term security issued by a community and repaid from the proceeds of planned permanent financing.

Bank range bonds. Short bonds; usually due in 1 to 5, or 1 to 10, years.

Basis, or basis price. Yield; average annual return on investment.

Basis point. 1/100 of 1% interest.

Bearer bonds. Obligations which are paid, principal and interest, to the physical holder. Not registered. Same as coupon bonds.

Bid form. A (usually) one-page sheet on which bidders officially enter proposals for new issues.

The Blue List. A daily publication of municipal bond offerings supposedly available from dealers.

Bond. A debt instrument through which a lender receives interest income and a borrower use of money.

A Bond, one bond. A unit of debt, $1,000 of principal.

The Bond Buyer. Our trade journal. Mostly concerned with the primary market.

Bond funds. Dealer-managed pools of fixed income securities.

Broker. In municipals, a company which acts solely as a middleman between dealers; also its individual employees. In stocks, it means a dealer.

Callable. Redeemable by the issuer prior to maturity at a price above 100. Optional is the same thing, but at 100, no premium.

Casualty company. An insurer against property damage; not a life insurance company.

C.D.'s. Certificates of deposit. Debt instruments which banks issue to borrow funds from customers.

Commercial banks. Full line money borrowers and lenders; not savings banks.

Common trust funds. Pools of tax-exempt bonds owned jointly by the subscribing customers of a bank trust department.

Competitive new issues. Bond deals sold at public bidding to the underwriter providing the lowest interest cost; not negotiated.

Concession. 1.) In the primary market, one of the two discounts members receive from their syndicates. 2.) In the secondary market, a discount one dealer offers another.

Confirmation. Advices sent out by dealers to their customers detailing purchases and sales of bonds, and showing the amount of money involved.

Corporate bonds. Long term securities issued by publicly owned companies.

Coupon. A bond's rate of interest in percentage per year. Also the part of a paper bond evidencing the interest payment.

Coupon and registered, interchangeable. Bonds which may be converted from either form to the other with minimal delay or charge.

Coupon bonds. Bearer bonds.

Cover. The second best bid, as in "Ours was a 7.95%, and the cover was a 7.99%"; or the difference between the high bid and the second highest (in this case .04%).

Current yield. The annual percentage return on a bond. Coupon divided by dollar price. An 8% bond at 80 gives a C.Y. of 10.00%.

Dated date. The formal birthday of a new issue, used to distinguish it from other securities of the same issuer.

Dealer. A professional investment banking company which buys and sells securities for its own account.

Dealer banks. Commercial banks with a municipal bond department.

Dealer sales. Sales made by one dealer to another.

Debt load. The total amount of G.O. bonds for which a community is responsible. *See* Overlapping debt.

Debt per capita. Bonds divided by population.

Debt ratio. Bonded debt divided by property valuation.

Debt service. Amounts necessary to pay the principal and interest of a bond issue.

Denominations. Units of bond principal, usually either $5,000 or $1,000.

Designated. A type of order for new issue bonds, placed for the benefit of two or more of a syndicate's members.

Direct debt. The total amount of a community's outstanding G.O. bonds, but excluding its overlapping and underlying debt.

Discount. Priced below 100% of principal amount.

Dollar bonds. Municipals which are traded in dollar price rather than yield. Usually term bonds whose exact yield is hard to calculate.

Dollar price. A bond's value expressed as a percentage of principal.

Double exempt. Interest income free from taxation from two different entities, such as state and federal governments.

Down .05. Higher in yield by 1/20%, resulting in an equivalent dollar price decrease.

Enabling laws. State legislation regulating local government units' ways of issuing bonds.

Equity. A security which represents ownership.

Face value. 100% of principal amount.

Federal Reserve System. The U.S. National Bank, composed of 12 regional banks and headed by a seven-person Board.

Financial advisor. A professional outside consultant who helps a community shape and market bond issues.

First National. A bank we invented to help illustrate a syndicate operation.

Full faith and credit. Unconditional obligation to repay debt.

G.O. General obligation bond. A full faith and credit debt instrument of a community, backed by all its resources, including real estate taxes. Not a revenue bond.

Good faith. An amount of money which an issuer requires from bidders to ensure they really mean business. Often 2%.

Group. A type of order for new issue bonds, placed for the benefit of a syndicate as a whole, and usually at its list price, net of concession.

High grade bonds. Gilt edge, usually Aaa or Aa rated.

Interest. A payment made for use of money.

Issuer. A governmental unit which sells bonds, pays interest, and redeems principal.

Johnson & McDonald. Our imaginary municipal bond dealer who bid on Vermont.

Joint managers. A polite term for dealer members who occupy positions just below the top of a syndicate.

Legal opinion. A written judgment by a securities lawyer that a bond is validly issued and tax-exempt.

Limited tax (L.T.) bond. A G.O., payable from all a municipality's sources, including a real-estate levy whose maximum rate is set by a special authorizing law. Almost indistinguishable from U.T.'s in market worth.

Liquidity. The probable degree of departure of a security's future market price from cost or present worth.

List. The offering price of a bond as set by a dealer who owns it.

Low grade bonds. Relatively weak debt securities; BBB rated, for instance.

Majors. Members of a syndicate account who take a larger than average share of the underwriting risk. In the ads they appear below the managers and above the smaller members.

Manager. The lead underwriter of a syndicate account.

Marketability. The cost of buying or selling a security at one point in time.

Maturity. The date principal will be repaid.

Medium grade bonds. Average strength, often A rated.

Members. All the underwriters of an account; also, the smaller ones only.

M.S.R.B. Municipal Securities Rulemaking Board. An independent 15 member committee which devised and revises the regulations under which the N.A.S.D. monitors municipal bond dealers.

Municipal bond. A debt instrument issued by a state or one of its local government units.

Municipal bond market. Dealer-operated channels which supply communities with money, investors with bonds, and in some years, the dealers with profits.

N.A.S.D. National Association of Securities Dealers. A self-regulating and self-financed organization which acts as a buffer between the S.E.C. and the dealers. It operates in tax-exempts according to a special set of municipal bond rules written by the M.S.R.B.

Negotiable. A security which can be resold.

Negotiated issue. A bond deal which a municipality sells privately to a single underwriting group; not competitive.

Net. At the list price, without a concession.

Net debt. Total amount of G.O. bonds outstanding, minus credits, such as for cash balances.

Non-litigation certificate. One of the closing papers for a new issue stating that no action in court threatens the bonds.

Notes. Municipal obligations, such as B.A.N.'s or T.A.N.'s, short in term and high in liquidity.

Notice of sale. An official set of specifications for bidding on a new bond issue.

Order. A commitment made by a customer to buy a specified number of bonds at the offered price.

Order period. The time after a new issue sale during which all orders are treated as though they had been received simultaneously.

O.T.C. Over the counter. The dealers' free-form, negotiated method of buying and selling securities, chiefly by telephone. Not on an exchange.

Overlapping debt. G.O. bonds, in addition to a community's own direct obligations, such as those issued by a county or school district in which it is located.

Par. 100% of face, or principal, amount.

Paying agent. A bank or public official who remits interest and principal to bondholders.

Point. 1% of principal amount. If we buy at 77, and sell at 78½, we make 1½ points, or a point and a half.

Portfolio. An investor's total security holdings.

Premium. Priced above 100.

Price restrictions. The minimum prices a syndicate sets for its bonds.

Primary market. The dealer-conducted process of buying new issues from localities and selling them to investors.

Principal. The dollar amount of loan to be repaid; the face, or par, value.

Private placement. An issue of bonds sold directly to an investor without a public offering.

Production. The average net dollar price of a new issue reoffering scale.

P.S.A. Public Securities Association. The municipal bond industry trade organization.

Public finance. The negotiated part of municipal bond dealers' activity; concerned with structuring and marketing debt securities for issuers.

Rating. A credit quality assessment of a bond made by a financial service company, and expressed as a letter or number grade; or that symbol itself.

Registered bond. One whose principal and/or interest is paid to a recorded owner.

Registered, fully. Bonds whose interest and principal are automatically mailed to the owner of record.

Registered, principal only. Obligations whose face value is recorded with the issuer, but with interest coupons attached to physical bonds.

Reoffering. A scale of yields/prices at which a new issue is offered for sale.

Reserve requirements. Set amounts of money which commercial banks have to send to the Federal Reserve System to restrain their lending capacity.

Return. Total income from an investment.

Revenue bond. A municipal obligation secured by a designated stream of income; not a G.O.

Run. In a new issue, the amounts of bonds remaining in each maturity.

S.E.C. The Securities and Exchange Commission. A federal agency which oversees and regulates stock, bond, and other financial markets.

Secondary market. The O.T.C. process whereby already issued bonds trade between investors and dealers.

Self-supporting bond. A G.O. whose debt service is paid from a revenue producing facility.

Serial bonds. Municipal borrowings whose principal is to be repaid in specified installments, usually once a year. Opposite of term bonds.

Settlement date. The day (conventionally five business days after the trade date) on which the price of a bond transaction is calculated.

Spread. 1.) Any of various differentials betweeen interest rates. 2.) Potential profit margin.

Stock bid. A dealer's proposal to buy bonds at a certain price (usually lower than list) for inventory purposes, rather than to fill a customer's order.

Stock company. A casualty company which is owned by and run for the benefit of its shareholders. Not a mutual company.

Strip. A condition set on an order, to specify that bonds in a number of maturities are linked together, all or none.

Syndicate. A group of dealers who underwrite an issue together.

Syndicate letter. A contract which binds underwriters together.

Takedown. The total discount at which member of syndicates buy bonds from an account; composed of two parts—the concession, and the additional takedown.

T.A.N. Tax anticipation note. A short term security against which expected future real estate levies are pledged.

Taxable equivalent. The gross interest rate needed to equal a certain tax-free return.

Tax-exempt. Of interest income: not subject to a levy (as by the Federal Government).

Term bonds. All, or a large part, of a new issue, carrying one coupon and due in a single year; opposite of serial bonds. Terms are usually designed to be retired in partial amounts before their stated maturity through a sinking fund or other device.

T.I.C. True interest cost. A method of calculating the winner of a new issue which factors in the time value of money. Canadian interest cost. Not N.I.C.

Ticket. A trader's or salesman's form describing a transaction of buying or selling securities. Used internally.

Time deposits. Savings accounts and C.D.'s.

Total debt. Direct debt plus overlapping and underlying debt.

Trade date. The actual date a security is bought or sold.

Traders. Secondary market operators, ranging from order clerks to large position takers.

True valuation. Market price of all real estate on an issuer's tax roll.

Trust departments. Separately managed sections of commercial banks, which handle individuals' and institutions' investments for a fee.

Underlying debt. G.O. bonds for which some, but not all, of the property owners of a governmental unit are responsible, such as those issued by one city, or one school district, within the same county.

Underwriters. Dealers who buy from issuers to sell to investors, usually taking a risk in between; primary market dealers.

Unlimited tax (U.T.) bond. A G.O., payable from all a municipality's resources including a property tax which has no statutory upper rate or amount.

Up .05. Lower in yield by 1/20%, resulting in an equivalent dollar price increase.

W.I. When issued; technically, when, as, and if issued, a conditional offering of bonds made subject to their actual delivery to the underwriter.

Yield (to maturity). Total return on a bond, considering its nominal interest rate (coupon), length of maturity, and dollar price. A 9% bond due in 8 years, 7 months and priced at 110, provides a yield of 7.40% to maturity.

Bibliography

The Blue List, New York, weekdays.

The Bond Buyer, New York, weekdays.

Carleton's Universal Bond Value Tables, South Bend, Ind., Carleton Financial Computations, Inc., 1970.

Census of Population and Housing, U.S. Department of Commerce, Bureau of the Census.

Lamb, Robert, and Rappaport, Stephen P., *Municipal Bonds*, New York, McGraw-Hill Book Company, 1980.

Moody's Municipal and Government Manual, New York, Moody's Investors Service, Inc., annual.

Municipal Finance Statistics, The Bond Buyer, New York, annual.

The Municipal Handbook, ed. Feldstein, Sylvan G., et. al., New York, Dow Jones-Irwin, 1983.

Municipal Securities Rulemaking Board Manual, Chicago, Commerce Clearing House, Inc.

Public Securities Corporation, *Fundamentals of Municipal Bonds*, New York, P.S.A., 1981.

Smith, Wade S., *The Appraisal of Municipal Credit Risk*, New York, Moody's Investors Service, Inc., 1979.

Standard & Poor's Ratings Guide, Standard and Poor's Corporation, New York, McGraw-Hill Book Company, 1979.

Statistical Abstract of the United States.

White, Wilson, Jr., *White's Municipal Bond Ratings*, New York, White's Ratings Inc., annual.

Index

The Municipal Bond Market

Designed by Lou Figliola
Composed by TypeArt, Inc. in Times Roman
Art and Production by The James Chin Group, Inc.
Printed by Command Web Offset, Inc.
Coordinated by Owl Graphics, Inc.
Jacket Design by Valerie Coll
Bound by Bookbinders, Inc.